SERGEANT YORK

SERGEANT YORK

HIS OWN LIFE STORY AND WAR DIARY

EDITED BY **TOM SKEYHILL**
INTRODUCTION BY **GEORGE E. YORK**
FOREWORD BY **GERALD E. YORK**

Racehorse Publishing

CONTENTS

LIST OF ILLUSTRATIONS

INTRODUCTION

Sergeant Alvin Cullum York, the third oldest of eleven children, was born December 13, 1887 in a one-room log cabin near Pall Mall, Tennessee and departed this life September 2, 1964, known as the greatest soldier of his time and a believer in Christ as his Lord. The story of those seventy-six years, eight months and twenty days is one of the most illustrious narratives of world history. The Old Testament gives no battle account more charged with miraculous victory than the event that occurred October 8, 1918 in the Argonne Forest of France. Nevertheless, in the story of this tall mountaineer there is more to be considered than that one miraculous battle about which so much has been written. A careful look at this man, his family, his community and his faith is an insight into the source of the strength of the American nation these nearly two hundred years of her existence. We shall endeavor in this account to relate the famous historical victory of the Argonne battle and likewise to acknowledge an even greater victory accomplished in the heart of this unusual Christian patriot. He fully believed that there is a purpose in everything and that "Mysterious are the ways of the Lord, His wonders to perform."

A TRIBUTE TO MY FATHER

On September 2, 1964, at 10:40 p.m. in Veterans Hospital, Nashville, Tennessee, God called to heaven the most wonderful man I ever knew. He was my father, Sergeant Alvin C. York. As most people know, he was an international figure, known around the world. Yet, he never expressed in any way a feeling of importance, or felt that he had really done anything to bring him world-wide fame and recognition. He would always say, "I only did my duty to God and my country, and every man should do this."

When my father returned from France where he had fought for his country and religious freedom, he refused many offers from various industries which could have made him a millionaire. What he had received prior to his enlistment in the Army was not for sale. He had found something at an old-fashioned mourners' bench that money could not buy. This experience was real and lasting, and it had kept him through the war. In his own words he said, "When God saved me, I quit my drinking, smoking, chewing tobacco, and playing cards." Of course, this happened before he and my mother were married. None of the children ever knew anything from my dad and mother but fine Christian character.

Dad was a man who believed in and established a family altar in our home. Every night before retiring, Dad would get the family Bible and read from its pages the promises of God which gave courage and inspiration to all of us.

The earliest thing I can remember about my father was his teaching the Adult Sunday School Class at York Chapel. This was the Church of Christ in Christian Union at Pall Mall, Tennessee, that he had helped to build. It was in this same chapel in May, 1941 that I was converted and received my calling to the ministry.

I was privileged to attend various kinds of meetings and conventions with my father. At these gatherings he always found a place to insert a statement concerning the importance of the individual and the nation turning to God instead of to men to solve their problems.

All the members of our immediate family are not Christians at this time, but I trust and pray that the influence of Dad's life will live on in their mind and thinking. This was his desire.

I do not think of Dad as one who is dead or sleeping, but the bodily form we laid away in the cemetery was only the house he lived in. I think of him having a new body and a new life in the glorious presence of our wonderful Lord. While writing this tribute to my Dad, these are the words that filled my heart:

Dad, it seemed so hard to give you up,
That day you went away,
But just a little while and then,
We'll all be home to stay.

So true to God we'll try to be,
As you have done before,
And when the mists have rolled away,
We'll meet on Heaven's shore.

REV GEORGE E. YORK

SERGEANT ALVIN C. YORK

TO

OUR OWN

LEAGUE OF NATIONS

The American-born boys and the Greeks, Irish, Poles, Jews, and Italians who were in my platoon in the World War. A heap of them couldn't speak or write the American language until they larned it in the Army. Over here in the training camps and behind the lines in France a right-smart lot of them boozed, gambled, cussed, and went A. W. O. L. But once they got into it Over There they kept on a-going. They were only tol'able shots and burned up a most awful lot of ammunition. But jest the same they always kept on a-going. Most of them died like men, with their rifles and bayonets in their hands and their faces to the enemy. I'm a-thinkin' they were real heroes. Any way they were my buddies. I jes learned to love them.

—SERGEANT ALVIN C. YORK.

FOREWORD

My grandfather, Alvin C. York, was one of ten children born and raised in a rural area of Tennessee. He learned to shoot early in life and always had a rifle or pistol handy. He hunted and shot in matches on Saturdays with his father. Those experiences served him well when he faced an overwhelming enemy force in France's Argonne Forest on October 8th, 1918.

When the fight was over, he and seven others had captured 132 Germans (128 soldiers and four officers). The other seven had been pinned down behind cover by machine-gun fire from the surrounding high ground and were unable to assist him in the fight. At one point, a German officer and five men charged him with fixed bayonets. He had only a half of a clip left in his rifle, so he pulled his pistol—a .45 automatic—and shot them one by one. He worked his way up until he'd shot the last one, who was leading the charge.

For his actions, he was awarded the Medal of Honor, the French Croix de Guerre, and numerous other medals. He returned to a hero's welcome in the United States after spending several months in Europe waiting to go home. During this time, he attended the inaugural meeting of The American Legion as a representative of his unit, the 82nd "All-American" Division.

He received many lucrative offers, but he turned them down because he felt he would be selling his uniform and service overseas. He returned to the mountains of Tennessee to marry his sweetheart, Miss Gracie, and raise his family on a farm in the Wolf River Valley of Pall Mall.

Because of his travels, my grandfather treasured education, which he had not had the privilege of receiving as a child and young man. He devoted time and effort to building and running a high school, the York Agricultural Institute. He worked tirelessly for the children of Fentress County and to bring education to the rural area where he was raised. On two occasions, he mortgaged his own home to make sure the school stayed open. He knew that the world was a larger place than the mountains and that to be competitive the children of his area needed an education.

When asked, my grandfather said that he'd like to be remembered for his work in education. In the late 1930s, he was persuaded to allow a movie to be made about his life and war exploits, as the world was once again facing war and patriotism in the United States was low. He was told that this would help the United States, so he agreed as long as the film was kept factual and did not "Hollywoodize" his story. *Sergeant York*, starring Gary Cooper, was released in 1941.

At the start of World War II, York volunteered for duty with the Army. Due to his age and physical ability he did not see active duty, but was commissioned a colonel in the Signal Corps (for which he did not wear a uniform or receive pay) and traveled around the country selling war bonds. A stroke left him partially paralyzed until his death on September 2nd, 1964. He is buried in the family cemetery close to where he was born and raised.

His life's work and legacy live on through the York Historic State Park, the York Agricultural Institute, and the Sergeant York Patriotic Foundation. Their mission is "legacy in action" by promoting educational opportunities and honoring veterans. Through this work, my grandfather's story teaches the next generation about history and heroes. More than his actions on the battlefield, the man behind the medals makes Alvin York's legacy so intriguing.

—Gerald E. York, retired Army colonel

PREFACE

THIS is the story of Sergeant Alvin C. York of Tennessee, the outstanding hero of the World War and one of the greatest individual fighters in the history of modern or legendary warfare. In the heart of the Argonne Forest on October 8, 1918, practically unassisted, he whipped an entire German machine-gun battalion, killing twenty-eight of the enemy, capturing thirty-five machine guns and with the help of a handful of doughboys bringing in one hundred and thirty-two prisoners.

For this extraordinary feat of arms he was awarded the Congressional Medal of Honour, the French Legion of Honour, the Croix de Guerre with palms, the Médaille Militaire, the Italian War Cross and a number of other high Allied decorations. General Pershing eulogized him as "the outstanding civilian soldier of the war." And General Foche, in decorating him, said, "What you did was the greatest thing accomplished by any private soldier of all of the armies of Europe."

Returning to New York City in May, 1919, he was tendered the greatest reception ever accorded an American soldier of subordinate rank returning from war. A few days later in Washington, D. C., both houses of Congress welcomed him in a joint session and cheered him to the skies.

He was offered fortunes to go into the movies, on the stage, to write for the big newspaper syndicates, and to sign advertisements. But he firmly refused to commercialize his fame, and with the naïve comment, "Wouldn't I look funny in tights?" turned his back on the world and "jes lit out for the old log cabin in the mountains and the little old mother and them-there hound-dogs of mine and the life where I belong."

Sergeant York was not a professional soldier, nor a member of the Regular Army, nor even a volunteer. He was a drafted man. He went reluctantly and with misgivings. He bore no hatred toward the Germans; he did not want to kill them or anybody else. In camp there were insistent rumours that he was a conscientious objector. And in the archives of the War Department in Washington, D. C., there are letters and applications asking for his exemption from military service on the grounds that his religion was opposed to war and fighting.

He tells the story himself that "he was worried a-plenty as to whether it were right or wrong." For two days and a night he knelt out on the mountainside and prayed to God for guidance. "And I received my assurance. I received it from God that it were all right, that I would go and that I would come back unharmed." And he scarcely ever doubted. He never once lost his simple faith, not even when the thirty-five machine guns were blazing almost certain death right into his face. He told his mother not to worry, that he was coming back all right. He told the same to his brothers and sisters, and to his friends. He wrote it in his diary. His faith was as immovable as the mountains of his native Tennessee.

He was born of good pioneer stock in a one-room log cabin in the mountains of Tennessee, off the railroad line. He was one of a family of eleven children, eight boys and three girls, all of them husky and strong and most of them freckle-faced and red-headed. One of his characteristic sayings is, "You may find a red-headed man in a penitentiary but you will never find one in an insane asylum."

He is the biggest of the York family. He stands over six feet in his woollen socks, weighs more than two hundred pounds, and is raw-boned, red-headed, and freckle-faced. He has never been whipped or knocked off his feet in his life and has the reputation in the mountains of being one of the deadliest shots that ever squinted down the long barrel of a muzzle loader and busted the head of a wild turkey or picked a squirrel off a distant tree. He has eyes of blue-gray; sky-blue and gun-metal gray; eyes, which pin-point when they look at you and seem to see through sham and make-believe. Withal, eyes which beam in the presence of little children.

Broad-shouldered, stout-chested, deep-dugged, thewed and muscled like an ox—a mountain of a man, York of Tennessee. And like the mountain he has his feet on the earth and his head in the stars. And like the mountain again he has emerged through cloud and storm to learn patience and "the peace which passeth all understanding."

In his youth he "went bad." He gambled, guzzled moonshine, cussed, and tore up things. This did not last long. Realizing he was missing the finer things, he gave up dissipating completely and forever. Since 1915 he has never tasted liquor, smoked, chewed, gambled, cussed, or even lost his temper. Again to quote him: "I am a great deal like Paul—the things I once loved, I now hate."

Before the war he "went religious" and was known in the mountains as the "Singing Elder."

He finished school with the equivalent of a second-grade education. It is doubtful whether he could have passed the second grade. He is not educated "in the larnin' that comes out of books." But he is a man of keen native intelligence.

He has turned his back on the outside world and is dedicating his life to the education of boys and girls in the mountains. He is building an agricultural institute in the heart of the mountains and off the railroad. He is planning to bring "a heap of larnin'" to his own people.

His is probably the most dramatic human story that has come out of the World War. It is one of the most significant spiritual documents in the world to-day. It has the stir and the sweep of an American epic.

Both Sergeant York and I feel it would not be right to end this preface without acknowledging our indebtedness to the officers of the War Department in Washington, D. C., and to Col. George E. Buxton, junior, of Rhode Island (official historian of the 82d Division), for their co-operation and permission to examine and publish many of the official "York documents."

We also wish to thank Mr. Maurice G. Hindus of New York City for his help in examining the documents and going over and checking the story.

TOM SKEYHILL.

Jamestown, Tenn.
1928

CHAPTER I

THE YORK COUNTRY

I FIRST saw Sergeant Alvin C. York in New York City the day he returned from France in the spring of 1919. What a day it was! What joy, what frenzy, what abandon had seized on the most hard-boiled city in the world! It seemed as if the floodgates of men's very souls had burst apart and all the pent-up passion of centuries had stormed forth in a mighty surge. Mobs everywhere, with banners, bands, bells, whistles, singing, screaming, clanging, whistling, and in every other way acclaiming the big hero of the day. Everybody's hero, everywhere. Ticker tape in endless waves streamed down from the tall buildings and flaked the streets until it seemed as though a blizzard had swept over them. The Sergeant himself, in commenting on this scene, or rather siege, or rapture, remarked: "There was a right smart crowd of people out and it seemed as though most of them knowed me."

Of course they "knowed him." How could they help it? They had read and heard so much of him. For weeks newspapers had printed endless stories of his extraordinary feat in the Argonne Forest. Marshal Foche and General Pershing had officially mentioned it in their dispatches. The returning doughboys guaranteed that it was true, every word of it, and there were the medals and other decorations on his chest for all the world to see.

More stories had poured forth of his exotic mountain background, his deadly skill with rifle and pistol, his amazing knowledge of woodcraft, his tender solicitude for the American wounded during the battle in the Argonne, his chivalrous treatment of the German prisoners, his great piety, and, most unbelievable of all, his having originally been a conscientious objector! Certainly a dramatic personality, fitting magnificently the scene and the spirit of the day.

I was one of the thousands that stormed the streets of the city. A returned wounded soldier myself, I felt poignantly the meaning of this uproarious welcome, its joy, and, almost as much, its undercurrent of sadness. I knew machine guns. I knew the staccato bark, the spitting yellow flame, the swish of bullets, and the double-distilled hell they sowed wherever they fell. I knew that they fired six hundred shots a minute in a steady stream like water from a hose. I knew that a skilled machine gunner could cut his initials on a sandbag. And I knew that German machine gunners shot straight. Again and again I had seen squads, platoons, and whole companies charge them and go down like ripe corn before the reaper's blade. And this big, gangling mountaineer had whipped a whole battalion of them!

At first I was sceptical. Who was not? It sounded too much like a fairy tale. It just could not be done. It was not human. Yet it was done. Therefore, it could be done and it was human. It was one of the best documented stories of the war. Appreciating that it was an almost unbelievable feat, the officers of his division very wisely lost no time in checking up and verifying it beyond the slightest shadow of a doubt. They carefully examined and took the affidavits of the surviving doughboys who were with York, but who, according to their own statements, took little or no part in the actual fight with the machine guns. They re-visited the battlefield and checked up the account of the battle the following morning and again after the armistice. Their report was thorough and convincing:

> The story has been carefully checked in every possible detail from headquarters of this division and is entirely substantiated. Sergeant York's own statement tends to underestimate the desperate odds which he overcame.

And there was the Medal of Honour awarded by a special act of Congress. No wonder that New York, after one glimpse of this sturdy and freckle-faced mountaineer with his flaming red hair, went wild with ecstasy.

The following morning I chuckled when I read in the newspapers that "he weren't a-going to commercialize his fame nohow. He weren't a-going on the stage or in the movies, but he sure would like a ride in the subways." It was the language of the mountaineer and the soldier, direct and decisive, and also of the boy, eager to play and see the wonder works of the world.

More than ten years have fled by since then. The

world has returned to its normal every-day tasks. Diplomats have resumed the old job of writing polite peace notes to each other and building armies, too, and new machines of war, the mightiest the world has yet known. Meanwhile, Sergeant York has slipped back to "the little old log cabin in the mountains and them-thar hound dogs of mine and the life whar I belong." Now and then there would be brief mention of him in some newspaper—of a lecture he had given in this and that city, of his interest in building schools and roads in the mountain country, and of his efforts to lead his people to some of the finer things in life. Once in a while someone would retell in a magazine the story of his Argonne fight. But that was all. Even his famous war diary, of which much had been written, had not, save for occasional excerpts, been put into print. The man himself had remained a mystery, possibly because he had already become a legend.

In the spring of 1927, while driving through Tennessee, I resolved to swing into the mountains to visit York in his own home. I wanted to see him in his mountain setting "in that-thar country whar I belong." I wanted to know how he was faring in his seclusion "far from the madding crowd," that had once so worshipfully acclaimed him. I wanted to get the feel of the man, the soldier, the mountaineer, the hunter, the preacher, the American. I had no thought at that time of writing with him his story. I just wanted to satisfy a personal urge, so deep-stirring that it had been part of me since that memorable day when I saw him in New York on his return from France.

On inquiry I learned that Sergeant York was living in Pall Mall, Fentress County, Tenn., in the heart of the Cumberland country. The town, if it may be so called, is off the railroad in the northeast part of the state, not far from the Kentucky line. Thither I went, and what a journey it was! What a road I had to traverse! Now it was a narrow ledge, dizzily skirting precipitous cliffs; now in the valleys, the bottom seemed to drop right out of it. It did everything a decent, civilized road should not do. It flitted up and down the mountain in unbelievable jerks and jumps. It led up creek beds. It forded streams. It most dexterously dodged stumps and boulders, with falling timber and landslides thrown in for added thrills. It was a primitive, barbarous road.

The country around was likewise primitive, but haunting in its picturesqueness, with second-growth timber and rock-ribbed fields. Scarcely a white man's country, certainly not a country of civilized humanity. It used to be the "Happy Hunting Ground" of the Creeks and Cherokees. Once it had abounded in bear, deer, and buffalo. The older mountaineers still regale each other with stories of Daniel Boone leaping on the backs of buffaloes and bringing them down with his bowie knife, and of Davy Crockett shooting more than one hundred "baar" in one season. But when the white settlers, Scotch-Irish, borderers, Covenanters, Cavaliers invaded the country, they whipped the Indians, slaughtered the big game and hewed down the forests. Now the Indian is banished from the scene. Big game is almost a memory only and timber is largely of second growth. But it is thick again, and rolls over the mountains in endless swells like ocean waves in a storm. It is really wondrous country! Sky. Pine. Rocks. Air that chills and buoys. Vista on vista of blue mountain peaks. Valleys shot with gold. Water everywhere, cool, clear, gurgling right out of the mountainside. Rhododendron bells. Laurel blooms. Redbud and wild dogwood blossoms, a profusion of both, and an endless variety of mountain flowers—a country to delight and thrill the seeker of adventure.

And still but sparsely populated. There were miles without a sign or sight of a human being. Now and then I would pass a cabin built of logs, with a flat roof and small windows, sometimes with broken panes or no panes at all, with a piece of cloth spread over the frame. Nowhere even a dab of paint. Nowhere a touch of brightness, save only what Nature in its bountifulness has provided. Dreary cabins, housing some of the poorest people in the country and the least enlightened. In the valleys there were groups of cabins, small, oft dilapidated, with withered shingles on the roofs, battered porches, sagging windows, sometimes twisted out of shape like the eyes of a cross-eyed man. Occasionally I would see a mountaineer toting a gun, rangy and raw-boned, with shoes twisted from wear, and a couple of hounds loping along behind. He would proffer the usual "howdy" and shuffle on. Once, right in the heart of the forest, I saw a man working in a field with a scooter plough which is all wood but the tiny point, and a woman stooping over a steaming black wash-kettle in a yard. I understood then why it was that Sergeant York had been seeking to bring schools to his people.

I drove on. Again woods, sky, rocks, enlivened with patches of riotous-hued flowers. The whine and rip of a sawmill, the clanging thud of the woodsman's axe, the crash of a falling tree rose now and then with reverberating echoes over the mountainside. Once I passed a logger's camp. Occasionally on a hillside or in a valley there would be patches of corn for hogs and cattle, and even more perhaps for moonshine, which is more profitable. It is not uncommon in the mountains for some wit to ask you when you call to buy corn whether you want it in a sack or in a jar. Tennessee "moon" is potent, overproof, and so clear, they say, that one can read the Constitution of the United States right through a gallon jar. Moonshining is still regarded, especially by the older folk, as a feudal right. The mountaineer insists that "hit ain't agin the Government nohow." Revenue men, like rattlers, and there are plenty of both, are not very popular in the mountains.

But conditions are changing. Improved roads, automobiles, and better organization work permit the Federal officers to penetrate deeper and deeper into the mountains, and with greater safety. Occasionally there is a fight, but only occasionally. The mountaineers have learned that it is bad business to shoot up Uncle Sam's men. They usually follow along without much fuss or bluster, or else "light out into the timber" where the Government agent, unless experienced in the ways of the woods, soon loses his trail. Meanwhile, a

younger and more enlightened generation is growing
up. In time "rev-killing" and feuds will fade into the
memory of a picturesque, if lawless past.

At last I came on an expanse of flat country. It was
the edge of the Cumberland Plateau, and, though I
knew I was up high, mountains were nowhere in sight.
A few miles farther I was in Jamestown, the county
seat of Fentress County, York's county. "Jimtown,"
it is called, and "hit is on top of the mountain." It
has a population of about twelve hundred and boasts
of an old courthouse right in the centre of the square,
a frame school house, post office, pool hall, several
stores, a prairie-schooner mail cart, and a weekly newspaper. Save for the York Highway, which runs
through the centre of the town, the streets are un-
paved, and what streets!—sand and rock, turf and
mud, ruts and hollows in which the water never seems
to dry out, and the sidewalks, when there are any,
are of split and rotted boards, with rusty nails sticking
up, tripping pedestrians and scratching up their shoes.

It is an unkempt, straggly town, with no sense of
style or even comfort. Cows browse in the side streets,
and so do pigs. Débris is never swept away except by
the wind. It is an old town, and it looks its age. It is
still dreaming of the Civil War and reliving memories
of bushwhackers, moonshiners, Indian fights, big hunts,
and other boisterous incidents of the frontier days. A
traveller passing through the town in 1893 wrote: "It
is one of the oldest towns in the state, and until the
last twelve months was also generally regarded by the
outside world as the deadest. It is said that for the

past sixty years the sound of the hammer or saw has not been heard there, and not a single nail has been driven into any new building."

The main show place, in a historical sense, is the hotel. It stands on the site of the old home of Mark Twain's parents. Jamestown, incidentally, is Obed's Town in *The Gilded Age*. The famous Tennessee Land Grant lies close by. Alvin C. York lives on a section of it. Mark's father, Mr. John M. Clemens, was a practising attorney in Fentress County, and was its first circuit court clerk. Mark himself was not born in Jamestown, his parents having left for Missouri a few months before he came into the world. In *The Gilded Age*, however, he gives the following description of the town:

"The locality was Obed's Town, eastern Tennessee. You would not know that Obed's Town stood on the top of a mountain for there was nothing about the landscape to indicate it—but it did. A mountain that stretched abroad over whole counties and rose very gradually. The district was called the Knobs of Eastern Tennessee, and had the reputation, like Nazareth, as far as turning out any good thing was concerned."

Still, the town is beginning slowly to stir into a new life. Only two years ago after a rain it was cut off from the world by rivers of mud. The few roads there were "begun and ended nowhere," as one of its citizens put it. But now, though still without a motion-picture house or dance hall, good roads are being built to the outlying world. Automobiles and radios are bringing it into closer touch with outside humanity, and the younger generation is beginning to learn something about college. There are indications that Jamestown is on the eve of big things and may yet play a dramatic part in the modernization of eastern Tennessee. To a very large extent, Sergeant Alvin C. York is responsible for this budding renaissance. He certainly is rubbing the sleep out of the town's eyes and shaking the life out of it, or, more properly, into it.

I stopped at a town restaurant, Suva's Restaurant, known far and wide for its culinary excellence. The usual unofficial court was in session there. Town folk, lumberjacks, mountaineers, in overalls, blue jeans, and ordinary street clothes, were gossiping with animation and were passing judgment on men and events. They all "knowed the Sergeant," or Alvin, as they call him. He lived nine miles away in Pall Mall, "right under the mountain"; that is, in the valley below. They hadn't "seed him around nowhere," but they guessed he was on the farm. Suva, large and radiant, with sparkling eyes, was York's most enthusiastic supporter of them all. It was she who directed me to the Sergeant's office across the street.

I clambered up the rough cement steps in the back of the bank building, traversed a dingy corridor, and entered a small furnished room where I met the Sergeant's secretary and his right-hand man, Mr. A. S. Bushing. Hailing from Brooklyn, Bushing had wandered into the mountain region, fallen in love with a native girl, and married her. For several years he had been a cashier in the bank, and it was there that he came to know the Sergeant. From the first he developed into an ardent champion of his person and his cause. In fact, he threw in his lot with the Sergeant, and by that I mean his time, his savings, everything. He never has wavered in his devotion to the big mountaineer, not even when sinister and powerful forces in the mountains held over him the threat of ruin and bankruptcy. No story of Sergeant Alvin C. York would be complete without the mention of this wiry little Northerner, whose official title is private secretary to Alvin C. York, but who is really one of the Sergeant's most intimate friends and most loyal champions in and outside of the mountains.

The Sergeant, Bushing informed me, had left that very morning for Florida. That was a grievous disappointment to me, especially as I had made this tortuous trip of nearly two hundred miles through the mountains on purpose to meet him. But Bushing's hospitality made up in part for the disappointment. The first thing he spoke of was the school. He offered to take me out and show me the site selected for it. It was evident that the school had already become as much a part of the Sergeant's story as his fight in the Argonne or the blue mountains amidst which he was reared.

We motored out along the highway, the very one on which York had at one time toiled as a labourer for one dollar and sixty cents a day, and which when completed was named in his honour. The school site stretched for a mile along this road, right outside of the town on the way to Pall Mall. No wonder the Sergeant insists that, "hit is going up right here." It is situated in the very heart of a clump of stately evergreens. It is to be a mountain school in a mountain setting for mountain boys and girls. It is to be the achievement of the life work of the big, red-headed, semi-literate mountaineer who faced all alone thirty-five blazing machine guns and "jes' teched them off" and then returned home, the greatest of all heroes of the greatest of all wars.

Bushing and I sat down under an inviting tree and talked and talked. He narrated to me the story of the big fellow's fight to build his school and to bring "a heap of larnin' " to the boys and girls he loved and who loved him; a fight to overcome suspicion, jealousies, petty politics, and small-town intrigue, a fight which, to quote the Sergeant, "was much more terrible than the battle in the Argonne," and in which he "couldn't use the old service rifle or the Colt automatic pistol nohow." But then, it ended well, for the present at least. The testimony of victory, mute but eloquent, lay before our very eyes—heaps of bricks, stone, lumber, all to go into the structure that is to be the fulfilment of a great dream. The small gang of misguided but powerful politicians, realtors, and county officials, bent on exploiting the cause of the school for purely personal benefits, has been completely routed, and the school is to be built "where and how hit ought to be, where the boys and girls want hit to be built, and where hit is a-going to be."

CHAPTER II

THE HOUSE OF YORK

SEVERAL months later, after an exchange of letters with Sergeant York, I received an invitation from him to come to the mountains again and be his guest for a few weeks. "Come right on down here," he wrote, "and I'm a-telling you we will show you what mountain hospitality is like."

This time, with memories of my first trip still fresh in my mind, I travelled by rail as far as I could—it was more restful for the nerves anyway. At Oneida, Tenn., I boarded the little logging train that runs into the Cumberlands. We literally crawled through the mountains, along precipitous ledges, across swaying trestle bridges, stopping every few miles to switch flats and box cars. The only passenger car was the caboose and there I sat with lumberjacks, surveyors, mountaineers, amidst heaps of mail sacks and parcels. The brakeman knew the passengers and the mountain people that turned out to meet the train. All of them knew Alvin York and the work he was doing, and all of them spoke of him with an esteem that bordered on reverence.

At the little station of Louvaine I was met by Bushing, and we drove together under the mountain to Pall Mall, the Sergeant's home down in Wolf Valley. A

magnificent valley it is, this dimple in the Cumberlands, with broad flat lands, towering rocks, and clus-
ters of woods, and threaded with creeks and springs.
Corn glistened in the sunlight; somewhere far away
hounds bayed, following apparently some scent in the
woods. In the near-by fields razorbacks were grunting
merrily and rooting for acorns.

It was Sunday, and the Sergeant was at church so
we drove there. We parked our automobile just off
the York Highway and, making our way through
mules, horses, flivvers, buggies, we entered the little
wooden structure that is the Sergeant's church.

Once inside we were face to face with a scene that
seemed to have crawled bodily out of a fairy story
by Hans Christian Andersen. The church was crowded
with boys and girls, tots all, sitting on hard benches
around the stove. In the centre, reading from the
Bible was the huge Sergeant. He had grown somewhat fuller of body since the day I had seen him in
New York. Little wrinkles had already begun to
make inroads into his face just under the eyes, and
traces of gray had begun to show in his hair.

I had often speculated as to what my first impression
of him would be after this lapse of years. I had pic-
tured him, of course, as a hunter, a woodsman, a dead
shot, a preacher on the mountainside, but somehow I
never had thought of him in the rôle of a guide to
children. He seemed too big, too strong, too severe,
too much of the fighter and the killer to fit such a rôle.
Yet, here he was in the midst of them, smiling and
quiet-voiced, with a radiance in his eyes. The eyes of

the children were on him. They followed his every movement. Around the little school he went, bending low over each little boy or girl and whispering in their ears a passage from the morning lesson, after which he called on them to read the passage aloud. When they faltered he smiled and helped them out.

Bushing and I slipped into a seat in the rear. We thought we were unobserved, but we were in error. Those blue-gray eyes saw us, pin-pointed at us, as is the wont of the Sergeant when he looks at people closely, and smiled a welcome. Then he introduced us to his Sunday-school class, and to our discomfort, especially to mine, asked us to recite from memory a passage from Isaiah. This, I suppose, he did to impress the children with the versatile knowledge of the Bible that grown-up Christians possessed. A pause followed. Neither Bushing nor I responded. It was a long time since I had peeped into the words of this ancient Hebrew prophet. I began to look around for the nearest exit, but the Sergeant's eyes were on me, and I knew there would be no escape. He repeated his invitation. Bushing acquitted himself with glory, and I stammered along and tried to bluff it out, but there was no bluffing the Sergeant. He looked at me as steadily as though he were squinting down the long barrel of a muzzle-loader, and when he realized my helplessness he rolled back his head and chuckled his inimitable "Ho! ho!" Then we sang a few hymns, the Sergeant leading and his own mellow tenor voice rising above the others. Now I understood why it was that he was known in the mountains as the Singing Elder.

At the conclusion of the service we strolled out to the highway, the children following on the heels of the Sergeant. He held one little boy in his arms, another was clinging to his hand, and the rest, laughing and shouting, trailed merrily behind. He looked for all the world like a modern Pied Piper of Hameln playing his pipes to another tune. At his automobile he told us that he could do little for the older people, for they were too set in their ways and beliefs, but he was sure he could lead the little ones toward a more enlightened future.

Then I left the Sergeant and went for dinner with Pastor Pile. A unique character this pastor is, known over the countryside as Rosier Pile. Farmer, storekeeper, hunter, he is of the earth, earthy, yet spiritual enough to have organized a parish in the valley of the Wolf and to have built a church there, the Church of Christ in Christian Union, said to be the only one of this denomination in the entire state of Tennessee. A handsome man he is, rather thick-set, with gray hair, keen eyes, and patrician features. He would grace the pulpit of any church. He is an extraordinary conversationalist, and his faith, like the Sergeant's, is the faith that moveth mountains. At first he was opposed to Alvin, as he calls the Sergeant, going to war. It was he who had sent affidavits to the county draft board and had written a personal letter to President Wilson seeking the Sergeant's release from military service. Alvin's going to war had brought him face to face with the greatest spiritual conflict in his life. He fought desperately to remain true to his faith.

But once the big fellow had definitely resolved to go, the gray-haired pastor of the Church of Christ in Christian Union "bowed to the will of God." He never ceased to pray for the safety of his soldier friend. He prayed in his little store, in his home, in the field, and of course in the church. To-day, as ever, Sergeant York has no more staunch supporter than this quiet-voiced preacher in the mountains.

We visited the cave or rock house under the mountains where Sergeant York's great-great-grandfather had originally lived, and where the Sergeant himself had once blacksmithed. We called in the little log cabin where the Yorks had so long been living. We passed the tree where Alvin and Gracie held their love trysts, and where they were later married by the Governor of Tennessee, in the presence of thousands of mountain people.

Then we walked to Pile's home and sat down to dinner. A sumptuous meal it was of beef, pork, chicken, beets, sweet potatoes, turnips, lettuce, homemade pie, and freshly drawn spring water from the mountains. While we ate Pile talked at length of Alvin's early days, of his "going bad and his being saved," of his church work before the war, of how he became known as a singing elder, and of his uncanny skill with rifle and pistol.

After dinner the pastor said grace and then we walked out on the porch. He took down his muzzle-loader, or "hog rifle," as he called it, and proceeded to tell us of his hunting trips, and of how he busted the heads of wild turkeys. Here they were then, the Bible and the musket, the hunter and the evangelist, so typical of the mountains.

I bade the gracious pastor good-bye and his son, a college student in Knoxville, drove me over to Sergeant York's home. The Sergeant lives on the big farm which the Rotary Club of his native state purchased for him. He himself built his house, a square two-story frame building with large windows, a spacious porch, and two gigantic fireplaces—a solid, comfortable dwelling place almost on the edge of Wolf River and within hearing distance of the roar of the mill dam.

As it was Sunday, the whole family had gathered together. Mother York was sitting before the blazing chunks in the open fireplace. She's an old woman, with a thin face that is criss-crossed from forehead to chin with deep lines. But her voice is firm and resonant as that of a person in full possession of physical powers. She wore an old bonnet and a plain calico dress with a blue checked gingham apron. Old as she was, she didn't seem to have outlived her mountain shyness in the presence of strangers. She spoke little and only when spoken to and always with a laconic directness. "I ain't hed much larnin'," she once remarked, "but I raised up a family of eight boys and three girls in a one-room log cabin and they's all eleven living. And that teaches you something about life."

She is a woman of few illusions. Fame and glory mean nothing to her. Love and faith and manhood and womanhood in the old-fashioned fundamental sense of the word she prizes above all else on earth. She cares not for the outside world at all. She has been in the city only once in her whole life, and that was in Nashville when her son, on his return from the front, was tendered an historic reception in the capitol of his native state. When she went to the city she wore the same clothes that she wears in the mountains—a split bonnet, a long dress, and the inevitable gingham apron. She would not even entertain the suggestion that she displace the bonnet with a hat and the sombre-coloured, old-fashioned dress with one that would have at least a semblance of modern style. She "wouldn't feel natcheral nohow in city clothes," and she "warn't a-going to change for nobody."

At that historic reception thousands of people crowded around her to shake her hand, but she was neither bewildered nor even impressed. She was pleased, of course, at the recognition accorded her, but her chief wish was to hurry back to the mountains.

She is proud of her soldier son, proud of his great war record, but proudest of all of his wholesome family life, his clean manhood, and his sterling spiritual qualities. She is especially pleased with the courage and the hardihood he showed when he resisted all attempts to draw him into the whirl of worldly life through the allurement of money and glory.

All of the Yorks were in the house, all tall, sturdy, somewhat unkempt, and five of them as red-haired and even more freckle-faced than the Sergeant. They, too, were extremely shy. In fact, they hardly said a word save the usual "howdy" when I was introduced to them. They just stood or sat around and listened, with mask-like expressions, betraying not an inkling of their real thoughts and feelings. Several times I turned and addressed them, but their replies were always brief, sometimes consisting of only the words "I reckon."

In the rear of the room sat the Sergeant's sister Lily, likewise red-headed and freckle-faced, with magnificent teeth and sparkling blue eyes. She was as reticent as her brothers. Not a word did she speak throughout the evening, though she listened with keen intentness to all that was being said in the house and now and then joined in a laugh.

Then there was Gracie, the tall, blue-eyed mountain girl whom the Sergeant married. Her luxurious mass of soft brown hair was done into two huge braids lifted to the ears and each fastened with a blue cotton string. Though she had given birth to four children, she had not lost her girlish glow or even her girlish ways. If anything, she was even more shy than the others, this despite her many contacts with the big outside world since her marriage to the famous Sergeant.

The four children were there, too, all sons, and all named for historic characters. Sam Houston, Woodrow Wilson, George Edwin Buxton, named for York's major (now Colonel Buxton, of Providence, R. I.), and Alvin, Jr.

The Sergeant himself by his sheer size seemed to overshadow all the other members of the House of York. He's the largest of the sons. He stands over six feet in his socks. He is easily the outstanding personality in the House of York. He would have been that without his war record, if only for his colourful career in the mountains prior to the war. He was clean-shaven, with a neatly trimmed moustache, as red as the hair on his head, and with the flush of a healthy child in his full cheeks. As he advanced to greet me, I noticed for the first time that he walks with a firm tread, bearing down with all his weight, first on the heels, and taking long measured strides as of a man accustomed to mountain climbing. So individual is this gait of his that it is easy to recognize him from a distance just by seeing him walk. Through contacts with men of the world he has acquired a certain outward fineness, almost polish, without, however, losing his mountain manner. He is slow of movement, but not awkward. He dresses well on occasions. Indeed, in a suit of gray tweeds he looks very much like an English country squire. He converses well, too, once he has overcome his shyness. He has not lost it all yet, despite his travels and his associations with strangers. Indeed, on first acquaintance he is almost as reticent as his brothers. He has to be led in conversation, but when he warms up to a subject his mountain reserve leaves him. He never argues in conversation, which doesn't at all mean that he agrees with everything the speaker says. It is just a way of his, and it baffles strangers, often making them think that he is either not interested or does not understand.

Here then they were, children of the House of York, three generations of them under one roof, and now for the first time in their lives in a real house, with a delco light plant furnishing modern illumination, with a little organ of their own on which to play accompaniments to hymns, and with several shelves of books. Shy, almost self-effacing, they withdrew as if by common consent into the background, allowing only the Sergeant to do the honours to the guest.

The fire blazed on the open hearth. One of the Sergeant's brothers carried in a fresh chunk, and it immediately began to smoke and then burst into a bluish flame. The Sergeant and I moved close to the fire, and we both talked away with much gusto. Not of the war—not yet—not of his dreams for the future—but of life and men and nature and rifles and dogs and hunting and children. When chore time came his brothers slipped unnoticed out of the house, and the Sergeant and I continued talking until long after dusk had settled over the valley. He invited me to stay around the country for several weeks so as "to git acquainted." He would show me around, tramp me through the woods with "them-thar hound-dogs of mine," take me out bee-hiving way up there on "Peevy Mountain" overlooking his farm, and perhaps arrange a shooting match in his own woods so that I could see the hill billies come together "with them-thar hog rifles of theirs and do some real shooting, busting turkeys' heads."

Of course, I accepted the invitation. I had to go back to Jamestown, and so late in the evening I bade the Sergeant farewell and left, he agreeing to meet me in the morning. It was a quiet night. Not

a breath of wind. Not a stir in the trees. The
mountains blurred and blended in the sky. The mill
dam back of the Sergeant's house roared in a ceaseless
monotone. Cow bells tinkled continuously, sometimes
in the valley and sometimes far, far away in the mountains. Dogs barked. Otherwise, all was quiet in the
Valley of the Three Forks of the Wolf, where lives
the most celebrated American soldier of the World
War.

CHAPTER III

THE STORY OF THE STORY

EARLY the following morning I met the Sergeant again in the office of the York Agricultural Institute. As if moved by common impulse, we plunged headlong into reminiscing of old days at the front. We yarned about camp days, rout marches, dugouts, fox holes, trenches, gas attacks, bayonet charges. In short, we were re-living and re-fighting the stirring days of the war.

The next time we met we did the same thing. We had now become "buddies" and told each other everything about ourselves. This we did again and again, now at his office, now at Suva's Restaurant, with pork and beef and cornbread and vegetables piled high in stacks before us, now tramping over the hills and woods, and now in front of the open fireplace in his home on the farm, with wise old Mother York and Gracie and some of his sturdy brothers around. The more I heard of his early life the more was I intrigued to learn more and more. The Sergeant willingly enough responded to all questions. He unravelled for me the story of his early days in the mountains, his love of shooting and hunting, his "bad days," his "being saved," his struggle with doubt when he was summoned to war, his training days in Camp Gordon, in Georgia, his "buddies" in the Eighty-second Division, his constant prayers in camps and at the front. The only episode he was always loathe to discuss was the Argonne fight. Whenever I would broach the subject he would dismiss it with a few abrupt phrases and pass on to some other topic. Not that it weighed heavily on his conscience. Most manifestly it did not, or rather, it does not. He is convinced that the hand of God was in it. Still, it is a story of killings and he prefers not to have memories of it stirred up in his mind. But he did speak, and always with animation, of his plans for the future, his dreams of good roads and schools in the mountains.

It was then that I suggested to him that the story of his life be written for publication. But he only shook his head. He would not hear of it. When he returned from France he was offered a huge sum of money for just such a story written by himself. But he had resolved not to "commercialize nohow," and turned down the offer without a moment's hesitation. At one time during his fight with local politicians for his new school he was so hard-pressed for funds that he was willing to have his war diary printed. But the diary was short and the publishers wanted him to build the story of his life around it, so as to make it a book of appropriate size. At first he agreed to do it. But on reflection he changed his mind. He would not lay himself open to the criticism of attempting to exploit for personal advantage his war prestige. However, I pressed the matter with vigour again and again. But of no avail. He was firm in his decision not to write his life story. He had no objection to my writing it myself. But he would have no hand in it. It could not be his story "nohow."

Once I asked to see his war diary. At first he refused. Only twice had he taken it out of the vault in the bank in which he has kept it since his return from the war, and that was to please two journalists who were determined to read it. However, he had them promise that they would not publish any of it, and when they did he was grieved. He was determined to keep it under lock and key until he was dead, so that his children could have it as a record of his war experiences. Not even Bushing, his closest friend, had ever read it. So, when I asked to see it, he just smiled and politely shook his head.

I had almost given up hope of seeing it when one morning he asked me in a way so jovial that I wondered if he was in earnest, whether I still cared to read his war diary. Of course I did, I told him. And to my unexpected joy he went out and came back with it. I was curious to know how he had managed to keep a diary, knowing only too well that the war authorities sternly forbade men indulging in such practices, and this was his explanation:

"Well, I kept a little notebook in America jes to remind me of places I had been. When I got to France I bought one of them little black French notebooks. I carried this little diary in my pocket. Every night I put down what happened. I wrote in it in camp, on the ships and in the fox holes and trenches

at the front. I wrote in it every night. Of course I
knowed no soldier in the American army was per-
mitted to keep a diary. It was against the rules and
anyone caught carrying it with him was subject to be
court-martialled. Because the carrying of the diary,
telling places you had been, what happened, and what
outfit you belonged to, if you happened to be captured,
would give such information to the Germans as we
did not want them to have. The Captain, when the
company was lined up, he would ask if any man in the
company had a diary. He was Captain Danforth of
Augusta, Ga. And one day he asked me if I was keeping a diary. And I told him I was not admitting
whether I was or weren't. And he told me it would
betray a lot of valuable information to the Germans
if I was captured. And I told him that I was not
figuring on being captured. That I didn't come to the
war to be captured. That I wasn't going to be captured nohow. And that if the Germans ever got any
information out of me they would have to get it out
of my dead body. And so the Captain kept a-going.
And I kept my diary."

After reading it I was more firmly determined than
ever to have him build the story of his life around
it so as to make it not only a record of his war experiences, but a picture of the life and culture and struggles
and hopes of the sturdy mountain folk from which
he springs.

Now I knew that he was in financial distress. He
had had some unfortunate setbacks on the farm. His
barn had burned, for one thing. He had told me all

that. He was also continually helping out his family and his plans for social improvements in the mountains could swallow many thousands of dollars. But I knew that money would not tempt him. It never had. He is a man of rigid principles and can be induced to accede to a demand or to embark on an action only if it is grounded in a principle in which he believes heart and soul.

So I appealed to his patriotism. The people, I argued, were entitled to know the facts of his stirring life. They had honoured him as they had few war heroes during their history, and in a way it was really his duty to draw them into his confidence and share with them the story of his whole life from his earliest days in a log cabin. His only reply to my pleas was: "I guess I'll jes keep it all for the children."

However, I persisted in my arguments. I pointed out to him that he could best draw attention to his school by drawing attention to himself, and this he could do best by having his story published. He admitted that he "shure would like to get the school known, but——" He was silent and sat dreamily looking out at the blue horizon. I continued the offensive. I knew he was primarily interested in boys and girls. His school was for them. His whole life he would dedicate to helping them. Very well then. His story would surely be an inspiration to them. He was now all attention. He always is when the subject of boys and girls is mentioned to him. He smiled, threw back his head, and laughed his good-natured "Ho! ho!"

He said he would think it over. He did. He kept
thinking it over, and he was a slow thinker. Most
mountain people are, except when they are face to face
with a crisis, and then their minds leap like lightning.
There's no use trying to hurry them. They have
their own way of deciding matters. However, once
they come to a decision they're for it with all the
verve at their command.

About a week later he came to me and declared
that he guessed it would be all right. He placed the
diary and the autobiography which he had begun
writing and all of his private letters at my disposal.
He dictated to me day after day. He gave me a
letter to the War Department, asking them to give me
access to his official records. "If you're going to do
it," he explained, "you might's well know everything."
Later he added, "Jes tell the truth, the whole truth,
and let it go at that."

I knew that such a story would have to be amply
documented with statements and affidavits from the
survivors of the fight in the Argonne Forest, and the
official records in the archives of the War Department in Washington. It was easy to find Major
Buxton, the first commander of York's battalion. He
had written an official record of the Eighty-second
Division and York had been in correspondence with
him since the end of the war. But how to locate the
other men, especially those who had been in the Argonne with York, was a perplexing problem. The
Sergeant himself did not know where they were, nor
even whether they were all alive.

We proceeded to search for them. We managed
to locate Sergeant Harry Parsons, at Hollis, L. I.
He had been in charge of York's platoon. And it
was he who had issued the famous order hurling
the eighteen doughboys against the German machine
guns. Of course, he remembered the occasion vividly
enough, and gladly submitted an affidavit covering all
of his knowledge of the fight. Parsons, a huge, mus-
cular son of Ireland, with flashing dark eyes and a
heavy mop of wavy, dark hair, had been a vaudeville
artist before the war, and after the armistice was
well known in France as the producer of one of the
most successful "soldier" shows. On his release from
service in 1919 he returned to the footlights. But
not for long. He had lost his power of amusing audi-
ences. He had left his laugh in the Argonne.

He became so interested in the project of this book
that he volunteered to help us search out the other
men we needed to make the record complete.
Through the Veterans Bureau we located Corporal
Bernard Early, in New Haven, Conn., where he
operates a restaurant. As the senior non-commissioned officer, he led the four squads behind the German lines and was in command when they captured
headquarters of the machine-gun battalion. It was
at this critical point in the fight that he fell with several bullets in his stomach and in the arm. He has
only a confused idea of what happened afterward.
His courage and initiative in the early part of the
fight played an important part in the outcome of the
engagement. Like Parsons, he submitted an affidavit

describing the activities of his command up to the point where he was rendered helpless. Corporal Murray Savage, the fourth non-commissioned officer, was killed during the first burst of machine-gun fire.

Captain Danforth, who knew Sergeant York perhaps more intimately than any of the other officers and who is now residing in Augusta, Ga., was interviewed and submitted his version of the Argonne encounter.

Of the eight privates who survived the machine-gun fire, the affidavits of seven have been obtained, either from the archives of the War Department in Washington or from the official records of the Eighty-second Division, in possession of Colonel Buxton of Providence, R. I. Thus, of the eleven non-commissioned officers and privates who were connected with the York episode, the affidavits of nine have been taken and incorporated in this story, together with the war diary. Likewise the statement of Captain Joseph A. Wood, Intelligence officer, describing the manner in which Corporal York brought in the one hundred and thirty-two German prisoners, and his receipt for them have been woven into the story, together with the report of Captain Bertram Cox, who, shortly after the silencing of the machine guns, led his platoon over the battlefield and stopped long enough to count, rather briefly, the number of the German dead.

This story is told in York's own way. Great care has been taken to preserve his mountain dialect, though it must be remembered that during the past ten years the Sergeant has read many books and has met people all over the country, all of which has made his speech more literary than that of the average mountaineer. Still this has not drained it of dialect peculiarities. Thus, like so many mountaineers, York observes no uniformity in the use of the past or the perfect tenses. Now he says "saw," now "seed," now "seen," now "have saw," "have seed," and "have seen." He is just as inconsistent when he uses words ending in "ing." Sometimes he uses the final letter and sometimes he drops it as in "telling," which he often pronounces "tellin'" or in "fooling" which is often "foolin'." Mountaineers say "hit" instead of "it." But the Sergeant forgets his h's now and then and pronounces the word as it is printed. This is a result of contacts with non-mountain people and their speech. The same is true of double and triple and quadruple negatives. The mountain people use them interchangeably, and so does the Sergeant, except when he speaks slowly and has time to think. The expressions "you-uns" and "we-uns" occur in his speech with liberal frequency though not so frequently as their correct counterparts, "you" and "we." The most extraordinary feature of his speech is its utter freedom from the least suggestiveness of profanity. Since the day of his conversion he has eschewed any words that relate, however remotely, to cussing. Not even army life has changed his speech in this respect. Once when the stenographer, in transcribing his speech, inadvertently inserted the expression "I'll be blamed," he ran his pencil right through it. Only on one occasion have I known him to use the name of the Deity in his speech, and that was when he learned that I had interviewed Everett Delk, his pal of hog-wild days. "Everett must have told you God's plenty," he remarked with a chuckle. When I remonstrated with him that he was swearing he shook his head and insisted that "God's plenty" was a thoroughly proper expression.

So this is his own story told in his own way and documented with his war diary, his little autobiography, and the affidavits and statements of his officers and comrades-in-arms.

CHAPTER IV

FIGHTERS

I AIN'T had much of the larnin' that comes out of books. I'm a-trying to overcome that, but it ain't easy. If ever you let life get the jump on you, you have to keep hiking to catch up with it again, and I never knowed the truth of this like I do now. It ain't my fault. It ain't nobody's fault. It jes happened. We were most all poor people in the mountains when I was a boy. We hadn't neither the time nor the money to get much larnin'. The roads were bad. There were creeks to cross. So I growed up uneducated. And I never will stop regretting it. Only the boy who is uneducated can understand what an awful thing ignorance is. And when he is suddenly pushed out into the world and has to live with educated people and has to hear them discussing things he can't understand, he then sorter realizes what he has missed. And I'm a-telling you he suffers a lot.

When I joined the army I immediately knowed what a terrible handicap my lack of schooling was. When I went over to Paris and visited all sorts of places and seed things I didn't know nothing about nohow, I jes wished I could have had my early life over again. I jes knowed I would have got some larnin' somewhere. Then when I come back home again and found so many people knowed and wanted to meet me, I kinder felt all mussed up about it. But until I begun this book I never fully understood how necessary an education is and how little chance you have to get anywhere without it. When I sit down to write I know what I want to say, but I don't always know jes how to put it down on paper. I jes don't know how to get it out of me and put it in words. I ain't had the training. Hit's no use kicking about it. I suppose I have to do the best I can. I can't do no more. All the same, I do wish I could have had the advantages of good schools and books and teachers.

I have promised myself that I am going to get these things for my children; and for a heap of other children too. I'm a-dedicating my life to building schools in the mountains. If it is necessary I'm going to build good roads and bridges and provide transportation so that the children can get to these schools too. If they can't afford it nohow, I'm a-going to give them a chance to work their way through.

Mountain people are not great readers. I don't mean the people in the towns and more settled communities in the mountain country, I mean we-uns right in the mountains. It is hard to get books and there ain't no libraries. But we're most all good storytellers. And we repeat our stories over and over again until they become sort of household news. Whenever you get two mountaineers together you 'most always get a story. Around the old blacksmith shop, at the store, or at the shooting matches you are 'most certain to hear a whole mess of them; and when

we visit each other and sit around the old open fireplaces on long winter nights we tell a right-smart lot
of them. Hunting and shooting stories are the most
popular.

And the best of them are remembered and handed
down from father to children, jes like the muzzle-loading guns and the old dresses. We never seem to tire
of hearing about old Davy Crockett's baar hunts and
Daniel Boone's fights with the Indians. And we have
all kinds of stories of Andrew Jackson and Sam Houston. They used to get around these parts. There's
a whole heap of Crocketts living in Jimtown to this
day. These old-timers must have been right-smart
men. We don't find the like of them around nowa-
days. But times have changed. Maybe we don't live
the sort of lives which make great men.

Since I was knee high to a duck I've heard tell of
these men. I guess what outsiders call history is jes
plain story-telling with us.

So you see we mountaineers, without having read
many books or studying the subject are tol'ably well
informed of what has done been in these parts since the
time of the first settlers. The records have been repeated in story form and handed down year after year
until it comes to us.

These-here mountains of old Tennessee, North Carolina, and Kentucky were once the hunting and fighting
grounds of the Cherokees and Creeks. They was jes
about the fightinest Indians that ever put on the war
paint. I guess the panthers and wild cats must have
studied their methods. Them-there Indians must have

been kinder fond of these-here parts. The bears and buffaloes must have attracted them. There sure must have been a mess of them around here. It was nothing for the early settlers to shoot a hundred bear in a single season. They say that Davy Crockett shot ten in one day. I'm a-telling you that's a lot of baar.

Daniel Boone once saw so many buffaloes grazing in the valleys of these-here Cumberland mountains that he shouted, "I am richer than the man mentioned in the Scripture, who owned the cattle of a thousand hills; I own the wild beasts of more than a thousand valleys." And there must have been a lot of deer on the hoof. Some of the old settlers in the mountains still have the fringed deerskin shirts and moccasins of their pioneer ancestors. And there were coon, fox, and panther and all sorts of other varmints. There still are.

But the white settlers come in and started things. The first to come were the fighting Scotch-Irish. They come from the borders of Scotland and from the north of Ireland. They were followed by the Cavaliers from the hills of Scotland and by the Covenanters from England, the Huguenots from France, and a number of Germans. But the Scotch-Irish outnumbered all the others. They were the first. They stayed right on and these mountains are full of their descendants to-day. These old settlers were the most independent, God-fearing and God-loving people in the world. They left the other side rather than bow down to kings and dictators and accept political and religious beliefs they didn't believe in nohow. So they come over here where they hoped to be able to govern themselves and worship God according to the dictates of their own conscience. They followed the Quakers over into Pennsylvania and then hiked down the Shenandoah Valley to the mountains of North Carolina, and from there they fought their way through the Smokies over into the Cumberlands and Kentucky. That's how Daniel Boone travelled.

He was a kind of trail blazer. Wherever he led others followed; that is, if they got past the Indians. They fought it out all over this country. It was tough fighting from the start to the finish. They tomahawked and shot and scalped each other until nigh every inch of these mountains and valleys was stained with human blood. "The Dark and Bloody Ground" begins only a few miles from where I live. There was no stopping them-there early pioneers. They gave the Indians the best they had. It was enough. When they started anything they stuck it out until it was done finished. They believed the only good Indian was a dead one; so they proceeded to make them all good. And they did a right-smart job of it. There are not many redskins left to-day; and them that are live by themselves on Government reservations. The trouble was there wasn't room enough for both to live in this-here country. What happened is what always happens, when two people fight—the strongest won. And the new settlers happened to be the strongest. That's the way of nature.

They were the fightinest men. They were always at it. If it is was not the Indians, it was the English

FAMOUS TENNESSEE SHOOTING MATCHES

"The long barrel, muzzle-loading type of rifle made in the mountains of North Carolina, Tennessee, and Kentucky were the best and most accurate shooting-guns in the world; and up to a hundred yards they still are."

or French or Spanish. The Tennessee Sharpshooters were in the thick of it at King's Mountain. They went up the slopes and sharpshooted Ferguson and his Red Coats until there was nigh on none of them left. That-there Ferguson was a tol'able hard-fighting man himself, and he and his troops were great favourites with Cornwallis. And our mountain men shot them all to pieces. That was one of the turning battles in the Revolutionary War. The Tennessee Sharpshooters were Andrew Jackson's favourite troops. Their old long-barrelled muzzle-loaders did a whole heap to whip the English at New Orleans. They were up against it there too. They were fighting the pick of Wellington's veterans, the ones who helped to bust Napoleon. And the mountaineers out-fought and out-shot them. They were well in it, too, at Pensacola and later on in Mexico. My grandfather, Uriah York, was in the Mexican War and took part in the storming of the heights of Chapultepec. Them-there old pioneers was always fighting. Whenever their liberty was threatened they went right at it. And once when they figured their own Government was not doing the right thing by them they up and founded the free and independent State of Franklin, which was in eastern Tennessee. If you step on a rattler he will strike, and if you step on a Scotch Irishman or a Highlander he will jes natcherly hit back until somebody gets hurt.

The descendants of them-there old pioneers are the mountaineers of to-day. We haven't changed so very much. Of course, we don't wear deerskin shirts and moccasins and coonskin caps. We get on tol'ably well now in overalls and jeans. The old muzzle-loaders are givin' way to the modern high-powered rifle and shotgun—but jes the same there are a right-smart lot of hog rifles, as we hunters call them, in the mountains even to-day. Most all of us know how to load them, with cap and ball; and up to one hundred yards prefer them to any other rifle in the world. The modern home is drivin' out the little old log cabin with the rough-hewn logs and puncheon floors, but they ain't all gone. You see them here and there through the mountains. My brother George still lives in the one in which we growed up.

Even if our clothes and guns and homes are changing, we still sort of hang on to the old pioneer's love of political and religious liberty. We haven't much use for rituals and prayer books. Our God is still the God of our ancestors—the God of the Old Testament. We still believe in His word as it has been revealed to us in the old Bible. In politics too we still hang on to the old ideals of liberty and states' rights. In our family life too we are much the same. Blood is still pretty thick around these-here parts, and we still stick together much like the clans of our ancestors.

The mountains have sorter hemmed us in along with our own beliefs and ways of living. We kinder live an Eighteenth Century life, in the middle of the Twentieth Century. You can kinder trace our pedigree in the names of the towns all through the mountains. There is Pall Mall, where I live; and James-

town, the county site; and Livingston, close by; and
Cookeville, and Crossville, and Rugby. Them's good
old Anglo-Saxon names. And to kinder balance
things, there is Possum Trot, Coon Gap, Wolf Valley,
Wolf River, and Burrville. There's the pioneer side
of us. And jes like the towns which are a mixture
of old Anglo-Saxon and the spirit of the frontier
days, so we-uns are a mixture of old Anglo-Saxon
stock, kinder seasoned and hardened in the roughness
of this-here new continent of ours.

So we people in the mountains claim that while we
are good Americans, the sons and daughters of early
pioneers, we are also the old Anglo-Saxon type and
among the purest in America. We still sing many of
the old border ballads and speak a heap of old English words, like "ain't," "we-uns," "you-uns," and
"afeared." We are big and rangy and raw-boned.
And there are 'most any number of red-headed people
all around. We have a saying that you may see a
red-headed man in the penitentiary, but you will never
see one in an insane asylum.

CHAPTER V

LONG HUNTERS

BEFORE the war, because I hadn't read many books, I was kinder ignorant of many of the things that people in the world outside of these-here mountains were arguing and quarrelling about. I had never heard tell of this racial superiority and never even knowed there was such a thing. I jes sorter imagined that people were more or less alike and that there were good and bad and all kinds among all peoples; and my experience in the World War bore out this belief of mine.

I was in the All-American Division, made up of boys from all over. In my platoon there were Greeks, Italians, Poles, Irish, Jews, and a German, as well as a few mountain boys and some Middle West farmers. It didn't occur to me nohow to look too carefully at their branding marks. They was jes American soldier boys to me and that was all; and I would be a heap bothered if I was to try to make up my mind which of them was the best. I didn't find out then, and I'm a-telling you I haven't found out since, that jes because a man comes from some particular place or country he's any better'n anybody else. It ain't where you come from, it's what you are that counts. But when I come home from the war and got to goin' around mixin' with people, I begun to run into this talk about racial superiority. I didn't understand it. It didn't mean nothing to me nohow.

So when I say that a heap of great men have come from these mountains of Tennessee, Kentucky, and North Carolina, I don't mean to say that we're any better'n anybody else; and I ain't admitting either that we're any worse. I am jes stating the facts. Daniel Boone, Davy Crockett, Andrew Jackson, Sam Houston, John Sevier, James Robertson, and Coonrod Pile—there they are, and that's a right-smart lot of real people. They weren't all "long hunters" and they weren't all born here, but most of them growed up and hunted and fought and explored through this mountain country, and have left their traces all around. Davy Crockett used to hunt coon in our valley, and as I said, there are to this day a lot of Crocketts in Jimtown. Over near Jonesboro there is a big beech tree with this inscription on it:

D. BOON

cillED   A BAR
in   ThE
YEAR   1760

When Andrew Jackson was public prosecutor for Tennessee he often had to come into these-here mountains and attend court; and over in Crab Orchard, which is only a few miles from Jimtown, there is an old hotel where he often used to stay on his way to and from Washington. Sam Houston, John Sevier, and

James Robertson also knowed these parts. If this is not enough, Hodgenville, where Abraham Lincoln was born, is over acrost the Kentucky line less than one hundred and fifty miles from our part of Tennessee. I might also add that Mark Twain's parents growed up in Jimtown. So I say that we have turned out a whole heap of most powerful fighters and hunters and statesmen, too. It kinder seems to me that the three used to go together in them days.

I'm a-thinking that larned people who believe in this-here "Nordic supremacy" would shout their heads off and say that this is because we're all good Anglo-Saxons in the mountains. We are, but jes the same John Sevier was a Frenchman, and if I understand it, Daniel Boone was of Welsh beginnings. I know, of course, that blood counts. I never yet have known a cur dog that was any good for coon or baar; a mixed-up steer is the foolishest thing on hoofs; and a scrub horse ain't to be reckoned with a thoroughbred nohow. I'm admittin' that you have got to have the right beginnings; but that ain't all. That ain't enough. You have got to have somethin' else besides—the right kind of bringin' up. The best bred hound in the world ain't goin' to earn a groundhog's pelt until it has been properly seasoned. And it don't matter what sort of blood great men have, they have to have the right sort of conditions to find themselves.

It's jes like our shooters to-day in Tennessee. I guess our mountain boys are among the best shots in the world. They can bust a turkey's head at sixty yards 'most every shot, and they can take the centre

out of a target at forty paces with the best shooters
in the world. But they wuzn't born sharpshooters
nohow. I'm admittin' they had it in them; and I'm
also a-tellin' you that they had to be trained and prac-
tised.

There's a muzzle-loader, or hog rifle we call it, in
most every mountain cabin. The rifle is mighty near
the first tool that a mountain boy learns to handle, and
there is always plenty of squirrels, turkeys, and foxes,
and coon for him to get his eye on. Even to-day
hunting brings tol'able good money in our country.
Coon skins bring around twelve dollars, fox pelts are
well worth the going after, and turkeys make right-
smart vittles. In between jobs there is a right-smart
amount of money to be picked up if you know how
to tote a rifle the right way. There you have one of
the main reasons why our mountain boys are such
good shots.

I am inclined to believe that this is why so many
great men come from around here. They had it in
them at the beginning and they had a right-smart
chance to develop themselves. Those old pioneers had
to be hard-fighting and courageous men. They were
always mixin' it with somebody or other; and they
had to get used to receivin' as well as givin'. It was
dog eat dog and the best won, or they jes kinder
passed out. And they had to be hardy. This was a
tough country a hundred years ago, with Indians,
Tories, bad winters and worse summers, and often
little enough food and a wilderness to travel in, often
with no roads and no bridges, and they had to be hard

and they were, harder'n hickory. They had to be resourceful. 'Most every man had to be his own blacksmith, gunsmith, carpenter, farmer, engineer, and doctor. They had to larn to stand alone.

This was a pretty lonely country and they was often alone in it. Daniel Boone once stayed out in the woods in Kentucky for several months without even a dog for a companion. So, them old-timers had to larn to stand alone and the man that larns that becomes the strongest man there is.

All of these things went a long way towards making these men the kind of men they was, great men. They was sort of shut off from other folks in the outside world and they jes had to go ahead and settle their own problems and kinder make their own country. So they went ahead and done it.

Next to a man who reads his Bible, we mountain people most admire one who knows how to tote a rifle. I riccolect that when I first went into the army and went out on the rifle ranges at Camp Gordon, Atlanta, Ga., and seed some of them Greeks and Italians shoot, ho! ho! I didn't have much respect for them nohow. They was the worstest shots that ever shut eyes and pulled a trigger. But later, when I had done been with them over there in France and seen them fighting in the front-line trenches like a lot of mountain cats, I kinder realized that there are other things in life besides using a rifle properly. But jes the same, I kinder like a man who knows how to squint down the barrel of a muzzle-loader and bring the bead up until it cuts the centre.

Most mountain people are like me. That's one of the reasons why we still think a tol'able lot of Daniel Boone. There was a shooter! Whenever he shot squirrels he never mussed them up nohow. He never even shot them through the head. He barked them. That is, he either shot so close to their head or between their body and the bark of the tree that they died from the concussion. That's shootin' I'm a-tellin' you. Of course, the big balls they used in them times helped some, but hit was shootin' jes the same. He was a right-smart man with a hunter's knife, too. Over in the Indian country, when he was hungry and wanted meat and dares'n fire off a rifle for fear of the Indians, he would leap on the back of a buffalo and cut him down. And they say that the buffalo is one of the meanest and hardest fighters that there is on hoof.

Daniel Boone come from Pennsylvania and settled on the Yadkin in North Carolina. After that he used to tote tobacco in the markets in Virginia. But he jes natcherly couldn't stay in one place long enough to make the ground warm under his feet. He had to be up and going, always to new country; and he never turned back, not for all the Indians in creation. He kinder had a hungering always for new ground. If he seed a new cabin going up or some new settlers coming in he sorter felt crowded and begun to search around for more room and the wilderness. He jes natcherly had to have game to hunt. No hunting and there was no Boone. I think the reason why he always whipped the Indians was because he could do anything that they could and could do it a heap better'n they could. He could out-shoot, out-hunt, out-run, out-fight and out-smart any of them. They often tuk him prisoner but they never could keep him long. Somehow he always seemed to be able to slip away.

Next to his shooting I most like him for the way he liked to be alone. On his first expedition through the mountains into Kentucky his companions were either killed or turned back and he stayed on all alone for several months. He was the only white man in the whole of what is now Kentucky. He hadn't any companions of any sort. He was all alone, by himself; he hadn't even any bread, or sugar, or salt. But he stayed jes the same. He hunted and explored and wandered around and had a right-smart time. It tuk a great man to keep a-goin' like that, all alone in the wilderness for months with the nearest white man hundreds of miles away. And the only time, so they say, that the Indians nearly ketched him off his guard was when he was a-standin' on the bluffs above the Ohio River lookin' kinder dreamy-like at the waters and the sun a-goin' down behind the trees; and while he was doin' this the Indians tried to jump him, but they never got him. As quick as a rattler he turned and jumped into a tree sixty feet below and got away. I guess them Indians wondered what sort of a man he was.

I would most awful liked to have seen him dressed in them-there black deerskins he used to wear, with his hair all platted up in the pioneer way, standin' lookin' acrost the river at the sunset with them-there

Indians a-crawlin' up behind him without a chance in the world to get their hands on him. And that jump down into the trees, ho! ho!

I guess hit's my love of good shootin' more'n the fact that old Davy Crockett once hunted coon with my great-great-grandfather that makes me like to listen in on any story, or read anything I can git a-hold of about him. Old Davy may not have been the explorer and statesman that Daniel Boone was, but to my way of thinkin' he was even a better hunter and fighter. If he was in the wilderness he jes natcherly knowed where to find game and to bring it down without wastin' powder and lead. They say that when he was with General Jackson's army and the men was starving all around him that he would always get something for himself and for a lot of others. He used to call his favourite rifle Betsy; and we-uns in the mountains think such a lot of old Davy that a right-smart number of us call ours after that old muzzle-loader of his.

Right down the line, Davy Crockett come from fightin' stock. He has Scotch-Irish blood in him. His grandfather and grandmother was killed by the Indians. His father fought in the Revolutionary War and David himself was a soldier with General Jackson and in the end died like a man at the Alamo.

He must have been jes about the greatest baar hunter that ever lived. When Davy with his muzzle-loader and baar hounds went out after them they hadn't much chance. He knowed their habits and their feeding grounds almost as well as they knowed them themselves; and in the winter time he knowed

how to locate them in hollow trees and in their cane
houses and harricanes. He was such a right-smart
hunter that he could always tell whether they were up
in the tree or not. He knowed that when they climb
up they don't slip a bit but when they come down they
leave long scratches.

One dark night Davy and his dogs got into a most
awful mix-up with a screamer of a baar which they
done treed in a big poplar. He shot the baar down
but it was only wounded. Then in the darkness they
all got mixed up and went to it. He couldn't use his
rifle when in the darkness. So he jes got out his
old hunting knife and went into it right. The dogs
chased the baar into a big crack in the ground and
Davy let fly with his old muzzle-loader gun, but instid
of killing the baar he wounded it in the fleshy part
of the back. That made it roarin' mad. It come
out of the crack and they went at it agin. In the
mix-up Davy lost his rifle, so he picked up a pole and
begun to punch the baar about until finally, with the
help of his hounds, he got it back in the crack again.
And they all got down after it. The baar was mussin'
up the dogs right smart, and Davy, like the good
hunter he was, didn't like that a bit. He must have
been jes about as mad as the baar. He jumped down
right on the baar's back, and in the darkness, with the
baar and the dogs barkin' and roarin' and fightin' and
scratchin' and bitin', he jes finished that old baar
with his hunter's knife, ho! ho!

It was a cold night and everything was too wet to
start a fire, but he got the baar out of the crack and

dressed it. He tended to his hounds the best he could. Then to keep from freezing he clum up a tree which hadn't a limb on it for thirty feet, and locked his arms together and slid down to the bottom. He done this all night, climbing up and sliding down over a hundred times; and he said that this sort of exercise made the inside of his arms and legs feel pretty good.

Another time his dogs found a baar in a hollow tree. Davy clum up a tree and looked into the hollow to make sure the baar was there. It was there all right. It poked its head out of the hole and Davy come down like a streak of lightnin' and the bear come after him. Davy was on his feet first, and with the help of his hounds and that old muzzle-loader that didn't know how to miss nohow he got the baar.

Once when he was down in Texas he got into a most awful mix-up with a panther. He was prowlin' round in the trees lookin' for a bed for the night when he almost ran head in onto the cat. But he beat the cat to it. He let fly with Betsy and in the mix-up only wounded the panther, and it kept a-comin' right at him with four claws and a mouth full of slashin' teeth and two hundred pounds of wounded, mean-fightin' cat. He hadn't time to reload, so he used his rifle as a club; but that was no use, so he throwed it away and went after the panther with his huntin' knife. They got into several clinches and mussed each other up, but Davy killed it dead. That's the sort of fighter he was.

Oncet around Christmas time when he was out of meat and other provisions and had run short of pow-

der he went afoot five miles through creeks and
flooded country, crawling over rocks and wading up
to his shoulders in half-frozen water to his brother-
in-law's for a keg of powder. It was way below
freezing and he was wet through; and several times
he was nearly drowned or washed away; and during
the last part of the journey he had practically no
feeling in his legs. But he got there.

He got the powder and he brought it home in much
the same way. Hickory was soft beside of old Davy
Crockett. He was even more fond of politics than
he was of baar-hunting. He was a right-smart poli-
tician, too. He knowed most all of the tricks of the
trade. Oncet when he was campaigning he come to
a town where the only way he could get the votes was
by buying whiskey for the voters. He hadn't any
money so he jes went out in the woods with that-there
gun of hisn and got him a coonskin which he was able
to turn in for the whiskey.

The voters drunk it up and wanted more. Davy
noticed the skin hanging over the bar. He stole that
same coonskin several times and kept selling it back to
the saloon keeper without him knowing nothing about
it. He got the whiskey and the votes too.

Like Daniel Boone, he didn't much like being
crowded. He often visited the big cities, but he was
more at home in the wilderness. It was the most
natcheral thing for him to go off to Texas. He knowed
what that Texas fight was all about. He wanted
to carve out a new career down there and help get
the state for Uncle Sam. Jes like water knows how

to find its own level, old Davy knowed how to find the hottest fightin'.

So he went straight to the Alamo. He was right with them when they was surrounded by the thousands of Mexicans. He fought like a baarcat and when the Mexicans broke into the fort in the morning he was one of the six men still living. He was backed up in the corner of the fort with a broken rifle in one hand and a big bowie knife in the other. There was about twenty Mexicans wounded or lying dead all around him, and he was yellin' at the others to come and get him. They jes bore him to the ground and he went down a-fightin'. After the surrender when they got out the wounded and the dead they found him very much alive and a-kickin', so they marched him out with the five other prisoners. They was takened before a Mexican general and his officers, who instid of treatin' them properly begun to most cowardly cut them down with their swords. When Davy seed this he let out a roar like a wounded baar and leapt at the Mexicans with his bare hands. But he had no chance. They jes hacked him to pieces. So old Davy died as he lived, a most awful brave and wonderful fightin' man.

Andrew Jackson, too, was another Tennesseean, who natcherly knowed how to shoot and fight. We kinder looked upon him as the greatest of them all; and even to this day they say that back of the cane breaks when the Presidential election comes around the people still go to the polls and vote for Old Hickory. Of course, that's only a story, but it sorter shows how really alive he still is. We talk about him jes as though he only lived a few years ago. He was the first state prosecutor for Tennessee and he had to visit every court in the state. They say he was pretty short on law and pretty long on fightin'. He was as full of fightin' as a mountain cat when the hounds have cornered it.

And Old Hickory's friend, Sam Houston, was another celebrated man in Tennessee. He stood near six feet six. He was a big one. In my home in Pall Mall we think so much of Sam Houston that we called our fourth son after him. Why shouldn't we? He was born right here in Tennessee. He was a twelve-pounder when he come into the world. And when our friends come in to see the baby I always introduce him as "Sam Houston, the man who conquered Texas." Ho! ho!

Of course, I know that a right-smart lot of books have been wrote about these old pioneers and many of these things are known. But as I said when I begun to write this, what's history with larned people is still a matter of story-telling with us, and I'm a-telling you that these people are not merely characters in books to us. We talk about them and we sorter feel them around us as though they were still alive. They are, of course, as much a part of our lives as these mountains here and the log cabins and the muzzle-loaders they used and we still have.

We have other great characters, too, John Sevier, James Robertson, Shelby, and still others not as well known. There was also my great-great-grandfather,

Coonrod Pile. He was the first white man to settle
in this-here valley and one of the first in the whole of
this-here part of Tennessee. He come in here in the
latter part of the Eighteenth Century. He was a
Long Hunter, and he come from over somewhere in
North Carolina, with two or three companions, but
they didn't stay. They kept on a-going, probably further West. That's the way most of them done went.
But Coonrod Pile, old Coonrod, as most of us speak
of him, stayed right here in the little valley. In them
times it was a cane break with the three forks of the
Wolf a-singing through, and a-plenty of springs bub-
bling out of the mountains.

He spent his first night, and most probably every
night until his cabin was up, in the cave or rock house
above the spring where I used to blacksmith when I
was a boy. It was good protection from the Indians
and wild animals. There was a-plenty of water and
the game used to come there to drink. It was a right-
smart place for settling in. There were a-plenty of
Indians around and the hills and valleys were alive
with baar, panther, and other varmints. And old
Coonrod was the only white man and he must have had
a heart made out of hickory and walnut. He jes went
right ahead and built him a home and put in his crops.
I guess he was a right-smart hunter and shooter, too.

Other hunters come in and joined him, and soon they
had a tol'able-size' valley settlement. And they called
it Pall Mall. I don't know why, but I guess Coonrod
Pile in the first place come from England, and maybe
it was jes his sense of humour letting itself go. But

Pall Mall it was called and Pall Mall it has stayed to this day. The little valley settlement went so far ahead and then it jes natcherly stopped, and here it is to-day, jes a sleepy, sparsely populated little place, sorter hid away in the Cumberland Mountains; but it was the beginning and what is now middle Tennessee growed up around it.

Pall Mall is older than Jimtown or Byrdstown or Livingston or any of the other places around this part of the state. In old Coonrod's time there were no histories kept here, and as the few old-timers who remember him were only little children at that time, a right-smart lot of what we know about him is jes hearsay, but there was court records and land deeds in existence which sort of bear out these hearsay stories.

Jes as he was the first, he always remained the richest and most powerful settler. At one time he owned 'most all of the valley and the present site of Jimtown and most all of Fentress County. He had a blacksmith shop and general store, farms, and a number of slaves. He was a hard worker and a smart trader and he had a lot of money for those times. They say he used to keep his money in a big safe in a special room. Uncle Jim Pile told me that old Coonrod, who was his grandfather, sharpened the prongs of a pitchfork and always threatened to fork anybody who come near that room where the money was.

Uncle Jim says old Coonrod was a big man and had a most awful temper. Most of the other settlers were a-feared of him, and when they went to him to buy corn or whiskey they held the money in one hand and the sack or jar in the other and jes said nothing. He must have been a man of mighty strong likes and dislikes. If you went to him for anything he would look at your trousers, and if the knees was patched and the seat was all right he figured you was always going ahead and he would help you, but if it was the opposite, ho ho! He figured you was lazy and always settin' down and he would run you out.

There are also stories in the valley, but of course they are only hearsay, that he was most awful a-feared of lightning and thunder, and whenever it stormed he would go right back in that-there old cave or rock house and shivver and cuss and wait until hit was over. The log cabin he built there by the spring, he built to stay. Hit is still there and until a few years ago was lived in by Will Brooks, my mother's only brother.

When old Coonrod died years before the Civil War he left a right-smart heap of money and land, but the war and the whole army of descendents that have come down from him have sorter broken it up until there ain't much for nobody to-day. Old Coonrod wasn't much heard of outside of these parts of Tennessee. He wasn't well known like Daniel Boone and old Davy Crockett and the others, but he was a big man, a pioneer of pioneers, and hit was men like him going alone into the wilderness and settling there and building up the community that helped to make this country great.

As I said before, and I'm a-saying it agin right here, I ain't trying to make out nohow that we're any better'n anybody else, but it has bothered me a lot in my trips around America that a heap of people sorter look at Tennessee as a sort of backward and ignorant state. I have heard them go so far as to say that Tennessee's one of the worstest states in the Union. I guess that-there trial at Dayton hasn't helped much to make them change their opinions. I ain't a-going to argue nohow about this-here evolution. I don't know much about it either way. I ain't read enough books to understand it. I ain't for it nor agin it. I don't care what it proves or don't prove. Like a lot of other people in the mountains, I have got my own beliefs about God and man and such things. They're real beliefs with me and they bring me a heap of comfort and help me at all times and I ain't a-going to change them for any trial at Dayton or anywhere else. But I am a-telling you that the state of Andrew Jackson, Davy Crockett, Sam Houston, and old Coonrod Pile ain't got to and ain't a-going to make no apologies to nobody nohow.

CHAPTER VI

FEUDISTS

ALTHOUGH we have much the same blood and live in the same sort of mountains and are a much-alike people, we-uns in the Cumberlands of Tennessee have never gone in for the killings and feuds like they have acrost the Kentucky line. I don't know the reason. I don't even know that there is a reason. I jes know that we have had very few feuds, while over there in the mountains of Kentucky and West Virginia they were baarcats for them.

I kinder figure that the mountains, because its hard for the officers to git into them, most powerful attract careless people. Then when they git located they try to run out the old settlers and have things their own way. Then they go to it and one of them is killed off and one of them survives. I'm not a-going to say that we don't have any lawless people or any killings where I come from, but I am a-going to say right now that the more decent people usually run things around our part of Tennessee. But acrost the line it has been a hard, cruel fight. But the decent people there seem to be getting control agin and the feuds are dying out.

The trouble with these-here feuds is that they have been exaggerated until the outside public thinks that all mountain people fight and kill each other when hit ain't so. Even in the feud districts, families not involved and even strangers, provided they keep their mouths shet, are not in any danger at all. But even so, the feuds are bad enough. To my way of thinking, they have been a disgrace, both to the people concerned in them and to many of the officers too. And then newspapers and writers have most often tried to make some of the feudists sort of mountain heroes, or mistreated people, or people who don't know better; and that, of course, has not helped much. Feuds are killings and that's all there is to it. I'm admitting, of course, that sometimes the feudists feel that they are defending their blood and their honour and their manhood and womanhood. It's a pretty narrow figuring out of these things, though. There are other and decent ways to protect these things without brawling and gunning and taking human lives and destroying valuable property and turning the whole mountainside upside down.

They generally start over some little thing. The terrible Hatfield-McCoy feud in Pike County, Kentucky, begun over an argument over some hogs. One of the Hatfields drove some razorbacks from the forests and put them in a pen in Stringtown, Ky. A short time after one of the McCoys saw the hogs and claimed them as hisn and demanded that they be turned over to him. That started things. First there were trials and then shootings and killings; and it didn't end neither till heaps of people were shot and a most awful lot of valuable stock and property mussed up right smart. Even women and children were beat up and killed. And although a most awful lot of people were shot down in this terrible feud only one of them was ever hung.

The Tollivar-Martin-Logan feud in Rowan County was jes as bad. They say that moonshine and politics was responsible for its beginnings. For years they went to it and bushwhacked and shot each other up until it's a wonder that there is any of them left at all. Families and relations and friends were drug in and sometimes even brothers were fightin' brothers. Often the officers, instid of going right after them, were afraid or sympathized, and sometimes they even took a part. Judges and juries were often corrupt, and the only law they knowed for a long time was that of the bullet and the killer.

And there have been lots of other feuds, most of them in Kentucky and West Virginia, a few of them in the Smokies of Tennessee and North Carolina, and jes a few here in the Cumberlands. Hundreds of people have been killed in these-here feuds. Families have been wiped out, homes burnt and destroyed, and hearts broken; and people in the cities outside the feud sections have come to regard 'most all mountaineers as ignorant, fighting, killing savages. And the awful thing about it is that so few of the real guilty ones has been punished.

I live in the mountains. I ain't never been in a feud, but I know about them. I know some people who have fought in them, and I say right here, they're all wrong. A feudist is a killer; and there ain't no other way about it. I know they often pose as wronged people, but jes because you are wronged doesn't permit you nohow to go a-gunning for vengeance: "Vengeance is mine, saith the Lord." "An eye for an eye and a tooth for a tooth" ain't part of the Constitution of the United States. So if people are wronged and the authorities are properly decent as they should be the wrongs should be righted and the wrongers punished; and if the officers are not honest, then hit's up to the people to throw them out and get honest ones.

The feudists are not heroes; they ain't never been. They are jes killers. Often they are jes cowardly assassins, hiding behind rocks or trees and bushwhacking and shooting people in the back or jumping them when they get the drop on them or ketch them unarmed or outnumbered. There is not much of this-here heroism in that and there ain't none at all in mussing up innocent people, or beating women and children, or burning and destroying. And you will find all of these-here terrible things in feuds.

But feuds are dying out. Larnin' is getting into the mountains. Roads are being built. Officers are going after the killers. And better'n all, the mountain people are beginning to understand hit's all wrong and don't profit nobody nohow.

CHAPTER VII

BUSHWHACKERS

BUT even if we-uns in the Cumberlands ain't been bothered to death with feuds, we've got to admit that we've had our share of bushwhackers. What a lot of baarcats they were! The hatreds of the Civil War are much to blame. Tennessee was a border state, and like most all the border states, it was all spotted with human blood. This-here northern part of central Tennessee was the raidin' and foragin' ground of both armies. It was a sort of no man's land, first occupied by one, then t'other. We got it from both sides.

Although Tennessee was a Southern and a slave-owning state, it weren't nohow all-fired in favour of the Confederacy. The mountaineers have always been free and independent. They have always kicked like steers if they were interfered with. They never could stand the Government telling them what they should do and what they should believe in and fight for. That's why they left the other side and come into these mountains and whipped the Indians and the British and founded their own civilization. They wanted to be left alone; and they have always jes bristled like a porcupine when anybody has tried to interfere with them.

63

Most all of them have been good Americans, too, and have proved it at King's Mountain and at Pensacola and New Orleans with old Andrew Jackson. So when the Civil War come on they weren't going to be ordered about by nobody nohow. So they got mussed up right smart. If they were for the North they suffered when the Southern troops come in; if they were for the South they got it jes as bad when the Northerners marched through; and if they was for neither and tried to be neutral they got it from both sides. I guess there ain't a cabin in these-here mountains, there ain't a road or a valley or a hillside that hain't seen blood and suffering and death as a result of the Civil War.

Around Jimtown was the scenes of some of the most awful fights of the guerillas and bushwhackers. The citizens first formed these bushwhackers to protect themselves against the raids and foraging expeditions of the soldiers of both armies. They were guerillas under independent commands and they were meant to protect the people and property from the regular soldiers and to do what they could to win the war. Around these parts the Southern Bushwhackers were led by Ferguson, a cold-blooded killer who was in jail in Jimtown awaiting trial for murder when the war broke out. He was then freed and took command of the Southern Bushwhackers.

The Northern Bushwhackers were led by Tinker Beaty, who growed up around here. At first they was tol'able good soldiers, brave and hard fighters. They protected the people and their property, and they done

done their best to win. But as the war went on and things become looser and looser and hatreds flared out worser and worser, like most undisciplined units, they kinder broke down and done jes as they liked. The more patriotic uns were killed off or left or went away and the bullies and the bedevilled uns become more powerful. Instid of protecting people, they jes went out to git whatever they could. Pastor Pile's mother-in-law, Mrs. Williams, remembers them right smart, and she's told me a right-smart lot about the bushwhackers, how they done got together and went around and takened everything they could lay their hands on.

Tinker Beaty led a big command of them, and there was a lot of little independent bunches who had no officers. They roamed around the country and whenever they caught enemy soldiers off guard they would kill them. They would kill sympathizers, too, and they would slip into homes and do their devilment. Everybody seemed to be killing in those days, but they was the worstest of the lot.

In the awful days after the Civil War when nobody seemed to know what was going to happen next and these mountain communities were the torn-downdest places you could ever think of, these bushwhackers bossed and bullied and killed and run things to suit theirselves. They often hunted out their own enemies and killed them on the spot. They run others out of the country and they never did come back. And one of their favourite games was to buy up for most nothing the property of soldiers who'd been killed in

the war, or who were in debt.   These places were sold
at public sales.   Some of the bushwhackers would go
out to the sales and threaten to kill anybody who bid
against them, and they would put in their own low bids
and get the places cheap.

One of the best known was Pres Huff. He was on
the Northern side around these parts. Old Jim Pile,
a grandson of Coonrod Pile, who lives in Jimtown,
knows a lot about Huff. Pres and his father was always quarrellin' and often near shootin' it out. He
was one of Tinker Beaty's men and most all of them
had an awful reputation.

The records of the United States Circuit Court for
the Middle District of Tennessee describes Pres Huff
as a "brigand of the most desperate character."

Well, in the midst of all these killings and goings-
on, young Jeff Pile, my own great uncle, was killed.
It was most common knowledge that Pres Huff done
it. Huff killed Jeff Pile on the Byrdstown road, right
plumb on top of the hill at John Pile's place, right
thar as you straddle the fence. He bushwhacked him,
shot him in the back, and the bullet went most through
and stuck against the skin on the other side. Old Jim
Pile's father took a razor and got that-thar bullet out.
Jeff was not a fighter in the war. He took no part in
it. But Tinker Beaty and Pres Huff and the other
Northern Bushwhackers considered him a sympathizer
on the Southern side. So they got him. At least, Pres
Huff got him.

Jes after the war, while the killings was still going
on, Will Brooks, a red-headed young Northerner, come

into the valley and located here. He fought in the
war on the Northern side. He was in a regiment of
cavalry from Michigan. When the war ended he jes
dropped out and settled here in the Valley of the Three
Forks of the Wolf. He fell in love with Nancy Pile,
poor Jeff's sister, and married her and settled on her
land.

He was a right-smart young man, around twenty-one
years old. He and Pres Huff were always quarrelling.
Brooks blamed Huff for bushwhacking his brother-in-
law, Jeff Pile. They say that Pres Huff had his eye
on the Pile property and thought if he could get Brooks
out of the way maybe he could get the land. Anyway,
they was always quarrelling. They met face to face in
Jimtown. Brooks was unarmed and had no friends
with him. Huff had his guns and a lot of his gang
around. Brooks had to get out. It was the only thing
he could do. He had no chance. Huff yelled after
him as he went that he would kill him the next time
they met. Some time after that Huff's dead body was
picked up on the road about a mile from his home. Of
course, everybody knowed that Brooks done done it.
My own kinfolks have been sayin' that most all the
decent people here sympathized with Brooks and
thought he done right, but the Pres Huff crowd didn't
see it that way. They went out to get Brooks. But
he slipped off to Michigan. A little later his wife
and baby followed him. They would have been all
right, but they wrote back to some friends and the
letter was intercepted and their address was found.
There was no real law nor order in those days, so

Pres Huff's friends jes organized and went up to Michigan, with papers, and brought Brooks back and put him in the jail in Jimtown. A few nights later they come in to see him and he jes knowed they was goin' to kill him. He begged them to have his little girl brunged to him. He wanted awful bad to see her. But they were not of a mind to be nice to him. They hooked him to the tail of a horse and drug him through the streets and jes filled him with bullets.

Well, Will Brooks was my grandfather, and the little girl, Mary, that he wanted most awful bad to see, was my mother!

My other grandfather, Uriah York, also lost his life as a result of the Civil War. He was first a soldier in the Mexican War. He fought many of the battles there. He went up to the Heights of Chapultepec and took part in the capture of Mexico City. In the Civil War he fought on the Union side. He went away from here and takened sick and stole back home and hid. While he was sick he heard that the Southern Bushwhackers was coming in and he got up out of his sick bed and stole away and buried himself in a canebreak where they hid the horses from the soldiers. He was sick with measles and it was wet and damp and he takened pneumonia and died.

So you see that both my grandfathers lost their lives as a result of the Civil War. One was lynched by the bushwhackers on the Northern side and the other died when he hid out in the rain and cold from the bushwhackers on the Southern side.

I'm a-tellin' you them must have been most awful

times. The hatreds and killings were terrible. There wasn't much law and human life and property weren't of much account nohow.

So you see that even if we haven't suffered much from the feuds, we have had a most awful time in these-here mountains from the bushwhackers and sufferings of the Civil War.

CHAPTER VIII

MOONSHINERS

THE people of the mountains always have made moonshine. Their ancestors larned to make it over there on the borders of Scotland and northern Ireland, and they brought the habit over with them, jes like they brought their Old Testament faith and their love of liberty and fighting. Even Daniel Boone and old Davy Crockett most liked to have a drink now and then. I guess they jes had it in their blood. But the mountain people hated to pay the revenue tax, which they thought was often most unfair.

So they done went ahead and made it in the canebreaks and back in the timber where the officers could not get at them. They used to make it like this long before there was any prohibition. Then when prohibition come along they felt they jes natcherly still had to have their liquor. It was profitable to make it for other people, too, for they always growed corn in these mountains and it was hard to get it out to market. Roads were bad and the towns and cities were a long way off. It was easier to turn it into liquor and move it out, or sell it to their neighbours. I ain't a-tryin' to excuse moonshiners. I don't drink liquor myself nohow, and I don't believe in moonshinin'. I'm a-tellin' you I would like to see them all cleared out. I am only tryin' to explain them.

A few years ago they sometimes used to fight and kill and it wasn't safe for an officer or a posse to try to get in and get them, but that's all changed now. Lots of folks still make moonshine. I guess they make more of it than ever, but they have larned that it doesn't pay to kill revenue men. So when they are caught they light out, or else give up without much trouble.

Our sheriff in Fentress County, Sheriff Livingston, who lives in Jimtown, is plumb fired up over moonshiners. He is always a-goin' after them. He has been an officer seven terms, about fourteen years, and I guess he has captured more liquor than the whole county could drink if everybody drunk all the rest of their lives. He knows more about moonshiners and their ways than 'most anybody else in these-here mountains. He goes right after them. He gets them, too. He's a brave man, I'm a-tellin' you, a hard fighter, and when he finds a still and squints down that old rifle of his, the moonshiners jes know the game is up.

He has been in a couple of killings. Oncet with a posse he went out to get some folks and he run plumb into them while they were driving along the road in a wagon. They opened fire right away. When the smoke cleared away they were all killed or wounded and the sheriff and his men were pretty badly singed with the powder, but they hadn't even been scratched. Another time he went out with the sheriff of another county to raid a "blind tiger" and there was a lot of shooting. In the middle of the fray he got a bullet in the shoulder, but he kept on a-fightin' and a-firin', and although wounded, he got the man that shot him and also the other one.

Sheriff Livingston is a brave and a pretty old man, but he has got a quiet voice and the softest eyes you ever seed. You would never think he would harm nobody nohow. But when you talk moonshiners to him, he sorter rares up. He has got some of them in his jail right now and one of his outhouses is plumb full of captured stills and worms and all the other stuff they use for making whiskey. He has to keep the door locked, too, to keep the moonshiners from coming right to the jail and stealing back their own stills, ho! ho! In the last twenty months he done captured thirty-six stills, and I guess there is that many more still operating. Moonshiners hain't never fired on him. A few of them are bad, but they won't shoot it out face to face. They prefer to waylay you in the bushes. But there's only a few of them like that.

They make their stills out of copper sheeting which they buy from the cities and then weld them together. They often use old oil barrels, or two washtubs joined together. Their worms are made out of copper pipes which they also buy and then wind around stumps until they get into correct shape. Some of them buy copper radiators from the mail-order houses. Most all the moonshiners are careless people and generally get mash all over themselves, so you can smell the stills for a mile. They put the most awful concoctions into their whiskey. They generally operate their stills away back in the woods where there is plenty of running water. They connect the worm to the still itself and distil the whiskey into kegs or sealed jars, which they put in water to keep them cool. They make most of their moonshine out of the ground corn. Then they add the malt and they call this mash. They put it in a barrel and add warm water and let it stand until it begins to work. Then they put in sugar and let it stand again until it sours. Then they put it in the still with a furnace under it and boil it. The steam escapes out of the closed still and comes through the worm and into the bucket or barrel. This is how the best and the purest whiskey is made. But very little of it is as good as this. Some moonshiners use concentrated lye or tobacco, or anything else to make the whiskey strong. Some put buckeyes into it, and that's plain poison. One still Sheriff Livingston found with a bunch of ivy tied into the cap. The moonshiner said it would steam and drip and make the whiskey bead. But the sheriff said it would poison the whiskey and the moonshiner allowed you can't poison whiskey with anything nohow. Well, the sheriff sent him to the penitentiary for "a year and a day."

I guess that old sheriff knows what he's talkin' about. He is the sheriff in one of the moonshiningest counties in the mountains; and that's our county, Fentress County. So I admit that there is still plenty of moonshine and moonshiners in the mountains. But I ain't a-goin' to admit that all mountaineers are moonshiners, or that all mountaineers even drink whiskey. They don't, but if you give a dog a bad name it's hard to git rid of it, and that's how it is around here.

CHAPTER IX

SADDLEBAGGERS

THE old-timers in these-here mountains sure must have believed that "man cannot live by bread alone." I mean whiskey alone, ho! ho! They had to have religion and they done had it. But jes as they couldn't git in over the bad roads and acrost the creeks to school, they often couldn't git in to church. So the church had to go to them. And it done went, at least the saddlebaggers went.

I'm a-tellin' you that them-there old Presbyterian and Methodist and Baptist preacher-men played a right-smart part in civilizing the people of the mountains. They were called saddlebaggers because of the big saddlebags they carried on their horses. They stuffed these bags with Bibles, song books, and religious magazines, which they sold or give out wherever they done went. The people in the mountains thought jes as much of their religion, and a little more, too, than they thought of their fighting and hunting, and they was most awful fond of them saddlebaggers.

The Scotch-Irish, Scotch Cavaliers, Lutherans, and Huguenots who pioneered this country were most awful religious people. But they believed in their own and not in other people's gods. That's why they lit out from the other side and come over here and takened on to the wilderness ruther than to live in comfort in their own homes. They knowed that over here they could find that political and religious liberty they were looking for. Even to this day you won't find many rosaries or Episcopalian prayer books in these-here mountains, and you won't find many rituals or liturgies either. The mountain people don't like them nohow. They don't permit anything except the Bible to stand between them and their God. They sorter like their religion plain, like their ancestors did and like the old Prophets did.

But they were so busy fighting and making their homes that they had no time nohow to do much preaching themselves. Then the saddlebaggers come. They was pioneers themselves, farmers, blacksmiths, gunsmiths, and hunters. They was jes plain people, earning their living by the sweat of their brow. But they felt the spirit of God telling them to go out among their fellowmen and preach His word. So of a Saturday and Sunday, and sometimes for weeks, they would git in the saddle and stuff their old saddlebags full of Bibles and hymn books and go a-ridin' through the mountains. If there was mountain churches they would hold their services there. If there was no churches they would hold them in the schoolhouse; and if there was no schoolhouse they would hold them in the cabins on the mountainside. Wherever they could get a few people together they would have a preaching. There was never a mountain cabin too far back for them to call at. There was never a family too poor for them to visit. They regarded all people alike as the children of God and themselves as His blessed messengers.

They not only held meetings everywhere they went, but they baptized and held marriage services and comforted the sick and buried the dead. They received very little salary or none at all. Preaching was not a profession or a business with them like it so often is now. It was the work of God. They looked forward to their reward in the next world. They was good men, sincere preachers. They worked most hard. They travelled through all sorts of weather, winter and summer. They rode over the worstest roads, up creek beds, over the mountains. They were greatly loved and respected by all the people, and though they never carried arms they were never touched. They used to stay at whatever mountain cabin they arrived at at nightfall, and they was always welcome, too. They were close preachers; that is, they clung closer to the word of God as it is written in the Bible than a coon to a tree when a hound-dog has chased him up there. They were what we would call fire-and-brimstone preachers. They believed in the reward of heaven for the good and the punishment of hell for the wicked. And I'm a-tellin' you theirs was the finest heaven there ever was and theirs was the worstest hell. They shore knowed all about the pearly gates and the everlasting flames.

There was many famous saddlebaggers riding circuits in these-here mountains. Jackie Brown was one of them. He come from somewhere over in North Carolina and sorter made his headquarters in our valley, and from here he would ride out through the mountains preaching and taking the word of God to the furtherest corners. Often he was the first preacher that the settlers away back in the mountains had ever seen. Sometimes he got so far back in that he found people that had never even seed a Bible before. Oncet at a famous meeting near Wolf River, in the valley, he said he would be happy to die at any time if he thought that by so doing he could save jes one lost soul. He meaned it, too, and the people listening knowed he meaned it.

About seventeen years later another preacher man named Bobby Burke come along with a new religion of the Gospel of Sanctification. He converted Jackie Brown to his new religion, and when Jackie was saved, as he called it, he told the congregation that he was awful glad that he hadn't died before, because if he had done so he shure would have gone straight to hell.

Jackie was saved between the saddle and the horse, so he used to say. It come to him sudden. He had been to a meeting and heard Bobby Burke preach and he was riding over to Jasper Pile's to get his dinner when he felt the power moving him and he knowed he was sanctified. He got off of his horse and laid on the flat of his back on the dusty road and slapped his hands and begun to holler. A man by the name of Jack Frogge was going down the road at the time, and when he saw Jackie Brown he thought it was some man drunk or crazy, and so he takened out around the other side and lit out for home and never stopped until he got there.

When Jackie Brown got up he run his hands into his pockets and pulled out his plug of tobacco and throwed it into the woods, and then he done went home to his farm, where he had half an acre of tobacco growing, and he takened a hoe and hacked it down and threw it over the fence. He said if it was not right for him to use tobacco it was not right for him to grow it and sell it to other people. His neighbours got after him and said that as he was poor he should have kept the tobacco and marketed it. But he said the Lord would not let him starve. They say he become a most powerful fine preacher after he was sanctified.

Another well-known saddlebagger was a man named Adams. He was blind. He couldn't look out into the world, but he declared he could look into people's souls. He was much loved and respected, as he should have been. They say that he was a Southerner and a very wonderful fellow. At about the same time that he was preachin' another saddlebagger by the name of Sam Greer come into the valley. He was a Northerner and a fire-eater. Long after the Civil War this-here Greer and Adams come together at a revival meeting on Wolf River. Sam Greer plumb forgot that he was a preacher man and he lit into Adams most awful for being a Rebel and a Southerner. So you see that often these saddlebaggers were human like most other people. They had their likes and dislikes. I'm a-thinking that is why they was so well received and loved wherever they went.

The most famous of the saddlebaggers was Ab

Wright. There was a man for you! He growed up in our valley and rode through these-here mountains for nigh onto fifty years. He is a-resting in his grave now, but I'm a-telling you his memory still lives in the hearts of the old-timers around here. They never tire of talking about him and his wonderful sermons and long rides and the great good he done.

Tennessee was a pretty tough place around seventy-five year ago when he begun carrying the word of God around. The roads were jes mountain trails. There were few bridges. Towns and even mountain cabins were a right-smart piece apart; and often Ab Wright was out all night in the cold and the rain on the mountainside. Agin and agin he was near drowned or bewatered by some sudden rising of creek or river.

Oncet he was lost in the wilderness. He was not like old Daniel Boone, who said he was never lost in the forest but he was once bewildered for a few days. He really was lost and he didn't know where he was nohow, and he had to do a most awful lot of praying before he found the road. Another time he was feeding a large herd of cattle when he was gored by a mad bull. It tossed him several times and he come near to losing his life. And worst of all, he was bit by a copperhead. He put his hand down in a sheaf of oats and the serpent got him on the wrist. It made him most awful sick, but he didn't lose his head. He bound his wrist above the wound to keep the poison from spreading, and then kept sucking the bite and spitting out the poison until he was a heap better; but jes the same he was not getting well nohow.

In them days they didn't know much about snake medicine, so they jes put another bandage on his arm, tighter than the first, to make shore the poison wouldn't spread. This bandage was so tight that it kinder cut off circulation and his shoulder and neck become so swollen that he couldn't hardly breathe; and then they begun to give him whiskey. That was about the only remedy that the mountaineers knowed for snake bite, and I guess hit was a pretty doubtful cure at that. He drunk three pints of raw whiskey in a few minutes, and then, so he said afterwards, he felt pretty drowsy and went to sleep—and while he was sleeping the whiskey and the poison fought it out inside of him and the whiskey won.

Next morning when he come to he was out of danger, but he shore was most awful sick—from the snake bite—ho! ho! For three seasons after that in the springtime, so he said, the bitten arm changed to the color of a serpent and shed off the outside skin. But he come round all right and was able to continue his preaching to the end of his life.

Ab Wright was a most awful good man. He had a good word to say for everybody, even for the criminals. Oncet he was praying with a condemned man the whole of his last night on this earth. It was in Jimtown. The man was James Calvin Logston. He was sentenced to hang for killing two women and a child with an axe. Ab Wright was with him most all of the last twenty-four hours. He done went and prayed with him in the cell and comforted him all he could. Well, when they were ready to hang him they put him in a shroud and placed him on a wagon with his coffin. Ab Wright and the doctor set beside him, and a heavy guard surrounded them all. They rode to the gallows, singing hymns as they went. The death warrant was read and Ab Wright preached the funeral service. He must have converted the condemned man, too, because after he done shaken hands with the people he told them he done come to his end through keeping bad company and warned them to keep away from the like. Then they stringed him up, but the rope broke and he fell to the ground. They got another rope and placed it around his neck and he was drawn up agin, but after a few moments the rope broke agin and he fell to the ground for the second time. Maybe they ought to have let him go then, but they didn't. They jes lifted him up agin, and as they done so he said a few words, but nobody knowed what they was. This time the rope didn't break and he hung twenty-five minutes and was pronounced dead. All through this terrible time Ab Wright and some other preacher men were there, singing hymns and praying to the Lord.

In one year this most wonderful old saddlebagger preached one hundred and eighty-one times, received one hundred and five persons into the Church, prayed with five hundred families, baptized fifty-four people and travelled over two thousand miles on horseback over the mountain country. He received no salary for this and only took up a few bits of collections. And during this year he had to look after his farm. That's a preacher man for you. In his whole life he baptized one thousand three hundred and twenty-three people, married eighty-seven couples, and held six hundred and eleven burial services. I know that our preacher men to-day do a lot of work, and most of them are sincere and godly men, but when I think of Ab Wright doing all of this in the mountains years ago when travelling was much harder and living was much worse than it is to-day, and never caring nohow whether he got paid or not, I kinder feel that him and the preacher men like him was among the anointed of the Lord.

Pastor Pile—Rosier Pile, we call him—who keeps a store to this day at Pall Mall and has a Sunday-school class too, used to be a saddlebagger. He used to ride through the mountains a-prayin' and holdin' meetings and a-visitin'. And he never received no salary neither and he didn't want none.

But jes like the feuds and the bushwhackers, these-here grand old saddlebaggers of the past are disappearing. Roads are coming into the mountains and people can get into church, and even if they can't go in they can build small churches a heap easier than before. So the preacher man on horseback with his saddlebags full of Bibles and religious books is passing out. There are a few of them left. These here modern times that are with us are sorter silencing "the voice crying in the wilderness."

CHAPTER X

GUNS

MOST all of the mountain people have jes natcherly growed up with rifles. From the cradle they are sorter used to the smell of powder and the presence of the old muzzle-loader, powder horn, and doeskin shot pouch hanging in a corner of the cabin. The mountaineer's arm has a sort of natural crook for an old rifle-gun.

The rifle played a big part in the conquering and developing of this-here mountain country. I ain't got much poetry in me, but any I have I sorter spill out on rifles and shooting and hunting. I am sorter used to these things. I understand them. I know how to make the most of them.

I am telling you I would much sooner take up my muzzle-loader than a pen or pencil, and I am much more useful with it, too. The early pioneers not only knowed how to use their rifles, but they knowed how to make them. The long-barrel, muzzle-loading type of rifle made in the mountains of North Carolina, Tennessee, and Kentucky was the best and most accurate-shooting gun in the world, and up to one hundred yards it still is. At the two last turkey-shooting matches held in our valley, seven out of ten of the turkeys had their heads busted with the muzzle-loaders and only

83

three with modern rifles. The distance was 'most always sixty yards, but the old muzzle-loaders also
brought down turkeys at one hundred fifty yards, although they are not so good as the modern rifle at that
distance.

Before the American pioneers made and sort of
perfected these-here muzzle-loaders there was really
no accurate rifle-guns in the world. The old flintlocks,
muskets, and blunderbusses which they used over there
in Europe were not much account nohow. They were
never sure of hittin' the mark. They were never even
sure of goin' off, and even when they did they made a
noise like a cannon. They often done more damage
to the shooter than to the one he was shootin' at. Most
often the powder flared back into the eyes of whoever
was squintin' down the barrel. Them-there guns might
have been all right over there on the other side where
a miss didn't matter so much and there was plenty of
time to reload and the more noise the better, but they
never would have got nothin' nohow over here. The
hunters who come into the American wilderness fightin'
Indians and shootin' game for food jes couldn't afford
to miss. They had to have a rifle-gun that they
knowed would shoot straight; that would shoot 'most
every time they fired it; that they could reload pretty
quick, and that wouldn't make too much noise for the
Indians to hear. They couldn't get these guns nowhere. There weren't any. So they begun to make
them themselves. And they made the first accurate,
dependable guns in the world. I guess the first real
good guns that come down here to the mountains were

the Decherds and the Leamans. They were made up
in Pennsylvania, but soon the mountaineers begun to
get busy and made their own.

Most all around this-here moutain country there was
blacksmiths and gunsmiths in them-there days who
learned how to make rifles that jes knowed how to
shoot straight. To this day there are men who can
make them. And if you roam around for a while you
can still see the ruins of the crude old blast furnaces
they used. I spent a heap of my time as a boy blacksmithing with my father. I never made any guns but
I often doctored sick ones. I know the heap of trouble and care you have to take when you are fooling
around with guns. And yet, these old Southern gunsmiths with crude forges and cruder home-made equipment turned out guns that served the purpose and were
in their time the best guns in the world and are even
now thought a heap of by our mountain marksmen.
These old mountain guns were made from ore dug out
of these-here mountains. Even the barrels were bored
or welded and then rifled on the ground. The trigger,
trigger guard, firing pan, flint chops, sights, and all the
other fittings were also made right in the mountains.
And the stock was generally carved out of grained and
seasoned woods, such as bird's-eye maple, or curly
cherry, or black walnut.

Some of the best known of these old mountain guns
were the Gibsons, Beans, or Duncans. Later on, of
course, the barrels and the locks were bought outside
and shipped in; and to-day nearly all the other parts
are bought and assembled. But jes the same there are

a heap of them old pioneer guns around, and there are a few mountain gunsmiths still left who can turn them out almost as good as ever. We don't use the flint-locks to-day. Hit is too hard to keep them dry. Out in the woods we always had to keep them covered with a sort of sleeve which we slip over the barrel. This sleeve was generally made from the skin of a steer or a deer's leg. Armed with these old mountain guns, not more than nine hundred mountain sharpshooters whipped and shot to pieces Ferguson and his twenty-six hundred trained men at King's Mountain. And it was these same old guns which made it possible for the six thousand men under Andrew Jackson down there at New Orleans to stop ten thousand British soldiers who once fought under Wellington and mussed up Napoleon.

Allowing for the times and the conditions and the purposes for which they were used, them-there native-made guns were the best rifle-guns that was ever made. I myself have used the Army service rifles and most of the modern high-powered rifles, but when I go hunting or take part in the shooting matches up to one hundred or even up to one hundred and fifty yards I much prefer my old muzzle-loading rifle-gun to any other in the world, and that's what I think of it.

They are very cheap to keep up. Loading ain't no bother if you know how. First of all, you stand the old gun upright with the butt resting on the ground. Then you pour the powder out of a powder horn, made from the horn of a buck or a steer, into the charger, which is generally carved out of the tip of

A TYPICAL CREEK-BED ROAD IN THE MOUNTAINS

"And there were only mountain trails and old dirt roads, that were no good nohow, and creek beds here before."

TURKEY-SHOOTING

"We tie the turkeys behind logs with only their heads showing and shoot off-hand; that is, from a standing position, sixty yards away. We pay ten cents a shot and get the turkey if we bust its head.

a buck's horn. The amount of powder you use, of course, depends on the distance you expect to shoot. Natcherly, a long shot takes a bigger charge of powder than a short shot. You pour the powder out of the charger down the muzzle of the gun. Many shooters are so expert that they can measure off the powder in the hollow of their hands and empty it into the muzzle, scarcely losing a grain. Then the patch is placed over the end of the muzzle. This-here patch is generally a piece of blue denim or bed ticking and it is best when it is greased or tallowed. The ball is then taken out of the shot pouch, which is made of soft doeskin and placed on top of the patch and pressed with the thumb into the barrel. Then the ends of the patch are trimmed off and the bullet and the patch are rammed hard down against the powder. The ramrod is generally a straight piece of hickory whittled into shape. A couple of whangs with this-here ramrod packs the ball into place. The patch lies on top of the powder and sorter packs the ball tight in the barrel so that the explosion can't escape. Last of all, the little percussion cap is put in place. Then the gun is ready for firing. All this takes jes a short time. Many of the old-timers can reload these old guns on the run.

Of course, if you're a hunter you have got to know all about guns and how to handle them. Guns are like hounds, they have a lot of this-here temperament, and you have got to kinder get acquainted with them. Sometimes you have got to kinder kid them. A gun will shoot a certain way one day and altogether different the next day. You have got to know whether they

shoot fine or full, or to the left or to the right; how
the wind affects them, and the sunlight and the clouds;
even how they shoot on damp days and dry days. I
have a whole collection of them at home. I have an
automatic shotgun and a twenty-five-twenty rifle and
that old muzzle-loader of my father's. It's the cap-
and-ball type. My father done used it in the shooting
matches, and that's what I use it for now. It's a sure
gun for that sort of work. It jes don't know how to
miss nohow. And I have a forty-five pistol. I sure
would like to have the one I used in the fight with the
machine guns in the Argonne. I tried to get it. The
War Department searched through about fifty thousand pistols for it, but I guess somebody got a-hold
of it and knowed it was a good one and decided to
keep it.

I kinder think that the reason why the mountaineers
are among the best shots in the world is because they
have growed up with rifles. They know all about
them. They know how to take them to pieces and put
them together again. They know how to doctor them
when they're sick, and many of them even know how
to make them. I am a-telling you that's understanding
a gun. Then they are always using them out in the
woods shooting at all sorts of game. Of course, that's
great practice. Then 'most all of them live pretty
healthy outdoor lives and go in for regular hours,
natcheral food, and the right amount of sleep. So
their sight and their nerves are 'most always good.

And then there's the shooting matches which are
always very popular in the mountains. Busting a

turkey's head and cutting the centre of targets makes
for expert marksmanship. A right-smart heap of the
men who went to King's Mountain and whipped Ferguson went right from one of these-here shooting
matches. They were a-having a big time of it. They
were shooting for beeves and turkeys at a big match
at Gilbertown, N. C., when they received word from
Ferguson, telling them if they didn't lay down their
arms and return to their rightful allegiance he would
come over them-there hills and smash their settlements
and hang their leaders. They was jes about the best
shooters in the mountains and they went straight from
that shooting match and connected with the backwater
men and went up King's Mountain and showed Ferguson how American mountaineers, armed with American muzzle-loading rifle-guns, can shoot.

CHAPTER XI

SHOOTING MATCHES

MOST every Saturday of late we have been holding these old-fashioned shooting matches on a hillside on my farm here in Pall Mall. Last Saturday we had one. We usually shoot for turkeys and end up the day with a beeve. We tie the turkeys behind logs with only their heads showing and shoot offhand; that is, standing up from a mark sixty yards away. We draw for positions and then take our turn shooting. We never know when the turkey is going to put his head above the log, or how long he is going to keep it there, or whether he is going to bob or weave just as you have drawn a fine bead on him. He pleases himself about that, and I am a-telling you a turkey gobbler tied behind a log is sometimes the contrarinest bird I ever knowed. He jes seems to know the right moment to duck.

We generally pay ten cents a shot and we get the turkey when we bust its head. Sometimes we do that right smart and the owner of the turkey don't get much out of it. Other times, when the wind and the light are agin us, he will collect a heap of dimes before anybody busts the turkey.

My father was p'int-blank certain death on turkeys' heads. He jes didn't know how to miss them. He really was a most wonderful shot. Often they ruled him down; that is, they made him shoot near the last, and sometimes they would never let him shoot nohow. They made him act as judge. I recollect a hill-billy from one of the back creeks brought in oncet two big turkey gobblers. He tried to raise a heap of money on them by laying down unfair conditions, but the mountaineers are pretty smart. They jes wouldn't shoot. He brought the price down to a nickel a shot. Still they wouldn't shoot. He had ruled my father out but at last he let him in to sort of start things; and he sure enough busted that old turkey's head the first shot. The same sort of thing happened over the second turkey, and my father had a pretty good day of it—two big turkey gobblers for ten cents. It is even better sport to shoot at the turkey at one hundred and fifty yards. We tie them to a stake out in the open and from a standing position have to hit them above the knee and below the gills. That's shooting too.

But the big event of these-here shooting matches is the beeve. "Beeve" is jes plain mountain talk for beef, and I guess 'most all over the world a beef means a steer. The beef is driven alive to the shooting ground. Its value is fixed by the owner, and then shots are sold at so much each until the price is made up. If the beef is worth fifty dollars generally fifty shots are sold at one dollar each. The owner takes the money. Each shooter can buy as many shots as he likes, but he has to pay for each shot. The first and second prizes are the hind quarters; the second and third the fore quarters; and the fifth the hide and tallow. That is generally how they are divided up.

The mark to shoot at is the dead centre of a criss-cross cut with a sharp knife on a board. Each shooter generally prepares his own board, and he prepares it according to his own liking. Some shooters blacken their boards over a fire of grass and twigs, and then put a little square of white paper either below or above the centre of the criss-cross according to the way they like to draw the bead. Others most like a plain white board with a black mark either under or above the centre of the criss-cross. The shooting is generally so expert that you 'most always have to cut the centre; that is, at least touch it with the bullet, if you hope to even get a smell of the meat; and if you hope to win one of the first choices, ho! ho! you generally have to take the centre out, bust it right out; and that's got to be a most powerful true shot. After each man shoots, his board is initialled and held by the judge until the prizes are settled. Often the shots are so close that the bullet has to be cut in half and placed in the hole and a compass used to determine which is the closest shot. My father 'most always was a judge and used to use the compass, and now that he is no more, my brother Sam generally does it.

At the last shooting match we had a right-smart crowd of mountain sharpshooters turn out. They come in from all over the mountains. They come in afoot, on horseback, in wagons, and in automobiles. They come in from away back in the canebreaks, from up the creeks, off the farms, and from the towns around. They come in in their blue jeans and overalls and all sorts of other shooting and business clothes.

They carried their old muzzle-loaders crooked under their arms and their powder horns and pouches slung over their shoulders. There must have been nearly a hundred of them and they were 'most all of the best shots around this-here part of Tennessee.

John Conatzer, a real hill-billy from back in the mountains, come in and declared he was a-going to eat turkey that night. He come in right off his little farm. He was dressed in his old overalls, with big patches on the knees and the elbows worn through. He had on an old slouch hat that hadn't any shape nohow. He had almost as much stubble on his chin as a wheat field after the mowing machine has been over it. He wore hobnail shoes and they shore give him a mean grip on the ground. John is jes one of the meanest men in all the mountains when it comes to drawing a fine bead under the centre of a target, or busting a turkey's head at 'most any distance. Winning the first prize is a sort of habit with him. He lives right up on top of a mountain, and he says it's that steep there he has to wear hobnails in the seat of his britches.

John Souders, one of the best shots in all this part of Tennessee, was on the ground early. He said he kinder felt it was his day and them-there turkeys was shore going home with him. I jes can't write well enough to describe his get-up, but I'm a-telling you it was even more *artistic* than John Conatzer's. Them-there two mountaineers seem to be rivals in everything, even in clothes, and they 'most always take meat home with them. John Souders comes from up one of the back creeks. Away in. He brought his old Dech-

erd with him; the same sorter gun they used at King's
Mountain. It stands over six feet and weighs twenty
pounds. You can still see the hammer marks on the
barrel. It sure is an old-timer.

Ike Hatfield was there, too. He is a descendant of
the bushwhackers who raised Cain around these parts
in the Civil War, and he is also a relation of the Hatfields who kinder set the fashion for feuds over acrost
the line in Kentucky. Compared with Ike's eyesight,
an eagle can't see nothing nohow. He said he was all
p'int-blank fired up to bust them old gobblers' heads
and to put his bullet inside of anybody else's.

Sheriff Livingston come in with a big crowd from
Jimtown. He is well over sixty years of age, but there
ain't nothing the matter with his sight or with his
nerves neither. That-there old sheriff has raided more
moonshiners than has 'most anybody else in these
mountains. He's shot bigger game than turkeys, too.
He has more'n once killed his man. Whenever he
squints down the barrel of a gun, he is jes going to hit
plumb in the centre.

Several of my brothers was there—Sam, toting my
father's old muzzle-loader, which is jes about the favourite gun around here; and Joe, who runs the store
at Wolf River; and George, who is jes the shootinest
fool when it comes to matches; and Henry and Jim and
Albert. They was all there. And they was all most
awful keen on carrying off some of them-there prizes.
And I am a-telling you I was there and I jes knowed I
was a-going to have a turkey dinner that night. I was
jes in the right mood for it.

It was a most awful bad day for shooting. The wind was a-blowing and there was a bright sunshine and a blue sky with jes a few thin white clouds kinder driftin' over. I was well down in the draw, so I jes set down and took it easy and kept my nerve steady. I felt plumb shore that I was going to get one of them-there turkeys. That-there first gobbler was jes the boldest bird that I ever seed. He jes stuck that-there red head of his up over the log and kinder looked lazily around as though admiring the landscape. The bullets of the first shooters pelted the log under him, knocked the dust out of his gills, or went whizzing past not a hair's breadth away, but not one of them drew blood. He shore seemed to have a charmed life. Every now and then he put his old head down to kinder rest or gobble up something from the ground, and then he kinder become interested agin and bobbed up to see what it was all about.

When John Souders stepped up to shoot, with that old Decherd of hisn I was even more interested than the turkey. He shore must have wanted that turkey most awful bad. He took a long time sighting, drew a fine bead jes above the turkey's gills—and then missed. His bullet whanged right past that old gobbler's head and cut up a streak of dust a few yards behind. I'm a-tellin' you that-there old gobbler blinked.

That tickled John Conatzer. He said that he knowed that the Lord Almighty was protecting that turkey from harm until his turn come. He took even a longer time than Souder. He jes stood there straight and still with his old muzzle-loader p'inting what looked like p'int-blank death at the gobbler. He stood there that long that it seemed that he would never fire nohow. We all sort of got tired holding our breath. Some of the other shooters tried to kid him, but they might jes as well have tried to kid a coon down the tree when the hound dogs are barking underneath. But in spite of everything he missed too, but only by an eye-lash. That old turkey was most awful close to being cold meat when John's ball whizzed past.

By this time we was all gitting fired up. Two of the best shots in the valley had fired and missed, and we shore made life miserable for them. It was even more miserable for them than for the turkey. That old gobbler didn't seem to care nohow. He still kept his old red head up, sorter challengin' like. Then young Oliver Delk, who lives back up one of the creeks, toed the mark. He looked pretty young and didn't stand much higher'n the muzzle-loader itself. We wasn't paying much attention to him and the turkey wasn't either. We all kinder counted him out as only a tol'able shot. He fired and that-there old turkey ducked, but he come up again right smart, bold as ever. Ike Hatfield was so surprised he swallowed his plug of home-twist and nearly had convulsions. Oliver had scratched it acrost the head. The skin was jes broken so he claimed it. The rules are that if you draw blood it is your turkey. So young Oliver, as proud as Solomon in all his glory, takened his turkey and another was placed behind the log.

My brother Sam was next to shoot. He complained that he had some dirt in his eye and that he couldn't draw a fine bead nohow. Jes the same he shot so close that I bet that new gobbler held his breath as Sam's bullet went past.

I was feeling pretty good when it come my turn. I told them hill-billies around to watch me right close and they would see what real shooting was. I looked that old gobbler right in the eye and he seemed to me to be looking right back at me and sorter challenged me to put his head down. I drew a pretty fine bead and allowed jes the least little bit for the wind. Then I recollected the sun was shining from the right. I allowed for that too. Then to make real sure I damped the foresight.

I sighted carefully. Then I lowered the rifle and told the boys that I could only have nicked him that time and I wanted to do better'n that. I sighted again and I figured on drilling him right through the head. I could already see that turkey on the table at home for supper. I drew even a finer bead and pressed the trigger, but that-there old gobbler didn't go down. He hadn't any sense nohow. A streak of dust spurted up just behind his head, and I shore enough had missed, ho! ho! My brother George suggested that maybe the bullet had bounced off of the gobbler's head, and John Conatzer 'lowed that I was gittin' old and shaky anyhow.

The next half-dozen shots also missed. That-there sunshine and them-there little white clouds shore made it bad for good shooting.

Mr. H. C. Cravens, who keeps a store in Jimtown, got the next turkey. He busted it right through the

head and it never did know what hit it, unless it
thought it was struck by a bolt of lightning.

And, after some more missing, Allen Brooks got the
third. It was a plumb good shot, too. After that we
lengthened the distance. We tethered the next gobbler to a stake, away under the hill, one hundred and
fifty yards away. He shore looked pretty, too, strut-
ting around on the end of the string, with his feathers
kinder glistening in the sunlight, and his big red head
held proudly up, jes like a peacock's. But he didn't
stay up long. My brother George, who is the most
awfulest man on long-distance turkey shooting, come
up with that-there old muzzle-loading gun of my father's. Some of the boys 'lowed that a hundred and
fifty yards was too far for that-there old hog rifle.
But George stood up there and hit that turkey that
hard it must have thought the hill had fallen on it. It
went right up in the air and then come down and
spread out all over the ground, stone dead. George
had shot it right through the breast with a hog rifle
at a hundred and fifty yards.

The turkeys were now going pretty fast. The boys
were getting their eyes in and were doing most wonderful things with their rifles. The next turkey we
tethered somehow or other managed to get loose jes
as one of the boys was taking aim. We all laughed
and suggested that he ought to shoot it on the run,
but he put down his rifle, spit out a plug of tobacco,
and remarked that hit was hard enough to hit them-
there fool birds when they were still and they was
harder to hit than bats when they was moving.

So some of the boys lit out and chased that old turkey through the woods, and run it up against a fence
and brought it back to its rightful place, where it spent
the next few minutes kinder contentedly picking insects
off'n the ground. Some other shooters fired and
missed. Their bullets tore up the dirt around the turkey, but he was busy hunting his dinner and didn't
mind nohow.

My turn come agin after a while and I was all fired
to make up for missing that first shot. I jes couldn't
figure on missing this time no way and nohow. I
squinted down the barrel of the old muzzle-loader and
I could see that turkey jes sorter on the end of it. I
drew a fine bead agin, allowed for windage and dis-
tances, and was jes going to pull the trigger when one
of them-there hogs of mine that had been feeding on
acorns somewhere in the woods, santered right acrost
my field of fire.

That kinder tickled the crowd. If it had been a
razorback I would have let fly jes the same, but it was
one of my prize Poland Chinas, and though I wanted
that old turkey most awful bad, I sorter didn't want
to ruin the future prospects of that-there hog of mine.
I kinder figured I could have cut a couple of his bris-
tles and got the turkey the same, but it ain't natural
for a farmer to take chances with hogs, so I waited
until he had wandered on a piece, and then I took aim
agin and whanged a bullet right at that-there old gobbler. I guess I must have had one eye on the Poland
China because I shore missed that turkey by several
feet. I didn't even scare it. The bullet kicked up the

dust somewhere between the turkey and the hog. So you see, that time I might have been a bad turkey shooter, but I was a most awful careful hog farmer.

The boys shot four turkeys in the next seven shots. That's shootin', I'm a-tellin' you. We kept the last one, a great big gobbler, the best of them all, for the last shootin' of the day.

Then we made up the beeve. But this time the beeve was a hog—a two hundred forty pounder. He was valued at twenty-four dollars and we paid fifty cents a shot until the amount was made up. Now, to me pork is right-smart better than turkey. Turkey is dry meat anyway. I had missed the old gobblers, but I thought I would get me that whole hog, so I bought five shots. John Souders bought in, and John Conatzer, and my brothers George and Sam, and some of the other best shots, too.

That shore was a mean day. Them-there experts jes couldn't cut the centre out of their targets. They laid a whole mess of balls within an eighth of an inch of the centre, but that was not close enough to git the meat. I was still feeling bad about the turkeys and I wanted to git my whole five shots right through the centre; I had done it before and I figured I could do it agin. I figured on driving that hog home on the hoof. That was a trick of my father's. He would most often win all the prizes and drive the hog or beef home alive. But, like the others, I got all around the centre, but I couldn't cut it.

At last I put a ball inside of the other shots, it jes broke the centre, and then that-there young stripling of a Delk boy that had busted the turkey went and cut the centre right out of his target and got first prize. He was the shootinest shooter of the whole bunch that day. I got second choice. They slaughtered and dressed the hog on the spot and I picked me a nice ham, which was not so bad after all.

John Conatzer didn't get none nohow, but he kinder consoled himself by saying that the pork would be sorter tough because it was killed in the soon of the moon—meaning, of course, when the moon was young. That's a mountain superstition.

Then we went back to finish off that last gobbler. He shore was the biggest one that ever come safely through Thanksgiving Day. John Souders remarked that he looked most as big as an ostrich. Jes as we were all gittin' ready to let fly at that last gobbler, a razorback sneaked in behind us and started in on George's dead turkey, which he had throwed down on the ground, and I am a-telling you, when George saw that hog calmly eating up his bird he let out a whoop like a red Indian. He started right after it, but the hog wasn't willing to let go. He picked up the turkey and lit out down the valley and over the hill and George kept a-going after him, and we all whooped and cheered, and finally George made a dive at the hog and the three of them went down in a heap, and there was feathers all over the place. But he got his turkey back, and when he returned he remarked that razorbacks never weren't good nohow.

Jes about this time Pastor Browne, who was holding a revival service in Jimtown, come out in the field. He

is only a young man, but he looked jes like one of them-
thar old fire-eating pastors that used to preach fire and
brimstone through these mountains in the old times.
He was wearing a sort of square black hat and a sort
of squared-off black suit, and he has a kind of square
head and a square figure, and I guess he has a square
mind; I mean he squares it with the Bible. He is a
mighty powerful preacher and a right-smart pastor.

We invited him to bust the turkey's head. He
hadn't handled a rifle for eight years, but he said he
guessed he'd try. He wanted that turkey worser'n
any of us, he guessed. Like a real preacher-man, he
stood to one side and prayed to the Lord that if it was
His will he would most awful like to have that turkey.
He stepped right up to the mark, clapped the rifle to
his shoulder, and prayed agin and then fired, and
shore enough he busted the gobbler's head. It was the
best turkey gobbler of the day, and his shooting was
the straightest and the best, too. And when he got the
turkey he told us that he didn't even see its head when
he pointed the rifle. It was the prayer that done it.
He was sure of that and we 'lowed maybe he was right.

Then he started for home in a hurry. The last we
seed of him he was striding off acrost the hills, going
back to Jimtown to hold his revival services that night.
He looked about the happiest preacher man this side
of Paradise. He was swinging the old turkey gobbler
with one hand, and he was shouting praises to the
Lord.

Ho! ho!

CHAPTER XII

LARNIN' FROM NATURE

THERE are two kinds of larnin'—the larnin' you git out of books and the larnin' you pick up from living close to nature. If you could only git both you shore would be what they call educated. It's most hard, though. If you get one you seldom get the other. That's the way of things. Life's fair. There's a sort of balance in things. The people in the towns and cities get to larn from books and schools and people in this-here mountain country sorter got to larn from nature.

Larnin' to know trees and flowers and animals and sunsets is like readin' a big book. You have kinder got to go to school to understand that sort of readin'. I mean to a sort of outdoor school where you have got to tramp round, hunting and shooting, and stay out and use your eyes and your ears and your power of reasoning, too. What you pick up from these things sort of larns you a most awful lot about life. What you pick up from dogs and horses and foxes and squirrels and coons and bees and hornets, and the little critters in the earth, and most everything in the woods, helps you understand people, too.

I've got a lot of dogs around my farm. I know them and they know me. We kinder understand and love each other. A few months ago a boy up in Jim-town killed one of my dogs. I felt pretty bad about it. I jes kinder moped around and missed that dog for a considerable time. Oncet I had a coon dog that got into the most rip-roarin' fight with a big coon. He got scratched and beat up, but he stuck it out, and after he whipped the coon he came to me all full of hurt and wagged his tail and kinder twisted his bruised face into a sort of human smile, and then I kinder got down beside him and petted and hugged him. I jes couldn't help it.

And I have an English Walker. There is a dog for you. He is pretty old now and getting grouchy but in his younger days I knowed him to trail a fox for forty hours without stopping. Then he'd come home, hungry and lame and worn out, and he would stand up and bark and whine and look at me with that knowing dog look in his eyes as though wondering if I was approving of what he'd done. I've got a couple of Red Bones, and when they git started after a fox they never stop. I'm a-telling you, you can larn a heap from dogs, and it makes you sort of more human to have them around.

Fox-hunting teaches you a lot. I ain't a-foolin' when I say that quite a heap of foxes have got a right-smart more sense than many human beings. The tricks they go in for to throw the hounds off the scent shore are astonishing. They circle and come back over their old trail. They go up creeks, jump from rock to rock, and walk along fences and rocks. They go in for all sorts of other contraptions; and they 'most always come home, too. They jes sorter circle away around

for hours and sometimes for days, and then, sure
enough, if they can throw off the hounds they come
a-loping and a-sneaking back to their homes. Foxes
think a heap more of their homes than a lot of humans
do.

I kinder like laying out under the trees watching
squirrels. They are the workinest animals. They are
never still. They are always up and a-doing, picking
nuts and whittling them to get the kernels out and
storing them away against bad times; and feeding their
young ones and teaching them to cling to trees and
travel over the tops of the forests. They're kind of
impudent, too, the way they chatter and scold. Squirrels sure have a heap of confidence in themselves and
they're pretty tricky, too. They don't seem to mind
you watching them, but they sure know when you've
got a gun around.

But if you want to know what real courage and in-
dustry is, just tackle a hive of wild bees in a hollow
tree on the mountainside. Ho! ho! They're right-
smart soldiers and they're the fightinest things.
They're great believers in this-here "rights of self-
determination." When they come to swarming and
buzzing around it ain't nobody's business to be too
close. You may get the honey, but you're going to get
a lot more, too, before the bees are finished with you.
They're most awful intelligent too. If a mouse gets
into their hive—Ho! ho! They sting it to death and
then seal hit off; that is, they seal it up in wax. They
shore have a whole heap of sense. And talk about
looking after their women folks! The way they fight

and work for their queen is right smart. And when you try to rob their hives, the way they will all get around and try to hide her or get her away is a most astonishing thing. Bees are the hardest working, fiercest fighting, and most home-loving and sensible things in the forest.

There's a moth down here in the mountains that can even out-smart the bees. Hit goes into their hives and eats up the honey. That's looking for trouble, I'm a-telling you. But hit does it jes the same. Hit spins a sorter web around the entrance to the hive and gets in without the bees being able to get at it. Once inside it kinder webs itself off and eats up the honey; all of it in time. And the bees either starve to death or swarm somewhere else. That moth's what you might call a genius. Ho! ho!

Coons are brave and good fighters, but they ain't got so much sense. When the hounds git right after them instead of dodging and doubling on their trail and trying to hide away in the woods they climb plumb up the first tree; and then you have got them. When you cut the tree down, instead of trying to get away they cling to it until it crashes, and then they do the foolinest thing; they climb down the tree again to the butt before they jump to the ground. They sorter haven't realized that the tree is down, and that is jes plain ignorance. The hounds have got more sense. As soon as the tree falls they rush right to the butt; they jes know the coon is coming that way.

Hogs, too, ain't got over-much brains. They do the craziest things. They let the dogs most often run them into corners where they can scarcely turn around and can't get away nohow, and when the dog gets hold of them, they sorter stand there looking silly-like.

If you want to know what real happiness is jes wander out into the woods of a moonlight night and listen to the whipperwill singing.   There is a bird for you, always good-natured, always happy, as if always glad for being borned.   There is only one other bird that's like it.   Hit's the mocking bird.   There is a bird with a heap of sense and what you'd call imagination. Hits always kinder foolin' the other birds.   There is folks here who say a mocking bird can make almost any sound and that sometimes they can whistle almost like a man and that way fool a dog.   I hain't never heard them do that myself, but I have heard them imitate other birds until you would think the forest was plumb full of almost every kind of bird.   Hit is no ordinary bird that can do that.   That's why I have always kind of thought a mocking bird the queen of all the birds in the forest.

You can larn a lot from birds and animals, but I kinder think you can larn most from the soil itself. I don't know much about philosophy.   I am not certain that I know what it is.   But I'm a-telling you that you do a heap of thinking about lots of things when you are following a plough and turning over great rows of all sorts of good soil.   And somebody told me that Bobby Burns, the Scotch poet, used to make up a lot of his rhymes while ploughing and harrowing; so I went and read me that one about the mouse.   That's poetry.   Only a man who knows about the soil and the little critters in it could have written that. That's what I mean.

I kinder think that even if you can't write poems you can sorter think them; and when you're sitting on a harvester with the ripe, golden-headed wheat stalks waving at you and going down as you go along, your mind sorter fills up and brims over, and all sorts of beautiful thoughts kinder sing in your soul.

I guess we have all got a little of this-here poetry in us and it takes old Mother Nature to bring it out. That's the way with me anyhow.

I am most awful fond of the woods after it's been raining. I like to stand in them and swing my arms and take deep breaths. There's scents there that jes make your soul bob with joy. And as for pictures, I ain't never seen none that could come up to a sunset in our valley, when the sky out there in the west is that full of colours that you sorter get drunk on them. And if you have never seen the woods when they are full of moonlight, all sorter soft and milky, you ain't never seen nothing nohow.

I am a-telling you you can larn a lot from nature. I ain't an artist nor a poet nohow. I don't know much about pictures and poems. I often don't understand them when I read or see them. But I kinder got a hankering after these-here natcheral things. I may be all wrong, but somehow, way inside of me, I kinder feel the best poems have never been written and never will be, and I jes know the best pictures in the world can never be made with paints and brushes.

I have been a heap criticized for what I done when

I come back from the war; for turning down all them-
there offers to go on the stage and into the movies and
in business. I knowed I was turning down fortunes. I
knowed I could never hope nohow to make a lot of
money like that agin. But I couldn't help it.

Even at that-there big banquet in New York City I
jes couldn't help thinking about them-there hound dogs
of mine. I kinder heard them baying and calling and
I couldn't get back to them quick enough. I seed the
lights of Broadway. I liked them. But I jes knowed
they didn't mean as much to me as the stars and the
moonlight and that-there little valley and the growin'
crops and woods and flowers at home. So I jes natcherly lit out on the first train.

I love being out-of-doors. I jes love it. I am used
to it, and all my people, way back to old Coonrod Pile,
and I am a-thinking away back beyond him too, loved
being out and foolin' around where there was plenty of
room to move in. I suppose everybody jes has different fancies. I ain't even questioning that. I ain't even
a-saying people are wrong for liking the cities and the
bright lights and the noises—if they get the most en-
joyment out of them, it's all right with me. But I
don't. And so I turned my back on them; and I am
back here on the farm with my own people, in the
mountains I love. I jes couldn't hope to be happy if
I couldn't hunt and shoot and tramp around these-here
hills with them-there hound dogs of mine.

I have got five of them, three English hounds and
two Red Bones. The English hounds are good for
most anything you want them for. They're the most

usable dogs. They're good for squirrels, coons, foxes, razorbacks and even rabbits. The Red Bones are no good for nothing except foxes. They won't yelp after nothing but foxes, but once they pick up the scent they sure will follow until they catch the animals, or get them back into their den.

The best coon dogs, though, has got to be trained for the job. They have got to be taught that they must follow a scent without yelping, because if they make a heap of noise the coon will hear them and keep a-going and never come near enough to be treed. You have got to understand dogs before you can get much hunting out of them. You have got to understand their ways and what they're good for, and you have got to understand the habits of the things they're hunting, too.

CHAPTER XIII

HUNTING

To be a right-smart hunter you have got to know not only about guns and hounds and woods and animals, but the right kind of clothes to wear. You have got to be comfortable when you are in the woods or tramping over the hills. You can't enjoy a hunt and you can't shoot straight or keep up with the hounds unless you are feeling all right. I have missed easy shots from being wet through and cold when I should not have been. And the wrong kind of socks or boots have made me miss more'n one fox or coon. I 'most always wear overalls and a hunting coat made of waterproof ducking. I wear light leggings and light hobnail boots and a good shady hat.

My favourite hunting is after fox. I don't mean riding the hounds. I mean following the hounds on foot, or sort of going acrost the circle to where you know they're most likely to be and getting them as they go by. You have shore got to know the habits of foxes and you have got to have good hounds and be a fair-to-middling shot if you hope to have any sort of success at this sort of sport.

We have two kinds of foxes here, the red and the gray. The red will run for two or three days before it circles back to its den, but the gray ones only take a few hours. When we go out after foxes we sorter hike along until the dogs hit the trail. Then they begin to bay. That's music, I'm a-telling you. We then get on top of a ridge where we can sort of locate things. We can most always tell whether it's a red or a gray fox by the size of the circle they're running. The gray keeps in kinder close, but the red goes from mountain to mountain and on through the gaps mile after mile. It shore takes a lot to tire them.

If we know it is a gray fox we go over on the edge of the plantation or on a bluff. It has a habit of making for those sort of places. If it is a red one we hide in the gaps in the mountains where we know it is most sure to go. Them-there red foxes is runners. They sure know how to wear the padding off'n a hound's feet and then lead him home all tired out. They sure enough are "dog tired" when they run a red fox. Foxes are very sly. They can see and smell a long way, and if the hounds catch up with them they will fight too.

Coon-hunting is 'most always at night. A dark night, or when there is about a quarter moon, is the best. It is good sport, if you have the right kind of dog. A coon lives in the woods, generally around the heads of the hollows. He feeds on corn, acorns, and chestnuts and the like. You take your coon dog out in the hills and turn him loose and you seldom hear of him again until he begins to bay. Then you know he's treed a coon. If it is in small timber sometimes you can shake the coon out and let him fight it out with the dogs. A coon's a good, hard fighter, much better'n a cat. It takes a right-smart dog to whip a coon. If you can't shake him out you have got to get busy with axe and saws and cut down the tree. That is, of course, if you want the sport; but if you don't care for the sport and only want the coon, you can shoot him out; that is, if it is not too dark and you can see him; and if it is dark, you can get out your electric pocket torch and shine the light around the tree until it reflects in the coon's eyes. He 'most always is looking down at you or the dogs. Then you can shoot with a fair chance of getting him. I have often stayed out all night and slept under the tree. It was too dark to see him and I didn't have a pocket torch or an axe along with me, so I jes had to stay with them dogs until the morning when it was light again and I could get me the coon.

Mountain cats are right-smart fighters, too, but the dogs don't seem to care. They rush in and soon kill them. I have knowed some cats that weighed forty or fifty pounds. I don't like cats. They ain't no sports nohow and when they get after lambs and pigs they shore cost a heap of money.

Hog-hunting is a favourite sport in the mountains. I have been in a heap of wild-hog hunts. The wild hogs around here are mostly domestic hogs that have been turned out and have sorter gone back on their kind. We keep hogs in the woods all the time. They get fat on the acorns, beechnuts, hickory nuts, and chestnuts. They jes grub around and find them or dig them up and have a right-smart time. Sometimes as many as fifty different farmers have their hogs running in the same woods. We all mark them with our own particular mark and fasten bells on straps around the necks of the leaders.

When a hog goes wild his whole nature seems to change. He lies up in the daytime and runs wild during the night, which is jes the opposite to the tame hogs. When we go hunting for them we trail them with our dogs, and then when the dogs bay them we go up and let loose a specially trained hound, which gets them by the leg and holds them or even throws them. I once knowed a dog, a sort of half bulldog he was. He used to grip the hog by the nose and then jes lie down. That shore was a sight and he wouldn't let loose nohow. The fool old hog would jes stand there and shake his head, and not know what to do. Hogs shore ain't got much sense. We generally shoot the wild hogs with our old muzzle-loaders. That's why we call them hog rifles.

Squirrel-hunting is pretty good. It's best in the fall when the woods is full of hickory nuts. The best way to get them is to locate your hickory trees, and then go in among them early in the morning. You have got to know how to slip in quietly and not disturb a leaf or twig. You have got to understand, to know the feel and sort of sense what I call the sounds of the forest. And in the forest every sound, every flutter of a leaf, every falling of a nut, every strip of bark fluttering down, everything means something.

The forest has its own way of talking. It has a language of its own, and the hunter jes has got to understand and learn that-there language, and he has

SPOILS FOR THE VICTOR

"I jes knowed I was a-goin' to have a turkey
dinner that night, ho ho."

HUNTING COMPANIONS

"I jes couldn't hope to be happy nohow
if I couldn't hunt and shoot and tramp
around these-here hills with them-there
hound-dogs of mine."

got to keep his eyes and ears open all the time, especially if he is out after squirrels. If you know these things and act natcheral you can go right in among the squirrels. I have seen as many as twenty in one tree. They set up there on the branches, whittling the nuts. They whittle off a hole and then they get the kernel out. They eat mulberries, acorns, chestnuts, and beech and hickory nuts. They eat the buckeye too. Part of that is very poisonous, but I am a-telling you the squirrel knows that. He knows which part to eat and which part to leave. Some animals shore have a lot of sense.

This country shore used to be full of deer, but they have been 'most shot out and there are only a few left. I have only shot a few deer, and I don't know much about it.

I don't know much about baar-hunting either. There's a few baars left, but they are back in the mountains and it's hard to get at them. It's more luck than skill, getting a baar in these mountains these days. A few weeks ago one of our mountain boys was driving a truck acrost a trestle bridge when he almost run p'int-blank into a baar which was going acrost the bridge from the other direction. That-there old baar jes kept a-going on. Hit warn't scared of that-there old motor truck nohow. So the boy went into reverse and backed up and give that old baar the right-of-way. That's sportsmanship for you. He jes warn't going to run plumb into that old baar and probably go over into the creek below. As he himself has said, baars are scarce enough, but if you have got the time and patience you can go into the mountains and get one, but you can't get another truck that way nohow.

The most exciting sport of all is cutting down a bee tree. I am a-telling you that's looking for punishment. Some men can get along with bees. I can't nohow. My brother Henry can handle them with his bare hands and do 'most anything with them; and they very rarely sting him, and when they do, it don't seem to bother him much. But they sort of have a natcheral dislike for me. They come at me right smart, and they shore make me do all these-here funny dances all over the mountain. Wild hogs are mean fighters and they often kill our dogs. Baars have got a bad way with them and coons and mountain cats ain't at all sociable, but the worst of them all are them-there wild bees. It kinder beats me how such a little critter can do so much damage when he sorter backs up against you and pushes.

But we mountain people are most fond of the honey and we will go to any length to get it. We hunt the wild bees jes like we hunt 'most any other animal, except, of course, we don't use dogs. A dog has got even less business than a human around a wild beehive. We put out bee bait on the trees. We generally use burnt sugar, or honey, or something else that's sweet. The bees come along and get at it and then we try and follow them up to their bee tree. They generally hive in a big hollow tree on the high ground on top of a mountain.

Once we have the tree located we begin making preparations. We sometimes get all dressed up. We wear bee bonnets, which are made out of something like mosquito netting, draped down over our hats and tucked into the collars of our coats. We wear gloves and thick woollen socks, or leggings. But, somehow or other, wild bees when you rob their hives know how to penetrate most any clothing. They sure find the open places, and then—ho! ho! But 'most all of the mountain boys, though they don't like bee stings no-how, generally go out without dressing in them-there special clothes. But they sure take a lot of punish-ment. My brother Sam tackled a hive oncet, and by the time he had felled the tree he was so wet with sweat that his clothes were jes clinging to him and the bees most nigh drove him off before he could even get near the honey.

The other night we cut down a bee tree and got one of the biggest hauls of honey we have ever known. We got out over two big bucketfuls, and there was even more'n that spilt or mussed up. It was a great big half-hollow oak tree on one of the mountains about three miles through the woods. We had a most awful time getting in over the rough places, sliding down mountains and climbing up others, and getting all tan-gled up in vines and thorny brushes. It was a very tall tree. We sawed it down. We tried to fall it on a small cedar so as not to smash up the trunk and spill the honey, but the cedar gave way, and that old tree cracked up and there was honey and bees all over the place.

I kept well back and held the dog. I don't like bee stings nohow. Besides, that-there dog thought it was

a coon tree and was rarin' to go. He would have
rushed in there and stuck his nose into the honey and
the bees would have stung every square inch of him.
It's right-smart funny, I am a-telling you, to see a
hound howling and prancing around, rubbing his nose
with his paws, but it's cruel jes the same, and it don't
do the hound no good nohow. So I clung to mine, and
later on I tied him to a sapling.

When the tree crashed the boys run along beside the
trunk until they located the hive. You couldn't miss it
nohow. It was jes a wild, mad swarm of mad bees,
and the sweetest, most golden honey you ever tasted.
My brother Henry turned in with his bare hands and
didn't seem to mind the bees nohow. My other brothers, Jim and Sam, went in with him, but in a few minutes they come out again, and they agreed that bees
never was no good nohow. Jim was so badly stung
around the ankles that he couldn't get his shoes on
next day. Worse than that, he was biting into a piece
of honeycomb and there was a bee in it and it bit him
on the end of the tongue and he hollered worse'n a
baar. Sam jes kinder sneaked out and got well out of
the firing line. He didn't want to admit that the bees
had whipped him, but they had jes the same.

But that-there Henry stayed with them. You could
hardly see him for the bees and honey. He filled himself full and said it was the best he had ever tasted.
Then he filled the buckets and the cans and a card-
board box, and there was a lot more running out and
jes as much was lost as was ketched. Henry always.

kinder believed that when you are robbing a hive you
are safer in the swarm than on the outside. He says
the fighters always skirmish on the outside and go
right after anybody who's straggling around, but if
you are in among them, and especially if you have
honey on you, they won't touch you unless you happen
to squeeze or pinch them, and then they let fly with
them-there torpedoes. They crawled all over Henry
and he jes lightly brushed or pulled them off and kept
right on after the honey. And then he poked about
among the bees looking for the queen. That stirred
them up, but he didn't seem to mind. That-there
Henry is the foolishest man that ever took honey out
of a hive. He don't seem to mind bees at all, and
their stings don't seem to bother him nohow.

After they had kinder recovered from the effects of
the first attack, Jim and Sam sorter slunk back in
among them, but their confidence was sorter ruined.
It don't take many bee stings to do that. But no
stings no honey, and they wanted more honey, and
they got it, and everything else that went with it. In
the evening we carried those old buckets and cans full
of honey back home. The next day we went out and
rounded up the bees. We wanted to take them home,
too. We took a gum along with us. That is a sort
of box-shaped beehive. We looked around for the
queen, to put her in the gum, but them-there bees sure
were on the warpath and we couldn't find her nohow.
We put some of the comb we had left in the box and
let it stand there and went away and when we come

back again they was swarming in the box and we was able to take them home and they're on the farm now. Bees sure have a lot of sense.

So I have growed up hunting and shooting and larning a few of the secrets of nature in these forests and mountains. And I'm a-telling you, you can larn a lot that way.

CHAPTER XIV

BOYHOOD

I WAS borned in Pall Mall, in Fentress County. Hit is under the mountain; that is to say, in the valley below. Hit is called the Valley of the Three Forks of the Wolf, because Wolf River forks into three branches not far from our home. Hit is in the Cumberland Mountains, in the eastern part of middle Tennessee, not far from the Kentucky line. I was borned in a one-room log cabin with puncheon floors, and the walls made of rough-hewn slabs. These walls was chinked with bark and mud, but jes the same, in the winter time the wind would whistle in through the walls and up through the cracks in the floor. Some of them-there floor cracks were so big we could look and see the chickens and pigs underneath.

I was the third in a family of eleven children, eight boys and three girls. Most all of them were big and red-headed; and I was borned and growed up the biggest of them all. There was a whole litter of us and we jes sort of growed up like a lot of little pigs. I don't mean we was allowed to be dirty like pigs. I jes sorter mean that we were 'most always turned loose out-of-doors on the mountainside, kinder running wild, playing and hunting around. We was sort of brung up by the hair of the head.

We weren't pampered. Mother and Father hadn't any time to pamper us. They was most awful hardworking people. They had to be to bring up eleven children like they did. Father was a blacksmith. His shop was in a cave or rockhouse, as we called it, at the head of the spring on the mountainside, just near our home. He knowed wonderful well how to handle mares and horses and never refused even the meanest of them. Some of the mules was most awful, but my father never backed up on them. I am telling you that shows character. But money was scarce in them times and he never made more than about fifty cents a day. I don't mean to say he averaged that much. He didn't. He was so fond of hunting that he would neglect his blacksmithing and go out over the hills for days to get him some deer or some turkeys. But he wasn't lazy and like the rest of us boys it wasn't natcheral for him to resist the baying of the hounds and the call of the woods. I guess we've got it in the blood. He was a right-smart woodsman. He could follow a trail anywhere, or go out through the wildest country on the darkest nights, and never get lost for a minute. He was the best shot in the mountains. Often I have seed him take the centre out of a target, shot after shot. I have seed him fire a dozen times at a target and put most all of the bullets through the same hole.

We most always had plenty of fresh meat from my father's rifle-gun. But jes the same, we was always poor. Mother used to hire out and work at other places, washing, spinning or weaving, or doing chores. She would earn about twenty-five cents a day.

So we growed up. We had our own log cabin and a little land. We raised chickens and hogs and some corn and we had a couple of cows and a whole heap of fresh air and plenty of room outside, but not much inside the cabin. Eleven children and mother and father take up a most awful lot of room, and that little one-room log cabin was kinder crowded at night, when we were all tucked in; but we was all under one roof, growing up good, strong, and healthy, and loving each other. Jes a mountain family. We children would all lie in bed, tucked in for the night. Mother would sit in front of the big open fire carding, or spinning, or weaving; and Father would sit in the corner in the light of a lantern or a grease lamp and clean and mend his guns; and that's the way we growed up.

We shore were pretty rough scrappers, and among ourselves and with the neighbours' kids we used to fight right sharp. Of course, a whole heap of children like that will get up to all sorts of mischief, but Mother jes knowed where the most stinging hickory sticks growed and Father had a mule whip, and they both knowed how to use them. I guess the reason I growed up so big was that I was such a roughneck and Father had to whip me so much that he sorter kept my hide loose so that I could fill out. When I was sixteen I was nearly six feet tall and weighed one hundred and sixty pounds.

Of course, they wanted us to go to school and we was most all anxious to get some larnin'. But we were very poor, and 'most all the other mountain people were poor too, and there was only money enough for the school to keep going about two and a half months each year, and that was in the middle of summer. It was too cold in the wintertime. The roads were bad. There were no bridges over the creeks and we couldn't get acrost; and we couldn't afford warm clothes neither. And even in the summertime they had to dismiss school for two or three weeks for crops and foddering. I went for about three weeks a year for about five years. I larned to read and write. I had about a second-grade education. I don't think I could have passed the second grade. The schoolhouse was a little frame one-room building over on the hill. There were about one hundred pupils and only one teacher. We used to sit on benches made out of split logs with two pegs mortised in them. The benches had no backs. They were so high that when I used to sit on them I could scarcely touch the floor with my feet. During the last year we had two or three desks.

I never read no books till I was about twenty years of age. Then I read only one and that was the life of Frank and Jesse James.

I begun to work almost as soon as I could walk. At first I would help Mother around the house, carrying water, getting a little stovewood, and carrying and nursing the other children to keep them from yelling around after Mother while she was trying to get a bite of dinner for us all. I would go out to the field with Father before I was six years old. I would have to chop the weeds out of the corn. Father would be ploughing with the old mule, and I and my brothers would follow after until he was out of sight, and then we would steal off and play and scrap around; and then when we would get home he would give us some hickory tea, as he called it.

And it didn't take much of it to make a fellow wish there never was no hickory in these-here mountains. Our clothes was very poor. When I first went to school I wore a home-made linsey dress, and I guess I worned it that long it couldn't stay on me no longer nohow, and jes dropped off as if by itself. As I growed older and larger Mother would get some clothes from the neighbours, old ones for washings she done for them, to make us boys britches and coats to keep us warm in the winter months. We had clean cotton shirts which we were only allowed to wear on Sunday mornings, but we had no coats. I shore do remember the kind of shoes we wore in the winter-time. Father made them. They was brogan shoes with brass on the toes, and when we would get up in the morning our shoes would be cold and stiff and we would have to warm them around the old log fire before we could put them on. They were most awful hard and stiff and would take the hide off our heels and they slipped up and down when we walked.

When I was sixteen Mother went to the little country store and bought me a pair of dress shoes. I called them Sunday shoes, for I only wore them on Sunday. They were number ten men's shoes. They were the first dress shoes I ever had. I was most awful proud of them. The next Sunday morning Mother and I started to the little church meeting. Of course, I put on the new shoes. I shore felt good in them. I kept looking down at them, and I kinder thought that everybody else was admiring them. Before I got to church it come up a rain and got muddy and the red clay was very tough and pulled off one of the heels. I scraped in the mud, got it, and put it in my front pants pocket. I kept on a-going with one heel on and one off. When I got almost to the church the other heel come off and I got it and put it in my other front pocket. My, what trouble I was in—my first pair of Sunday shoes and both heels off before I got to church where I could really show them off—and I had no coat and my shirt was all wet and muddy too! And there was a girl friend there that I kinder admired. So there I was with my first pair of Sunday shoes and my first time to wear them, and this trouble had to come, and I was slipping all over the road with those number tens with no heels on them, and that shore spoiled the pleasure of the day.

As I growed up I begun to look around for some work, but there wasn't much of it in the little valley. Father took me into the rockhouse, where I helped him to blacksmith. He taught me to handle them-there mules and not to back up on them. I got to know horses and mules right smart, and I picked up the blacksmith business. But I most loved getting out with Father to help him shoot. We would hunt the red and gray foxes in the daytime and skunks, possums, and coons after dark. Often we would hunt all day and do the blacksmithing at night. I did a heap of farming too. I worked for Mr. E. J. Williams and others for forty cents a day.

In 1911 my dear father takened sick and died of typhoid fever. He was kicked most awful bad by a mule he was trying to shoe. She lashed out and got him. She was the only one that ever out-smarted him. She would not have done it nohow, only he didn't know she was mean. He was most awful sick for some time and I think it led up to his death.

That left my mother with a family of eleven small children. Although I was only a young boy, I had to go out and work with the men to help support Mother and the smaller children.

CHAPTER XV

HOG-WILD

AFTER my father died in 1911 I sorter went to pieces for a few years. I know I shouldn't have. I ought to have hewed to the line closer than ever, but I didn't. I was at that age, too, when a young man thinks that it's right smart to drink and cuss and fight and tear things up. I sort of felt that that was the right-smart way to come into my manhood. And coming into your manhood is like suddenly coming into a lot of riches—you may not appreciate it at first, and sorter squander it.

I begun to drink and gamble jes a little at the start, but it growed on me. I got in with a crowd of gay fellows and before long I sure was drifting. There was plenty of liquor around. It was very cheap; about sixty-five cents or seventy-five cents a quart. Poker and other gambling games were pretty popular, and smoking and chewing was supposed to be the thing. I was a big fellow, strong and hard, too, from blacksmithing and farming and hunting. I didn't know my own strength. I thought I could whip anybody.

At the beginning we used to have a few drinks of a week-end and sit up nights, gambling our money away; and of course, like most of the others, I was always smoking and cussing. I don't think I was mean and bad; I was jes kinder careless. But the habits grew stronger on me. Sorter like the water that runs down a hill—at first it makes the ravine, and then the ravine takes control of the water—that's the way it was with me. I jes played with these things at first, and then they got a-hold of me and began to play with my life. I went from bad to worse. I began really to like liquor and gambling, and I was 'most always spoiling for a fight.

There was a bunch of us. There was Everett Delk, Marion Leffew and Marion Delk, who is dead now, and a couple of my brothers. We were a wild crowd; wilder than wild bees when they're swarming. Of a week-end we would go across the Kentucky line and get drunk and look for trouble, and we shore enough found it.

Back in the days before the World War the Kentucky-Tennessee state line was a tough place. There were drinking shacks, "blind tigers" we used to call them, 'most every few miles. I am a-telling you Sodom and Gomorrah might have been bigger places, but they weren't any worse. Killings were a-plenty. They used to say that they used to shoot fellows jes to see them kick. Knife fights and shooting were common, gambling and drinking were commoner, and lots of careless girls jes used to sorter drift in. It shore was tough. They used to build these wooden shacks right on the line, half in one state and half in the other. If you come from Tennessee and wanted to buy liquor and booze you went across to the Kentucky part of the building. If you come from Kentucky you crossed over to the Tennessee side. That was to befool the law and sorter protect yourselves and the people who were running the places. We used to go over there 'most every week-end and after we was filled up with liquor we would go back in the trees and gamble and roam around, or go dancing and looking for trouble.

The liquor we used to drink in those days was most often jes plain Tennessee or Kentucky moonshine. That's powerful liquor. There was plenty of it; and we jes natcherly knowed how to put it away. We would often drink over a quart each a night, and two or three quarts each over a week-end. That's a lot of liquor. We used to think it right smart to drink each other down.

I ricollect oncet a bunch of us got us each a quart of moonshine whiskey and a quart of apple brandy, and we had a sorter drinking bout. We would drink so long as we could stand up, but when we fell over or passed out we would what you might call disqualify. The one who drunk the most and stayed on his feet the longest got all of the liquor that was left. We bought the liquor at Ball Rock, which is right on the line, and then we come back around Caney Creek and went to it.

There were six of us and we shore put away a lot of that-there liquor. My brothers Henry and Albert didn't last long. They each put away about three quarters of that apple brandy, and that was the end of them. Everett Delk and me guzzled up a quart each, and then I am a-telling you we were rarin' to go.

We started out for Jim Crabtree's house. There was some right-smart girls there; fine girls and good-looking too. And though we could hardly stand no-how, we kinder thought we would like to have a little dance with them. We crossed over through a sage field and drunk some more liquor. I guess that old field was pretty flat country, but it seems most awful hilly to me. I knowed I was a-going; and sure enough, another drink and I was flat on my back; but Everett kept a-going and a-drinking.

He went to the house and swallowed a most awful lot of buttermilk, which sorter brought him around. He then went back around the field and collected up all the liquor that was left and took it back to the house and hid it upstairs. Then he kinder kicked and shook us awake. We was scattered here and yonder, jes wherever we give up. We began to come to and go into the house all the way from seven o'clock till midnight. Next morning we didn't none of us know what we had done with our whiskey. We thought we drunk it all. We felt like it, too. But Everett went upstairs and got it and we went to it again. That was the kind of drinking we used to do.

Another time we had to light out from home and go over near the state line and hide us from the grand jury which was after us. They wanted us for liquoring up and fighting and carrying weapons. They didn't have any specific charges against us. They jes wanted to get us before them and question us. And we jes knowed if they ever got us before them and got to questioning us we shore would give each other away and be indicted. So we went over there near the line and jes drinked and gambled and played around until it kinder blew over.

Once they got me for being mixed up in carrying and selling a weapon. I used to always tote a gun around with me and a knife, too. I went before the jury and got out of it right smart. I pleaded my own case and proved to them that it was not my gun, that I was jes delivering it for somebody else. But hit shore was close and they come near getting me. Another time I was riding home on a mule, drunk as a saloon fly, and sorter wanting to shoot things up. It was in the very early morning. I saw some turkey gobblers sitting on the fence and up in a tree. I had a pistol with me. I jes couldn't resist seeing if my nerve was all right. I jes fired six shots from a long way off, and the air was full of feathers, and there was six dead turkeys stretched out on the ground. Now that was one time that my marksmanship got me in bad. I was brung up before the court, but was able to buy out of it. Turkeys are pretty valuable around our way, especially when it's near Thanksgiving, and it's a pretty serious offence to muss them up.

Once Everett and I were full of booze and riding home on the same mule, both of us, one behind the other. How we done it I don't know; neither of us could sit up straight. But we done done it. In the darkness we saw something white sorter floating on Caney Creek. Everett thought it was a white pillow, and I didn't know what it was. We were that full that we couldn't see straight. I got out the old gun again and let fly and we heard an awful squawking and fluttering about in the water, and whatever it was begun to float off. Everett went down to investigate. He said there was feathers and blood all over the water. Then we knowed I had killed a tame goose. I had shot it plumb through the breast. So we thought we had better get out while the going was good, and we did. It was Mr. Moody's goose, and I guess he doesn't know to this day who it was that bumped it off.

Not having no money never bothered us much. We could make it all right at shooting matches. I sure could bust a turkey's head at 'most any distance and cut the centre out of a target and win the prize money 'most any time. I used to do the shooting and Everett would do the betting and then when we won we would buy us some more liquor.

I am a-telling you I kept going from bad to worse, drinking more and more, and gambling whenever I had the chance or the money, and fighting a whole heap. I was never oncet whipped or knocked off my feet. I jes kinder thought I could whip the world and more than oncet I set out to do it.

I was in a couple of shooting frays too. You see the only book I had read was the life of Frank and Jesse James. It made a big impression on me. I used to practise and practise to shoot like them James boys. I used to get on my mule and gallop around and shoot from either hand and pump bullet after bullet in the same hole. I used to even throw the pistol from hand to hand and shoot jes as accurate. I could take that old pistol and knock off a lizard's or a squirrel's head

from that far off that you could scarcely see it. So
you see I was kinder handy when it come to hitting
the mark. I never did kill nobody. I never did really
fire at anybody; that is, not to hit them. I often shot
a few bullets in their direction to frighten them off.
Once we hired to a fellow to take some cattle from
Wolf River to Chanute. We got four dollars for
that. So we took it to Lick Creek and bought us that
much whiskey. That was enough to make us pretty
full. We was riding along on our mules and we met
up with Will Huff, and we decided to have some fun
with him. I got out my little pearl-handle revolver
and began to shoot at the ground underneath his
mule's belly. That sorter knocked the rocks loose and
they flew up and hit the mule and it got to bucking
and throwed Will off. He was not hurt, but he was
most awful mad.

Then we got to firing under my mule and it bucked
me off. I was that wobbly I couldn't sit straight and
I jes sorter fell off, and I lay where I fell, too.
Everett got him a paling off'n the fence and proceeded
to bring me around by slapping me with that old
wooden paling. I come to and, thinking somebody was
after me, I jumped on the old mule and galloped like
an express train through the trees. I guess an express
train couldn't have catched me. I lost my hat, but
I kept on a-going, shooting and hollering and cussing
as I rode. After a few miles I fell off and went to
sleep again.

I got into a knife fight, too, with one of the boys
in our valley. It was on a Sunday morning after

church and that made it worse. We were both full
of moonshine and that started it. We sure would
have cut each other up, but some of the other boys
got between us and separated us. It was over a girl.
I am a-telling you that wine and women make a bad
mix-up.

Then there was a fellow named Maxey. We had
a most awful argument down at a stave mill, and he
said next time we met he was going to get me. A
few days later I decided to wait for him on the road
and run him off. So when he come along I fired a
few shots near his feet, and knocked up the dust, and
told him to go; and he done went, too. I never seed
him again.

I ain't a-boasting of these days. I am kinder
ashamed of them now. They was most awful bad.
They couldn't have been worser without me killing or
hurting somebody; but I never did that. I did enough
just the same. I drunk liquor whenever I could get it.
I was drunk 'most every week-end. I gambled away
most of my hard-earned money. I was always chewing and cussing. I was always wanting to whip somebody.

I am a-saying again that old Kentucky line was a
tough place, and the boys around there was tough too,
tougher than hickory; and I was one of them. I was
always in trouble, or looking for trouble, and it looked
as if sooner or later I would get it and get it right
smart.

I was hog-wild.

CHAPTER XVI

MOTHER

'Most like all boys, I think my mother was the best mother in all the world. I jes think so much of her that I don't know how to say what I want to say. I guess sometimes you can feel things so deep you are sorter lost for words to express them.

We mountain people are pretty clannish; that's the Scotch-Irish blood in us. We sorter hang together, 'most like bees when they are swarming. I sometimes think that our feelings are nearer the surface than they are in 'most all city people. We don't try to keep them down. We let them go. When we love we love right out, and we ain't ashamed of it, and when we hate it takes a lot to make us forgive and forget.

Both my father and mother were honest, God-fearing people, and they did their best to bring us up that way. They didn't drink, or swear, or smoke themselves, and they didn't believe in us doing those things. They didn't have no use nohow for people who told lies or broke promises. They believed in being straight out and aboveboard. I'm a-telling you they honoured the truth so much that they wouldn't hide it nohow for nobody even if they was to suffer an awful lot.

I have told about my father. It was sorter easy for me to talk about guns and hounds and horses and all those things he loved and taught me to love. Hit's different talking about Mother, but I jes got to. Her story is jes sorter mixed up with mine and mine with hers, and I can't jes tell where one ends and the other begins, and I can't look into my own life nohow without finding her always mixed up with my affairs. And always for the better. I have generally taken her advice as being most helpful. When I have failed to do it, I have 'most always got into a heap of trouble. I can't remember us ever having a short word.

She has sort of been through everything. She has had 'most all the trials and tribulations they write about in the Scriptures. She has always had to work hard, and she says that is why she has always been happy. I guess she has never really had time to be unhappy. I am a-thinking that she sorter knows what life's all about. Long ago she had come through most all of the fool notions, and she sorter understands now.

When her father, William Brooks, was killed by the bushwhackers in Jamestown, she was jes a little baby in her mother's arms. Her brother was not borned then. He come into the world a few months afterwards. The three of them went on through life clinging to each other jes like a three-leaf clover. My grandmother never married again. She jes went back to her people in the valley and give her whole life to bringing up her babies. She had to be both mother and father to them. Maybe it's because my mother never had a father she growed up so independent and strong-willed and knowing. She had to larn to look after herself without a father and to find out heaps of things alone.

There was no man-person at the house and they all had to work, and her little brother was sickly at first. She went to school and larned how to read and write and that was about all. She never read no other books but the Bible. She larned to card and spin and weave and knit and to make clothes. She milked the cows and even larned how to plough. She used to hitch up the horses and go out into the field and do a good day's work. She had some cattle of her mother's, and she often used to go out in the fields and hitch them to logs and do her share of hauling. She worked right smart from her girlhood up.

She must have been full of life, too. I'm a-telling you she still is. She used to go in for all the goings-on in the valley. In those old days there was a lot of this what you would call community spirit. If a couple would marry and wanted to set up for themselves, or if some strangers come in and takened up some land, most all of the mountain people around would turn out and give them a good start. There would be log-rollings and house-raisings. The men would do that. They would come from all around and cut the timber and roll in the logs and clear up the brush and burn it off, so that the new settlers would have some good crop land. Then they would build them a home, a regular log cabin; and while they was doing this, the women folk would get together and do a right-smart piece of quilting. That is, they would cut and sew and make quilts and other things for the new couple to help begin a home.

And after the day's work was done they would all get together and dance on the new puncheon floor. They would often dance all night, them square dances with banjo music and fiddles. They jes paired up and hit the floor, the young and old, married and single, and all. The men sometimes would drink a little hard cider and liquor but they seldom got drunk.

Then there were corn-shuckings too. Somebody would put up a crib of corn and maybe put a bottle of liquor in the centre. The men folks would come in from all around and shuck until they got right in the centre where the liquor was. Then there would be some drinking, and after that there would be some dancing. In them days they all worked hard from sunup to sundown; and they knowed how to play, too. Their enjoyments might be different from ours, but they was kinder wholesome and sorter fitted in with this-here mountain life.

Roads were bad in them times and travelling was hard. Anyone who went into Jimtown more'n once a month was considered to be a regular gad-about. The first time my mother ever went into Jimtown she drove a yoke of cattle with a load of fodder. It was a little place then, but it was a new world for her, for she had been used only to the little mountain place. They used to raise sorghum cane in them days and grind the stalks into molasses and cut the heads off, and then they would take them heads that was left and fill up the bottom of the cart and then pile up bundles of fodder on top until the cart was full. It was a load like this that she took into Jimtown.

Mother and Father most growed up together. They both lived in this-here valley. They first got to going together when my father decided to move house and Mother did the moving for him. This was long before they were married. They was both most young then. She took her cattle and wagon and went and moved him from off the mountain where he was living to his new place, which was within shouting distance of her own home. She drove the oxen and he walked along the road, toting a rifle, with a dog following him. That was the beginning of it.

They had to run off to be married. You see her people were opposed to him. They jes couldn't see him nohow, so they went and eloped. They ran across the mountains to her uncle's. He was a squire and in them days the squire could issue a licence and marry people himself. He married them. Mother's wedding dress was made of mixed linsey. She spun the wool, wove the cloth, and made the dress herself. They stayed over at her uncle's for a week. They spent their honeymoon helping the old people. Then when they kinder figured that Grandmother had got over her fractiousness, they returned.

About a year later Father built the log house at the spring, and that's where most all of us were borned and growed up. The children kept coming right smart until there were eleven of us. Mother had to work hard from sunup often until ten o'clock at night to keep us clothed and fed. Of course,

Father had his blacksmithing and was the head of the house, but thirteen's a big family, and there just couldn't be no idle hands nohow. Until we was old enough to help, Mother had to do 'most everything around the house. She milked the cows, made the butter; she looked after the hogs and chickens. She made the soap and the tallow candles and fixed the grease for the lamps. She carded the wool and spun and wove the cloth and made all of our clothes. She was a good mother to us, and with Father she brought us all up, and we are living to-day. We're all strong and healthy and well and she enjoyed every moment of it. She enjoyed life much more in those days, so she says, slaving and working for us, than she does to-day, jes quietly living with us with not much to do or to bother about.

She jes didn't have time to worry or be unhappy. Life tried to crowd in on her and bust her up right smart and she jes wouldn't let it nohow. She knowed what she wanted—she wanted her home, her husband, and her own children, and she knowed she would have to pay for these things with work and sacrifice, so she was willing. That's a mother for you! And that's what she's done done for me.

And here I was running hog-wild around the country, keeping her up late nights and worrying the heart out of her. No matter how long I stayed away and how late I come home, no matter how drunk I was, no matter how much I had gambled away my money, no matter how much I come home shouting and whooping it up, she never had a short word for me, never.

She would shake her head and look at me, with a hurt look in her eyes, and sometimes she would cry and always she would beg me to give it up and lead a better life. Sometimes I would come home from a big drunk or from a wild party, and I would find her sitting up in the lamplight waiting for me. And when I would ask her why she hadn't laid down or gone to bed, she would kinder look at me and say she couldn't sleep, because she was afraid I would get killed or something would happen to me.

Often she would remind me of my father, of how he never drunk, or gambled, or played around with bad company, and of how he would not like it nohow if he knowed what I was doing; and she used to meet me at the door and put her arms around me and tell me that I was not only wasting this life, but I was spoiling all my chances for the next. She used to say that she jes couldn't bear to think of where I would go if I died or was killed while I was leading this wild life.

All of this was making me feel kinder bad. I jes knowed I was wrong. I jes knowed there was no excuse for me, and I was beginning to make up my mind to cut it out, when she begun her praying for me. She told me of the Good Shepherd in the Bible who left the whole flock of sheep to go and look after and bring in the one that had strayed. She prayed and prayed. So I made up my mind to finish it. It was hard though. When you get used to a thing, no matter how bad it is for you, it is most awful hard to give it up.

It was a most awful struggle to me. I did a lot of walking through the mountains and thinking. I was fighting the thing inside of me and it was the worstest fight I ever had. I thought of my father and what a good man he was and how he expected me to grow up like him, and I sorter turned over in my mind all the sacrifices Mother had made for me. I ricollected that I had never asked her to do anything which she refused if it was right. I knowed that she had given up 'most all of her life for her children. I knowed she would have given her whole life for me. I knowed how she loved me. And now she was asking me to give up all of this wild life and bad companions and be a good boy again.

So I thought and struggled and prayed more and more. And then, jes as I was making up my mind and getting control of myself, a preacher-man come into the valley. He was the Rev. H. H. Russell from Indiana. He preached very close. I mean very close to the word of God as it is revealed in the Bible. He fought everything that any preacher could have fought. He fought everything that was not right. His meetings were at the Wolf River Church. The people come in from all around. They come from the river flats and from the back creeks and from the mountains. They come most in farm wagons and on horseback, and some of them walked. It was a wonderful crowd. The church could scarcely hold them all. There were great meetings every night, and that preacher man had more conversions, in the time, than any other man that had ever been through the valley.

Sometimes I used to walk out on the mountainside and do a heap of thinking and praying before the meetings. Then I would go and listen and pray and ask God to forgive me for my sins and help me to see the light. And He did. In that-there little church, out in the hills and at home with Mother, I begun to see how wrong I was and how terrible it was for a man to be wasting his life like I was. I begun to see that I was missing the finer things. I knowed in my heart that when you miss the finer things of life you might jes as well be a razorback out in the mountains for all the good you are to yourself and anybody else.

So I decided to change and go in for the finer things. And I have done it. I give up smoking, drinking, gambling, cussing, and brawling. I give them up completely and forever. I give them up the first of January, 1915. I have never backslided. I have never done any of those things since. I have no desire any more. I am a great deal like Paul, the things I once loved I now hate. I went through the World War without drinking, smoking, or cussing.

After I changed my life everybody around me was happy. My mother was most happy of all. I found out the truth of what the Bible says: "There is more rejoicing over one sinner that repenteth than over ninety-nine just persons that need no repentance." But I was not yet saved. I knew there was something else. I continued to pray and go to church, and then it come to me that not only must a man not do bad, but he must also do good to be truly saved. I joined the church. It was called the Church of Christ in

PREACHING ON THE MOUNTAINSIDE

"I hed been living for God and working in the church work
sometime before I joined the army."

YORK AGRICULTURAL COLLEGE
(The Grade School)

"I'm goin' to give all the mountain children a chance
to get a heap o' larnin'."

Christian Union. It hasn't any rituals or anything like that. Its only creed is the Bible. It accepts the Bible as it is written. I gave most of my spare time to it, and with Pastor Pile I helped teach a children's class at Sunday school. I also led the singing. I have a natural tenor voice. I went to Byrdstown and takened lessons. I became known as the Singing Elder.

So I was saved.

And that is the greatest victory I ever won. It's much harder to whip yourself than to whip the other fellow, I'm a-telling you, and I ought to know because I done both. It was much harder for me to win the great victory over myself than to win it over those German machine guns in the Argonne Forest. And I was able to do it because my mother's love led me to God, and He showed me the light, and I done followed it.

CHAPTER XVII

WAR

LIFE's tol'ably queer. You think you've got a grip on it, then you open your hands and you find there's nothing in them. It doesn't go in straight lines like bees to their hives or quail from the covey. It sorter circles like foxes and goes back again to where it begun. After I had given up liquoring and gambling and fighting and the wild life, I kinder thought I could settle down in peace and make amends for my sins by working hard and doing all the good I could. I got me a job farming with Rosier Pile. I worked from sunup to sundown. I kept up my singing lessons, and I spent any spare time I had reading the Bible and doing church work.

Of course, often the old longing to go out and bedevil around would come over me, but I jes prayed and resisted the temptation. Sometimes Everett or Marion or some of the other boys would drop around and tell me they were putting on another gay party and invite me to join them. Then it was that I was most sorely tempted. I prayed most awful hard and got a good hold on myself and didn't go. Each time I refused, it was so much easier next time; and every day it became easier. In a few months I got them. there bad things out of my mind. I was thinking of

better things, more worthwhile things. I was beginning to find peace in my soul.

So I was happy, living and working and learning
to love my fellowmen and trying most awful hard to
help anybody that wanted help. My mother was nigh
to the happiest woman in the valley. She was always
smiling and putting her hands on my shoulder sorter
loving-like whenever I was around. That made me
feel good. Most all of my friends were glad too.
That encouraged me. I worked harder than ever.
I read the Bible. I led the singing in the church, and
I helped in the Sunday school. I jes knowed I was
saved.

I truly felt as though I had been borned again. I
felt that great power which the Bible talks about and
which all sinners feel when they have found salvation.
I felt in my soul like the stormy waters must have felt
when the Master said, "Peace, be still." I used to
walk out in the night under the stars and kinder linger
on the hillside, and I sorter wanted to put my arms
around them-there hills. They were at peace and so
was the world and so was I.

And, of course, there was a girl; a little slip of a
girl. I knowed her since she was a baby. We sorter
growed up together. She was younger than me, and
it may have been on account of that or because I was
careless and didn't notice things, when I was drinking
and sinning around—anyway, I hadn't noticed how she
had growed up from girlhood to womanhood. But
when I was saved and working hard and going in for
the decent things again, I begun to watch her comings

and goings pretty close. I didn't see much of her at
first. I guess she had heard of my wild life and
sorter wasn't interested and kept out of my way, but
when I got religion the church work brought us together. We did not speak to each other much **at**
first. She was kinder shy; she hain't never been out
of the mountains and hain't been used to strangers.
But she had a nice way about her, always kind to
folks and always doin' things for the church. There
hain't been nothing flighty about her nohow. And
I'm a-tellin' you she was pretty, always as fresh as
a flower in the mornin' with the dew on. I kinder
noticed her hair. You jes couldn't help noticing it.
I jes couldn't nohow. It was sort of soft and silky
and there was so much of it, and she done it up nice
in two big braids wound up in the back with a blue
ribbon woven in. And I seed her eyes was blue and
big and kinder shined with goodness, and though
I never thought of it before, I jes knowed blue was
my favourite colour. I am a-tellin' you there was
somethin' grand about her, the way she talked in that
quiet voice of hers that sometimes got shaky, she was
that shy, and the way she looked at you with those big
blue eyes as though she was jes trying to see inside
of you and help you be good. I jes wanted to be near
her and talk to her; and there was many a time when
I was out tramping in these-here mountains with
them hound dogs of mine and scouting for coon when
I would jes sit down on some log and look over the
valley on that-there mountain where she lived and
wish I could be there and tell her how much I thought

of her and how there was nothing in the world I would not do for her if she'd only let me. That's how much I cared for her.

Her parents were agin me. I couldn't blame them nohow. But I wasn't in love with them at that time. I was in love with Gracie, and we managed to steal meetings, and nobody but us knowed much about them nohow. There was a long winding lane between our homes. It was lined with big shady trees. And there was wild honeysuckle there. And, best of all, it sorter dipped out of sight between the two hills. It was sorter made for us to meet in. So of an evening Gracie would come along this way to get the cows for milking, and I most awful sudden found out there were a heap of squirrels along that old lane. So I would tote the old muzzle-loader and go hunting down that way. I don't recollect getting many squirrels. But I kinder used to always go back there every evening.

I was happy. I was happier than I had ever been before. You see I found love, too. When you have found that and peace of soul you are beginning to find out what life is all about. I guess them-there two things, love and peace, are what folks call the fundamental things.

The World War done broke out, but as you don't pay much attention nohow to a cloud when it first comes up in the sky, so I didn't pay none to the war. I scarcely heard or seed it. It didn't touch me. It didn't mean nothing to me. I knowed it was in Europe, but that meaned nothing to me. I knowed

big nations were fighting, but I didn't know for sure
how many and which ones. I didn't know what they
were fighting for. I didn't know what it was all
about. It was a long way from our peaceful little
valley to them-there battlefields way across the sea.
I read a little about it in the papers, and I heard them
talking about it around the store. Not much, though,
jes a little now and then.

So I went on with my farming and my church work
and trying to court Gracie, when people were not
around and I was lucky enough to meet her there in
the lane. And I am a-telling you that kept me
a-going. I had no time nohow to bother much about
a lot of foreigners quarrelling and killing each other
over there in Europe.

I had had fighting and quarrelling myself. I had
found it bad. I had larned that it didn't profit a man
nohow, and I had given it up forever, I hoped. I
didn't want to go in for it again nohow. I jes wanted
to be left alone to live in peace and love. I wasn't
planning my life any other way. I didn't see that I had
anything to do with them-there things away over in
Europe. I kinder figured out that if some people
were quarrelling and fighting in the valley next to ours
it wasn't none of my business to go over there and
interfere, and Europe was so much farther than any
neighbouring valley. That's what the war meant to
me.

I didn't think our country would get into it nohow.
I didn't think we had anything to do with it. I never
even dreamed that we would go over there and fight.

Even when we got into it in 1917, it seemed a long
way off and I didn't figure on being called. But the
little cloud was growing blacker and bigger, and even
in our little valley there was a heap more of this war
talk. Some of the boys were talking of going away
and fighting, and there was a tol'able lot of talk of
the draft and of how we would all have to go. I
couldn't see it that way. I couldn't sorter get interested, and I just didn't want to fight nohow.

I wasn't unpatriotic or disloyal or anything like
that. I knowed my people for generations back had
always fought for their country. I knowed we were
all good Americans in the mountains, but that-there
World War seemed such a long way off. So I didn't
pay much attention to it. I didn't let it bother me.
I jes kept on a-going as I had been ever since I had
been saved.

One summer afternoon I got my old squirrel gun
and went down the lane as usual and met Gracie. I
disremember what we talked about or how it happened, but I know we come to an understanding. I
walked back home the happiest man that ever could be.
I was kinder drunk with happiness. I had Gracie's
promise that she would marry me. Her folks were
agin me but she was for me. I sorter lived in a dream
for the next few days. And then all of a sudden, out
of nowhere, so it seemed to me, life sorter took me
by the back of the neck and tried to lift me out of
our little valley and throw me into the war over there
in France. I received from the post office a little red
card telling me to register for the draft.

I can't tell you how I felt. I just can't describe it. I was all mussed up. Everything was going from under me. Fight! Kill! And I'd been converted to the Gospel of peace and love, and of "Do good for evil."

That's how the war come to me, in the midst of all my peace and happiness and dreams, which I felt all along were too good to be true and just couldn't last.

CHAPTER XVIII

CONSCIENTIOUS OBJECTOR

In my records in the War Department in Washington, D. C., there is a little narrow pink slip, marked:

Conscientious Objector
YORK, ALVIN C.

Desires release as he is conscientious objector.
A. G. 383.2 Exemp. Religious sects.
4-19-1
1918

So as long as the records remain I will be officially known as a conscientious objector. I was. I couldn't have been anything else nohow.

At first I jes couldn't imagine I would have to fight. The war seemed too far away to be mixing me up in it. And I didn't want to be in it nohow. I never had killed nobody, not even in my bad days, and I didn't want to begin now. I turned my back on all of those rowdy things and found a heap of comfort and happiness in religion. I joined the church. It was the Church of Christ in Christian Union. I had takened its creed and I had takened it without what you might call reservations. I was not a Sunday Christian. I believed in the Bible. And I tried in my own way to live up to it. It was the only creed of my church.

To be a member I had to accept the Bible as the inspired word of God. I did. And the Bible said,
"Thou shalt not kill." That was so definite a child
could understand it. There was no way around or
out of it. So you see there were two reasons why I
didn't want to go to war. My own experience told
me that it weren't right. And the Bible were agin
it too.

But Uncle Sam said he wanted me and he wanted
me most awful bad. And I had also been brought
up to believe in my country. I knowed that even in the
Civil War, when Tennessee was a doubtful state, my
two grandfathers had both fought straight out for the
Union. I knowed that my great-great-grandfather,
old Coonrod Pile, had been one of the pioneers who
done helped to build up this-here country, and he
hain't never hesitated to use a gun, and I kinder felt
that my ancestors would want me to do whatever my
country demanded of me.

So you see my religion and my own experience sorter
told me not to go to war, and the memory of my
ancestors jes as plainly sorter told me to get my gun
and go and fight. I didn't know what to do. I am
a-telling you there was a war going on inside of me
and I didn't know which side to lean on. I was a
heap bothered. Hit is a most awful thing when the
wishes of your God and your country sorter get mixed
up and go against each other. One moment I would
make up my mind to follow God, and the next I
would hesitate and almost make up my mind to follow

Uncle Sam. Then I wouldn't know which to follow
or what to do.

I wanted to follow both. But I couldn't. They
were opposite. And I couldn't reconcile them nohow
in my soul. I wanted to do what was right. I wanted
to be a good Christian and a good American too. I
had always figured that the two were sort of connected. And now I was beginning to find out that they
were kinder opposed to each other. If I went away
to war and fought and killed, according to my reading
of the Bible, I weren't a good Christian. And if I
didn't go to war and do these things, according to
Uncle Sam, I weren't a good American.

So I was the most bothered boy in all of these
mountains. I didn't know what to do or where to
turn. I walked the mountains night after night, trying
to figure it out. I read the Bible over and over. I
prayed and prayed, often late into the night. I got
away off in the woods and I got out that little Government card telling me to register for the draft. I
turned it over. I read and studied it. I jes couldn't
make up my mind that the Bible were wrong. And
I couldn't make up my mind Uncle Sam were right.
I was a soul in doubt. I'm a-telling you, I was most
unhappy.

Pastor Pile was the registrar. He had a store and
the post office at Pall Mall, and the Government done
instructed him to take the registration for the draft.
I went to him and we talked it over, and we read the
Bible and prayed together. No matter how we looked

at it, we always come up against "Thou shalt not kill."
That was the word of God and that was how it was
revealed in His Holy Book.   There was no gitting
past that nohow.

So when I registered I claimed exemption from the
draft. I wrote on the paper: "I don't want to fight."
And that-there paper with that statement on it is now
in the War Department in Washington, D. C.

A few weeks later I filed this application:

August 28, 1917.

To Local Board
County of Fentress.

I, Alvin Cullum York, Serial Number 378, hereby
certify that I am 29 years old and reside at Pall
Mall, Tenn.

I hereby respectfully claim discharge from selec-
tive draft on the following ground, that I am——

(1) A person who was a member of a well-
recognized sect or organization, organized
and existing May 18, 1917, whose then
existing creed or principles forbade its
members to participate in war in any form
and whose religious principles are against
war or participation therein in accordance
with the creed or principles of said well-
recognized religious sect or organization.

But the Local Board refused to exempt me.

LOCAL BOARD FOR THE COUNTY OF FENTRESS
STATE OF TENNESSEE
JAMESTOWN, TENN.

Serial No. 378   Order No. 218

ALVIN CULLUM YORK

Denied, because we do not think "The Church of Christ in Christian Union" is a well-recognized religious sect, etc. Also, we understand it has no especial creed except the Bible, which its members more or less interpret for themselves, and some do not dis-believe in war—at least there is nothing forbidding them to participate.

Then I was bothered more than ever. I done done what I thought was right. I followed God, so I thought, even against the judgment of my country. I done wrote to the Board that I didn't want to go to war because I didn't want to kill; and because I belonged to a church which was opposed to war. And they done refused my appeal. But that didn't convince me nohow. I couldn't accept the written word of man against the written command of God. So I appealed against their decision. I wrote them:

LOCAL BOARD FOR THE COUNTY OF FENTRESS
STATE OF TENNESSEE
JAMESTOWN, TENN.

To LOCAL BOARD

I, Alvin Cullum York, Pall Mall, Tenn., now hereby claim an appeal to the District Board for Middle District of Tennessee, Nashville, Tenn., because you denied my claim for discharge which was based upon the ground that I am a member of a well-recognized religious sect or organization existing May 18, 1917, whose then existing creed or principles forbade its members to participate in war, etc.

A. C. YORK,
Pall Mall, Tenn.

And I also forwarded two affidavits, one from Pastor Pile and one from myself:

1. Affidavit of Person Whose Discharge Is Sought.

State of Tennessee,
County of Fentress, *to wit:*

I, Alvin Cullum York, do solemnly affirm that I am 29 years old and reside at Pall Mall, Tenn., and that Serial Number 378 was given me by Local Board L. B. for County Fentress, and that claim for my discharge was filed with said Local Board on the 28th day of August, 1917, on the ground that I was a person who was a member of any well-known religious organization, organized and existing May 18, 1917, whose then existing creed or principle forbade its members to participate in war in any form and whose religious principles are against war or participation therein, in accordance with the creed or principle of said religious organization.

I do further solemnly swear that I am a member, in good faith and good standing of the Church of Christ in Christian Union, which, on the 18th day of May, 1917, was organized and existing as a well-recognized sect or organization whose existing creed or principles forbade its members to participate in war in any form.

I do further solemnly swear that my religious convictions are against war or participation therein in accordance with the creed or principles of said religious organization.

I do hereby bind myself to report in person and to notify said Local Board, at once, whenever the conditions entitling me to discharge cease to exist.

A. C. YORK,
Pall Mall, Tenn.

Subscribed and affirmed to before me
this 1st day of Sept., 1917.
> Blaine Williams,
> Notary Public,

State of Tennessee, County of Fentress.

2. Affidavit of Clerk of Minister in Support of Claim for Discharge.

State of Tennessee,
County of Fentress, *to wit:*

I, R. C. Pile, Minister, do solemnly affirm that I am the minister of the Church of Christ in Christan Union, and I hereby certify that A. C. York, who is personally known to me, is now a member of said religious sect or organization.

I do further solemnly affirm that the said religious sect or organization was organized and existing on the 18th day of May, 1917, and was then a well-recognized religious sect or organization, and that the then existing creed or principles of said religious sect or organization forbade its members to participate in war in any form.

I hereby bind myself that if the said person whose discharge is now sought ceases to be a member of said religious sect or organization, or if the existing creed or principles of said religious sect or organization are changed so as not to forbid its members participating in war in any form, or whenever the conditions entitling such person to discharge cease to exist I will at once notify said Local Board and will also request my successor in office to give such notice.

R. C. PILE,
Church of Christ in C. U.
Pall Mall.

Subscribed and affirmed to before me
this 3d day of Sept., 1918
Blaine Williams,
Notary Public,
State of Tennessee, County of Fentress.

But it weren't no use. They denied my appeal:

Notice of Decision of District Board on Claim of Appeal Filed by Person Called

To ALVIN CULLUM YORK,
Pall Mall, County of Fentress, Tenn.

You are hereby notified that this District Board, having considered your claim of appeal from the decision of Local Board for County of Fentress, and having considered all affidavits and the record with respect to said claim of appeal, has, this 6th day of October, 1917, affirmed said decision.

DISTRICT BOARD FOR MIDDLE DISTRICT OF
STATE OF TENNESSEE

By ERWIN L. DAVIS
(Chairman)

W. H. HANFORD
(Secretary)

I was now most awful worried. I was sorter mussed up inside worser'n ever. I thought that the word of God would prevail against all of the laws of man and of nations. I thought there must be some mistake somewhere. I knowed those words in the Holy Book come from God. I knowed He meant them and I knowed they must be right. I thought that I would not be a good Christian if I did not do all in my power to stick to them oncet I done accepted them. So I appealed to the Board again. I was sorter fighting against fighting. I mean I was fighting hard so I would not have to go to war and kill. It was sorter like a forest fire, when you fight fire with fire. I didn't understand it all. I only knowed I was troubled more'n I ever'd been before. I was up against the biggest thing I ever'd been up against. I'd used God's holy command in order to get an exemption from war. And now men who claimed they were jes as good Christians as I was, and were good churchmen too, although they didn't belong to my church, disallowed the words of God, as I had sent them in, and told me that I would have to go to camp and learn to fight and kill for my country. So I appealed again:

Form No. 151, prepared by the Provost Marshal General.

Notice of Claim of Appeal by Person Certified to District Board

To District Board for Middle District of Tennessee
Nashville, Tenn.

I, Alvin Cullum York, Pall Mall, Tenn., hereby give notice that on the 13th day of September, 1917, I filed with Local Board for the County of Fentress, State of Tennessee, Jamestown, Tenn., a claim of appeal to your Honourable Board from the decision of the said Local Board, wherein said Local Board denied my claim for discharge, which claim was based upon the ground that I am a member of a well-organized Religious Sect or organization, existing May 18, 1917, whose then existing creed or principles forbade its members to participate in war in any form and whose convictions are against war or participation therein in accordance with the creed or principles of said well-recognized religious sect or organization.

A. C. York,
Pall Mall, Tenn.

So you see how I fought against going to war. I didn't hate nobody; I didn't want to kill nobody. I jes wanted to live and let live. I jes wanted to live my life in peace and I jes wanted to be let alone to love God and my fellowmen; and though the Germans were a long way off and I didn't know them, I figured jes the same they were my fellowmen.

For the third time the Board refused to exempt me and wrote confirming their decision that I would have to go.

Form No. 157, prepared by the Provost Marshal General.

Notice of Decision of District Board of Claim of Appeal Filed by Person Called.

To ALVIN CULLUM YORK,
Pall Mall, Tenn.

You are hereby notified that this District Board, having considered your claim of appeal from the decision of Local Board, County of Fentress, and having considered all affidavits and the record with respect to said claim of appeal, has, this 6th day of October, 1917, affirmed said decision.

DISTRICT BOARD FOR MIDDLE DISTRICT OF
STATE OF TENNESSEE
By ERWIN L. DAVIS
(Chairman)

W. H. HANFORD
(Secretary)

I wrote it in my little diary:

JUNE 5, 1917

Pall Mall, Tennessee. Well, the first notice I receved was to go and register. So I did. And then I begun to think that I was going to be called to be examined.

I was lean and hard at that time. I'd been hunting, farming, blacksmithing, and driving steel. I had no fat on me at all. I was all bone and muscle. And I knowed I was physically fit.

OCTOBER 28, 1917

Jamestown, Tennessee. I was called to report to the Local Board for examination. So I went and when they look at me they weighted me and I weighted 170 lbs., was 72 inches tall. So they said I passed all right. Well, when they said that I almost knowed that I would haft to go to the army.

NOVEMBER 10TH

Pall Mall, Tennessee. So I just went on with my work and I receved a Little Blue Card that told me to be ready for a 24 hour call at any time.

I didn't pass judgment nohow on the members of the Board. I knowed it was written, "Judge not lest ye be judged." I was not even angry. I larned to kinder hold in my anger. I was only sad and sorry and bothered deep down in my soul. I thought that if I wanted to follow God and do His blessed will that was my own affair, and I would be left alone to do it. And I wanted to be left alone. I told them this again and again. I wrote it in my application. I swore it out in my affidavit, and they said jes the same I had to go! And worst of all, Pastor Pile, who was my friend and spiritual adviser, and who didn't want me to go any more'n I did want to go myself, had to be the one to register me. I often wondered why we have got to do things we don't want to do nohow, why, when we want to live in peace, we have to go away to war; why, when we say we are Christian nations, we don't try to live in peace and kinder respect people who love peace instead of sending them off to fight and kill, like they were going to send me.

And the worstest thing of all was that it was my country that was sending me. I'd always loved my country and believed in it. I was willing to live and work for it. If it wanted me to, I was willing to die for it. I hain't never been afraid to die, I am a-telling you. But my country wanted me to do more'n that; it wanted me to go and fight and kill others, and it said that it was right for me to do this, and God said it was not right. And there I was that way—I didn't know what else to do but pray for the light.

Then I received word to report.

NOVEMBER 14, 1917

Jamestown, Tennessee. So later I sure receved a card that said report to your Local Board. So

I went to Jamestown, Tenn., and reported to the Local Board and I stayed all night that night with Doctor Alexander.

I knowed that I had to go. Of course, I could have run away and hid in the mountains, but I hain't never run away from anything before, except sin. I hain't never run away from my country. I hain't never done anything agin my country so I would have to run away. So I didn't. I could have stayed in Pall Mall and jes waited to see what happened, but then I knowed what would happen. The soldiers would come for me and takened me, and if I resisted there would be a fight, and maybe a killing, and that's jes what I didn't want to happen. I didn't want to fight or kill at home or anywhere else. So I reported.

NOVEMBER 15TH

Oneida, Tennessee. The morning of the 15th I started for the camp, which was Camp Gordon. I went to Oneida, Tenn., and stayed there until about 2 o'clock A.M. the next morning, when I entrained for Atlanta, Ga.

I jes went to that old camp and said nothing. I did everything I was told to do. I never once disobeyed an order. I never once raised my voice in complaint, but I was sick at heart jes the same. I heard the boys around me talking about what fun it would be to go over seas and fight in the trenches. I heard them telling of how many Germans they were going to kill if ever they got a chance. I heard all sorts of things about the glory of war. But I couldn't see it like they seed it nohow. I prayed and prayed that God would show me His blessed will. And back there in the mountains Pastor Pile prayed and Mother prayed, too, and I jes knowed that all of those prayers would not be in vain. I jes knowed it.

CHAPTER XIX

THE SWORD AND THE BIBLE

I WAS detailed to Company G, 328th Division. That was a fighting division and was soon to be ordered overseas. I knowed that unless something happened I would have to go up into the front-line trenches and shoot and kill my brother men. I knowed that would be soon, too. And I didn't want to do that nohow.

So at last I went to my company commander, Captain Danforth, of Augusta, Ga., and I told him everything. I told him I belonged to a church that was opposed to war and that I didn't wish to be placed in a position that it might be necessary for me to kill a fellowman. I told him I hain't never talked about this in camp or disobeyed orders. I hain't never shirked my duty at no time. I hain't never refused to do anything he had ordered me to do, and I wasn't planning on refusing. I told him I knowed I was in the army and would have to obey. I would continue to be a soldier if I had to. I would go overseas. I would go in the front-line trenches. I would even kill Germans if I was ordered to. But I told him I wanted him to know I didn't believe in killing nohow, and that it worried me a-plenty. I told him all of this as man to man straight from the shoulder.

The Captain told me that there were several conscientious objectors in the camp, but that he sorter
believed I was honest and sincere. I told him then
how I had prayed and prayed. He assured me that
he would consider everything I had told him and give
me a right-square deal. A few days later he told me
he done spoken to the battalion commander, Major
Buxton, about me, and that the Major asked him if
he believed I was sincere and when he said he believed
I was, the Major done told him to bring me to his
headquarters for questioning.

Major Buxton was from Providence, R. I. He was
the first New Englander I ever knowed. He was a
very good man, but at that time I was most troubled
for his soul. I disliked to think that such a good man
as he appeared to be would be willing to go to war
and lead other men to fight. I couldn't understand
how he could sorter square war and killing with his
professed religious beliefs.

So one night Captain Danforth took me to Major
Buxton's room to discuss these things with him. Before I done went I prayed to God for guidance. I
took my Bible along with me. We all got together
in his room there in Camp Gordon, which is in Georgia
not far from Atlanta. The Major's room was like
most of the officers' headquarters, jes a plain, small
room. There was a little bed in it and some camp
stools. There was a trunk in the corner and some
military clothes hanging up or scattered around, and
jes one light, a small electric light that hung down
from the ceiling. The Major was very friendly-like;

he always was with us boys. He told us to sit down.
He said he didn't want to discuss this question as a
battalion commander discussing it with an officer and
a private. He wanted us to discuss it as three American citizens interested in a common cause. He said
he respected any honest religious conviction and would
be glad to discuss things as man to man. He asked me
why was I opposed to going to war. I told him that
I belonged to a church which disbelieved in fighting
and killing. He then asked me what was the creed
of the church. I told him the only creed was the Bible,
and I also told him that I done accepted the Bible as
the inspired word of God and the final authority for
all men. So he then asked me what did I find in the
Bible that was agin war, and I told him it was written,
"Thou shalt not kill." He kinder looked at me for a
moment and then asked if I accepted everything in the
Bible, every sentence, every word, jes as completely
as I accepted the Sixth Commandment, "Thou shalt
not kill." I told him I did.

He then begun to read other parts of the Bible
which he said proved that a man under certain conditions could go to war and fight and kill and still be
a good Christian. He read a number of quotations.
He read them well and accurate. I was kinder surprised at his knowledge of the Bible. It made me
happy in my soul to know that my battalion commander was familiar with the word of God. I always
thought Major Buxton was a good man, and now I
knowed he was. Jes the same, he was for fightin'. I
remember he begun by p'inting out that Christ once

said: "He that hath no sword, let him sell his cloak and buy one." I 'lowed that was in the Bible. But I reminded him that Christ also said: "If a man smite you on one cheek, turn the other to him." He admitted that, but he asked me if I believed that the Christ who drove the money changers from the temple with the whip would stand up and do nothing when the helpless Belgian people was overrun and driven from their homes.

By this time he was at it right. We both knowed the Bible. I knowed now that I was on the right track. I knowed that if we studied the whole business through the words of the Lord, we must come to a right understanding. We talked along these lines for over an hour and every now and then Captain Danforth joined in. We didn't get annoyed or angry or even raise our voice. We jes examined the old Bible and whenever I would bring up a passage opposed to war, Major Buxton would bring up another which sorter favoured war. I believed the Lord was in that room. I seemed somehow to feel His presence there. I disremember a heap of what we said, but I know that I mentioned that when St. Peter struck off the ear of the high priest's servant, Christ, in restoring the ear, told Peter to put up the sword: "They that live by the sword shall die by the sword." But that-there Major Buxton knowed his Bible right smart. He come right back at me and answered that at the same time Christ also said: "For my kingdom is not of this world; but if my kingdom were of this world, then would my servants fight."

The Major then went on and said that the United States of America was an earthly government and its servants must fight for it whenever its liberties was threatened, and he reminded me that Christ said we must render unto Cæsar the things that are Cæsar's. And the Major 'lowed that Christ meant by this to emphasize the duties of Christians to their government. Major Buxton ended by quoting from *Ezekiel:*

When I bring the sword upon a land, if the people of the land take a man of their coasts, and set him for their watchman:

If when he seeth the sword come upon the land, he blow the trumpet, and warn the people;

Then whosoever heareth the sound of the trumpet and taketh not warning, if the sword come and take him away, his blood shall be upon his own head.

He heard the sound of the trumpet, and he took not warning, his blood shall be upon him. But he that taketh warning shall deliver his soul.

But if the watchman see the sword come and blow not the trumpet, and the people be not warned, if the sword come and take any person from among them, he is taken away in his iniquity; *but his blood will I require at the watchman's hands.*

The Major made a great impression on me that night. A right-smart impression, too. He had kinder opened my eyes to things which were in the Bible, which I knowed were there, but which I hadn't thought of as he had thought of them. I ain't admitting that he had convinced me. He got me to thinking more and more. And more than ever now I didn't know what to do. I jes sat there and prayed and thought. He must have knowed it, too. He sorter looked at

me and smiled, jes like my father used to. Then I
told him that I would like time to think it over, and
that in the meantime I would go on jes as I'd been,
doing everything I was told to do and trying to be a
good soldier. He shook hands with me and told me
to take as long as I liked, and to come to him whenever I wished to. Then he said good-night, and Captain Danforth takened me back to my lines.

I spent considerable time turning the Major's arguments over in my mind that night and I worried and
prayed 'most all through the night until reveille. The
next morning I wrote in my little diary:

MARCH, 1918

Camp Gordon, Georgia. Oh, these were trying
hours for a boy like me, trying to live for God
and do His blessed will, but yet I could look up and
say:

> O Master, let me walk with Thee
> In lonely paths of service free,
> Tell me Thy secret, help me to bear,
> The strain of toil, the fret of care.

And then the Lord would bless me and help me to
bear my hard toiles.

But I couldn't get no understandin's around that-
there old camp. I hain't been used to that. I sorter
can't get alone with myself when there's crowds about.
And I knowed I jes had to be alone to fight it out
with myself. Hit was one of them-there sort of battles
where nobody can help you nohow. You have jes got

to help yourself. And I kinder knowed that the only place where I could do that was back there in the mountains where I belonged. There's heaps of peace there. I jes knowed I had to go back, or else I would always be sorter twistin' in torment like them-there lost souls that can't never see the light nohow.

So I applied for leave and I was given a pass for ten days.

MARCH 21-31ST

Pall Mall, Tennessee. So I got a pass after a while for 10 days. So I went home and while I was at home we had several services at Greer's Chaple, and the Lord blessed us and we had a fine meeting. Rev. R. C. Pile and others were helping, and there were a number of people saved during this little meeting. So the Lord was with us. Bless His holy name.

I knowed now that if I went back and told the Major I was still opposed to fighting he would let me out or have me transferred into another branch of the service where I wouldn't have to kill. He knowed now that I was sincere. He was a good man. He would help me. But something in me had kinder changed. I was beginning to see war in a different light. I had takened to heart and read over and over again them-there passages from the Bible he had read to me. I kinder balanced them against the passages that made me a conscientious objector. I had tried to bring the two together. I knowed the "Lord worked

in marvellous ways, His wonders to perform." I
knowed that He had His own way of saying and doing
things. I knowed that if it was His will He would
even use war as an instrument in His hands. I tried to
look at it this way. I talked to Pastor Pile again and
again. But all I got from all of this was to get more
and more confused than ever. I jes didn't know what
to do; whether to want war or peace; and I didn't
know which He wanted me to do.

So I went out on the mountainside and asked Him
sorter straight out from the shoulder. I went off to
a quiet place not far from my home. I knelt down and
I prayed and I prayed all the afternoon, through the
night and through part of the next day. I asked Him
to have pity on me and show me the light. I begged
Him to comfort me if it was His will and tell me what
to do. And as I prayed there alone a great peace
kinder come into my soul and a great calm come over
me and I received my assurance. He heard my prayer
and He come to me on the mountainside. I didn't see
Him, of course, but He was there jes the same. I
knowed He was there. He understood that I didn't
want to be a fighter or a killin' man, that I didn't want
to go to war and hurt nobody nohow. And yet I
wanted to do what my country wanted me to do. I
wanted to serve God and my country, too. He understood all of this. He seed right inside of me, and He
knowed I had been troubled and worried, not because
I was afraid, but because I put Him first, even before
my country, and I only wanted to do that which would
please Him.

So He took pity on me and He gave me the assurance I needed. I didn't understand everything. I didn't understand how He could let me go to war and even kill and yet not hold it agin me. I didn't even want to understand. It was His will and that was enough for me. So at last I begun to see the light. I begun to understand that no matter what a man is forced to do, so long as he is right in his own soul he remains a righteous man. I knowed I would go to war. I knowed I would be protected from all harm, and that so long as I believed in Him He would not allow even a hair of my head to be harmed.

I arose and thanked Him and went home over the mountains, singing a hymn.

I told my little old mother I was going and not to worry. I was coming back safe and sound. I told my brothers and sisters and I told Pastor Pile. And for a while I was happy and at peace with myself and with my God.

But when I went back to camp and seed all the boys there getting ready to go to the war, some of the old worries come a-piling back on my soul. I knowed I was all right. But I kinder got a-figurin' that the whole thing was a heap bigger than my own personal peace of soul. I might be safe myself, but in going over there and fightin' I might be helping to have them killed and a heap more of others, too, and that worried me.

I knowed He was going to watch over me, because I done done what I thought was right. But I wanted Him to watch over all of us, and I knowed He would only do that if we were all right and if our cause was right, too. I kinder felt now that it was right. But I wasn't sure. It's most awful hard for a weak human being, all sort of torn up with doubt and worry, to walk his way in perfect faith and understanding.

Pastor Pile wrote direct to President Wilson and explained things to him and asked him to release me. The letter come on down to our camp in Georgia. But I didn't follow it up. I didn't make any more claims for exemption. I didn't try to get out nohow. I knowed I was to go, but—I was still worrying about the war in general.

We moved up to Camp Upton, N. Y., and prepared ourselves to go overseas. So I went to the Captain again, Captain Danforth of Augusta, Ga., and asked him to please explain to me what we were fighting for and why we were leaving our homes and going over there to fight people we didn't even know and had never met before. The Captain kinder looked at me, funny like, as though he had thought he had settled all of that with me once before. But jes the same he was patient. Lieutenant Stewart, who, later on, was killed in the Argonne, was there in the orderly room with him and he was patient, too. They explained to me how the Germans done broken their promise to Belgium and done overrun those countries over there and put so many people to the sword; that unless they were stopped they would keep on until they done overrun the world. They jes had to be stopped and we Americans were going over there to help stop them.

Then I begun to understand, not clearly yet, but kinder like.

We were to be peacemakers. And it was written in the Bible, "Blessed are the peacemakers"——— That was we-uns. We were to help make peace, the only way the Germans would understand. But I couldn't help a-wonderin' why there wasn't some other way to get peace except by fightin' for it.

CHAPTER XX

SOLDIERING

AND all of this time while I was struggling with my doubts I was going on with my training and sorter fitting into camp life. I obeyed orders. I did everything I was told to do. I tried my best to be a good soldier.

NOVEMBER, 1917

Camp Gordon, Georgia. I was placed in the 21st Training Bn and there I was called out the first morning of my army life to police up in the yard all the cigarette buts, and I thought that was pretty hard as I didn't smoke but I did it just the same.

I hain't never travelled much before going to camp. I hain't never been out of the mountains before, and I'm a-telling you I missed them right smart. It's pretty flat and sandy country down there in Georgia, and there ain't no strength or seasonin' in it. Hit shore needs hills and mountains most awful bad.

DECEMBER, 1917

Camp Gordon, Georgia. So I stayed there and did squads right and squads left until the first of February, 1918, and then I was sent to Company G 328 Bn. 82 Div.

The Eighty-second Division was known as the All-American Division. We wore the insignia A A on our shoulder. We were made up of boys from 'most every state in the Union. There were some mountaineers. Not many of them, though. Jes a few. There were Jews from the East Side of New York; there were English and Irish boys from the mill towns of New England; there were Greeks and Italians from some of the big cities in the East; there were Poles and Slavs from the coal mines of Pennsylvania; there were farmers from the Middle West; there were cow punchers from Oklahoma and Texas; and there were even some German boys. One-fifth of our men were of foreign birth, and several hundred were not even citizens of the United States. A right-smart number of them couldn't speak or understand the American language. And a whole heap couldn't read or write or even sign their own name.

FEBRUARY, 1918

Camp Gordon, Georgia. So there they put me by some Greeks and Italians to sleep. Well, I couldn't understand them and they couldn't understand me, and I was the homesickess boy you ever seen, ho! ho!

I had never had nothing to do nohow with foreigners before. When I first heard them talk I kinder thought they were angry with each other; they seemed to talk so fast and loud. I couldn't pronounce their names nohow. There was a great big Pole in our out-

fit whose name was Private Feodor Sok. That was
easy. We jes called him Sok. There was another,
Private Maryan E. Dymowski. I never could get the
straight of that nohow. And then there was Private
Joe Konotski. I couldn't do much with that either.
And there was Private Mario Muzzi and Michael Saccina. These are only a few of the foreigners we done
had in my platoon. But they kinder give some idea
of what a mixed-up gang we had in the All-American
Division.

Our battalion commander was Major George Edward Buxton, Jr., from Providence, R. I. He was a
New Englander. His beginnings went away back; so
far back that I guess he can scarcely trace them himself. He was one of the finest men I had ever met.
He was one of the most larned men too; and he was a
right-smart mixer. He was one of the best soldiers I
ever knowed. Before America come into the war he
was over there on the other side writing for the Providence, R. I., *Journal*. When he returned home he jes
knowed America was coming in, so he got busy doing
everything he could to prepare us for when our turn
came. He takened part in the Preparedness Cam-
paign with ex-President Roosevelt. He went to Platts-
burg and he was one of the first officers to be commissioned there. He went all over the country preaching preparedness.

He was a most wonderful man at handling soldiers.
He had a battalion mixed up of all sorts. And yet he
knowed most all of us and understood us and figured
out the way to handle us. He was young for a com-

manding officer, in his early thirties, I reckon. He was handsome, and in his major's uniform he looked a right-smart soldier. He had a kinder habit of getting us soldiers together and talking to us, something like a father talks to his sons. I'm a-tellin' you he sorter looked upon us as his sons, too. And in quicker time than it takes a coon to jump out of a tree he made that torn-up battalion all around us into a happy family.

I ricollect a heap of our fellows were sorter short on this saluting business. So one day the Major got us together and talked to us. He told us that we were soldiers and we had to salute. Then he explained to us that when we saluted an officer we weren't admittin' nohow that we were under him or inferior to him; we were jes letting him know that we were his friends. He told us how the salute began. It was over there in England. They had a big Civil War something like ours here in America. The side that was beaten was mussed up awful bad. Some of them were killed. Some of them were put in jail, some of them were shipped away acrost the seas, and a whole heap of them were driven into the forest where they were hunted jes like wild animals. They had to keep moving jes in order to keep alive. Their sufferings sorter drew them together. Of course, they were desperate and did a lot of killing. But not among themselves. Whenever they come together in the forest they would hold out their right hand to show they didn't have a gun in it and that they were friendly. That was the beginning of it, so the Major explained to us. And

after a while it was sorter takened up by the English
army and made over into the salute. And so Major
Buxton pointed out that if we didn't salute him and his
officers he would take it that we were not friendly, and
if the officers didn't salute us back we were to take
it that way.

After that there was no more trouble about this
saluting business. Our boys were so friendly they
would salute every chance they got, and the Major had
to sorter slow us down. I ricollect another little talk
he gave us. He said in every war there was always
one famous battalion that come out of it and sorter
lived forever. He hoped that battalion would be ours.
And every war always produced its outstanding hero.
He didn't know where that hero was in the American
Army, but there was jes as good a chance of him being
in our battalion as anywhere else. And I'm a-tellin'
you after we heard him speak like that we all kinder
made up our minds to be better soldiers and maybe try
and be that outstanding one ourselves. His favourite
advice to us was "Keep moving and always use your
head." I'm saying here and now that's right-smart
advice.

Captain E. C. B. Danforth, Jr., was my company
commander. He come from Augusta, and was a
Georgia "Cracker." He was a Harvard man. That
didn't mean nothing to me in those days. It didn't
mean much to the other boys either. All we knowed
was that like the Major he had a heap of larnin'. He
was tall and tough jes like a hickory pole. He must
have been about twenty-three or twenty-four years old,

and he had as much sense as a much older man. He was the fightinest man, too, and when he was in action our boys used to say he was that hard that the bullets used to bounce off'n him. The Major and the Captain together were as good a combination as a pair of Red Bones when you have them out after the foxes. They ran together. If ever I have to go to war agin I'm a-telling you I wouldn't ask for anything more than to have them two leading me. Wherever they go I am willing to follow. And that's jes about how most of the other boys under them feel.

My own platoon was made up of a gang of the toughest and most hard-boiled doughboys I ever heard tell of. There were bartenders, saloon bouncers, ice men, coal miners, dirt farmers, actors, mill hands, and city boys who had growed up in the back alleys and learned to scrap ever since they were knee high to a duck. They were mixed up from 'most every country. They were as hard as a forest full of oaks and they were meaner and more full of fight than a hive of wild bees. They could out-swear, out-drink, and out-cuss any other crowd of men I have ever knowed. They sorter looked upon leave-breaking as a divine right.

Our sergeant takened forty-eight hours' leave and stayed away ten days. He was busted for that, but later on he got his stripes back. He had to. He was the only one who could drill and keep us in hand. One of our corporals went on leave and missed the boat and had to follow us to France.

They were always spoiling to have it out with somebody. They were fighters and that's all about it. If you looked at them sorter sideways for even a second you were in danger of being on the wrong end of a punch. If you didn't drink they kinder regarded you as being ignorant; and if you didn't cuss a blue streak every time you opened your mouth you were considered to be most awful illiterate.

A heap of them couldn't talk our own language at all, and any number of them couldn't sign their own names. The only way the Captain could get them to larn to write was by telling them they couldn't get their pay unless they could put their signatures to the pay sheets. Ho! ho!

But jes the same, they were my buddies. I didn't understand them at first. I didn't know nothing about them nohow. I didn't cuss or drink or smoke or fight. I didn't go A. W. O. L. [absence without official leave]. And I was a conscientious objector. So they didn't understand me either. But most they left me alone. And that's all that I asked for. So they let it go at that.

I guess Major Buxton and Captain Danforth must have lost a heap of sleep over there trying to figure out how to handle that-there gang of wild men. But I'm a-thinking them-there officers knowed in their hearts that if ever they got them safe overseas and into the front-line trenches they would have a bunch of fighters under them that never would stop until they done mussed up the Germans right smart and busted a hole right through that-there old Hindenburg Line. But the puzzling thing was to keep them together and to handle them in the right sort of way until they were overseas. That was a job, I'm a-tellin' you, and I ain't a-foolin' nohow. Them-there boys jes had to fight.

The sergeant in charge of our platoon was Harry Parsons, of Brooklyn, N. Y. He'd been an actor and he was jes a natcheral-born entertainer. He used to lead us in singing. He used to entertain us at night, and when we were out on a long route march and were tired out he would gather us around and go to it and then we would all get to laughing and singing. That's one of the ways he handled us. He was a big husky sort of fellow. He knowed how to handle that platoon. He didn't fight unless he had to, and then he had a habit of biting his teeth together and putting his chin out and letting fly with both hands at the same time. And when he did that somebody went down, and it was never him. But he never manhandled our fellows unless he had to. But when he had to he made a right-smart job of it. Something must have happened to him over there in the Argonne, because when he come home he was changed. He went back on the stage but he done lost his power to entertain.

Then we had two of the wildest fighting corporals that ever knocked them down and dragged them out. One of them was Bernard Early. He used to be a bartender in Connecticut. The amount of liquor he could put away was most amazing. And when it come to fighting he jes couldn't be beat. Early come from Ireland where they jes natcherly breed fighting men. In and around the camp, in the saloon or over in the

front lines in France, it was all the same to Bernie.
If there was a fight he was happy. If there wasn't he
was kinder always looking for one. But he was a
friendly chap, and he had a sorter way with him. He
was a right-smart soldier, too, most awful brave. I
guess he hain't never known what fear was.

His particular buddy was another corporal, William S. Cutting. He was a Pole from around Boston
and New York, where he used to be an ice man. He
was always rarin' to go. You ought to've heard him
talk. He was funny—oncet he said that when he got
into the front-line trenches if the Germans ever threw
bombs at him he would jes eat them-there bombs for
breakfast. These-here two corporals were jes about
the hard-boiledest soldiers I ever knowed. It took me
a long time to understand them, and I'm a-thinkin' I
ain't never really done it. But jes the same, once they
done gone into action, they shore enough cost the Germans a heap more bother than a whole swarm of
hornets or bumblebees ever could have.

Among the privates was that-there Sok. For a long
time I didn't even know that was his real name. I
thought it was a nickname. When he went berserker
over there at the front it looked as if he never would
stop nohow until he got right through to Berlin.

Then there was Michael Saccina, a little Italian. I
think he come from New York. After the fight in the
Argonne he likened the German Major's whistle to the
little whistle on a peanut stand at home in New York.
That sorter speaks for itself.

And there was Joe Konotski and Walter Swanson

and Muzzi and Beardsley and Johnson and a heap of others; all of them most awful hard fightin' men and most awful tough soldiers. Most of them were always causing a lot of trouble; but they bothered the Germans a heap more than they bothered anybody else. I ricollect, too, we had a couple of farm boys from the South with us. Ho! ho! When we were in New York, before sailing, they got their safety razors. They didn't understand them nohow. One of them fixed up his razor and tried to shave with it, but it weren't no good. He looked at it and said: "Anything the Government gives you for nothing ain't never no good," and with a sort of disgusted look on his face he throwed it away. The other one tried several times without even cutting a hair. Then he throwed his away too, and said he "never had no use for the Democrats nohow," and now they were in power they had to go and buy razors that wouldn't shave. Ho! ho! They were trying to shave with the wax paper on the blades!

So these were the sort of soldier boys that I was in with in the Eighty-second Division. Jes a bunch of hard-living, hard-fighting doughboys; always spoiling for a scrap. But when you got to know them, they were jes about as fine a bunch of buddies as ever got together and did squads right and squads left, and when they got into it over there they jes kept on a-goin'.

Of course, it takened me a long time to get to know them. In camp I never did think I would larn to understand them, and I guess they couldn't figure me out

nohow. They knowed that I was a conscientious objector, and they hadn't much use for that. They jes
didn't understand. Sometimes they got to teasing me
most awful bad, but I never done any arguing with
them. I hadn't anything to say or any fault to find,
and I wasn't going to quarrel or fight with them no
matter what they done. I didn't want to fight nobody
and least of all American doughboys.

So we went on training together through the early
months of 1918.

MARCH, 1918

Camp Gordon, Georgia. Well, they give me a
gun and oh my that old gun was jes full of Greece
and I hed to clean that old gun for enspection. So
I had a hard time to get that old gun clean. So
when I got this gun I begin to drill with the gun, and
we had to hike once a week. So I have seen many
boys fall out of the hikes. We would haft to take
long hikes with all our stuff on our back and carry
that gun. Ho! ho! And we would haft to go out
before daylight and have sham battles. So I begin
to want a pass to go home.

That first army rifle that was issued me was all full
of grease, gun grease of some kind. Of course, I
didn't like that. The rifles we used in the mountains
we always kept clean. They were most all muzzle-
loaders. And I'm a-tellin' you up to one hundred
yards they could out-shoot them-there army rifles any

time. But, of course, a muzzle-loader wouldn't be no good nohow in a modern war. It takes too long to reload. It don't carry far enough, and it's too heavy. So I had to get used to the army rifle. And I did. I cleaned it up. I takened it to pieces. I put it together agin. I nursed it and doctored it. It larned all about it.

Then we went out on the rifle ranges to practise shooting. Them-there Greeks and Italians and Poles and New York Jews and some of the boys from the big cities hadn't been used to handling guns. Some of them didn't even know how to load them, and when they fired they not only missed the targets, they missed the backgrounds on which the targets were fixed. They missed everything but the sky. It shore was dangerous scoring for them boys. Of course, it weren't no trouble nohow for me to hit them great big army targets. They were so much bigger than turkeys' heads. And an army bull's-eye is about a million times bigger than a criss-cross cut with a sharp knife on a piece of board or a tree; and that's the target we most often used in our shooting matches at home. We had to cut the centre right out to win anything. That's the sort of shooting I was used to. So I made a tol'-able score on the shooting ranges in camp.

I got my pass to go home in late March. I takened the train as far as I could and then I hiked the last twelve miles over the mountains, alone. I had to carry my suit case, too. Ho! ho!

It kinder hurt to say good-bye to Mother. And I jes knowed I would never forget that-there last meeting in the lane with Gracie. But I ain't a-writing about those things. There are some things in your life that you can't do nothing else with but jes sorter feel deep inside of you. And that's the way it was with me.

MARCH 29TH

Pall Mall, Tennessee. So I had to start back to my company, and that was a heart-breaking time for me, as I knowed I had to go to France. But I went back to my company, trusting in my God and asking Him to keep me, although I had many trials and much hardship and temptation. But yet I could look up and say:

> O God, in hope that sends the shining ray,
> Far down the future's broadening way;
> In peace that only Thou canst give;
> With Thee, O Master, let me live.

Then it was that the Lord would bless me, and I almost felt sure of coming back home, for the Lord was with me.

APRIL 19TH

Camp Gordon, Georgia. So we left Camp Gordon in the afternoon.

APRIL 21ST

Camp Upton, New York. We got to Camp Upton, N. Y., so we stayed there a few days and drilled.

APRIL 30TH

Boston, Mass. We went to Boston, Mass.

MAY 1ST

Boston, Mass. About 4 o clock am we got on board the old Scandaneven ship and started for France.

We left Boston and sailed down around to New York Harbour and we stopped there until we got our convoy, and then we lit out. And that was the first time that I had ever seed the open sea. It was too much water for me. Like me, Mark Twain, whose parents come from Jimtown, was borned inland. And he never seed the open ocean until he growed up. And when he stood on the beach and seed it for the first time, his friends asked him what he thought of it, and he said, "It was a success." But when Mark said that he weren't on the ocean. He were on the shore. And when our old boat got away out and begun to pitch and toss I jes knowed Mark was wrong.

The Greeks, Italians, and Poles, and New York Jews stood the trip right smart. That kinder impressed me. It sorter made up for their bad shooting. I sorter got to like them more.

CHAPTER XXI

OVER THERE

MAY 16TH

Liverpool, England. We got off the boat in the evening.

MAY 17TH

Camp Knotteash, England. We stayed at a little camp called Knotteash on the 17th.

MAY 18TH

Southampton, England. We went to Southampton.

MAY 19TH

Southampton, England. Stayed there the 19th.

MAY 20TH

Southampton, England. We started from England to France.

So you see I didn't see much of England. I'd travelled over three thousand miles from my home to get there, and when I did get there all I did was hike and catch trains and keep moving. I might jes as well have been in Georgia, only the English country was more beautiful. It was sort of rolling-like and the parks and fields were so neat and tidy that it 'most looked as though they had special gardeners to look after every few acres of them.

Of course, we were all anxious to get to France. We wanted to get into it and get it over. We had a sorter idea that they would rush us right to those old front-line trenches and let us get at the Germans without losing any time.

MAY 21ST

Le Havre, France. So we got to France at Le Havre there we turned in our guns and got British guns.

We crossed the English Channel on the H. M. S. *Viper*. It was more like a bucking mule than a boat. We were only on it for a few hours, but that was a-plenty. Long before we landed I didn't care whether we stayed up or went down, whether we got there or didn't get there. I didn't care about anything. I was kinder miserable. I missed the mountains of Tennessee more'n ever.

We spent our first night in France in a little camp outside of Le Havre. We had to turn in our guns and get British guns. I had takened a liking to mine by this time. I had takened it apart and cleaned it up so often that I had learned every piece and could almost put it back together with my eyes shut. The Greeks and Italians and Jews and Poles were improving. They had stayed continuously on the rifle range for a month or two, and got so they could do shooting.

They were fairly good pals, too. But I missed the mountain boys. I was the only mountaineer in the company. I was the largest in our platoon.

We got our first gas masks in Le Havre. That brought the war a whole heap closer. I never did like those pesky gas masks.

We travelled in box cars. They were marked, "Forty men or eight horses." One of our boys who was detailed to load the cars went to the Captain and said: "Captain, I loaded the forty men all right, but if you put the eight horses in too they will shore trample the boys to death." Ho! ho!

MAY 22D

Eu, France. Taken the train at Le Havre and come to a little place called Eu.

MAY 24TH

Floraville, France. We eat our Breakfast at Eu and then Hiked to Floraville, and we stayed at floraville a few days.

Field Marshal Haig and his staff inspected one of our battalions here. The British commander made a right-smart impression on the boys. While he was with them he went and inspected one of the kitchens. One of the cooks was a great big fellow from Tennessee, and the Field Marshal asked him if everything was all right, and he said, "No, everything is all wrong, most awfully all wrong—there is no salt." The Field

Marshal turned to the Quartermaster General, who was with him, and asked for an explanation. The Quartermaster said the two last salt ships were torpedoed and there was a shortage. The Field Marshal then instructed him to immediately send some salt to the American kitchen. That kinder tickled our boys.

Our own General Pershing also inspected us. We were anxious to make a right-smart impression on him, because we knowed if we did we would get up to the front-line trenches so much quicker, and our boys were jes rarin' to go. General Pershing made even a better impression than Field Marshal Haig, and he seemed sorter satisfied with us. So you see here we were in France. And we were inspected by two commanders-in-chief and we got by all right. We shore were a different outfit to the rambunshus crowd of half-wild men that first got together in Camp Gordon, in Georgia.

Anyone who thinks that soldiering is jes goin' back in again and fightin', is jes plumb foolin' himself. Weeks passed and we never even seen a trench except the training ones. We never once heard the sound of guns. All we did was hike, and hike, and hike—and then hike again. They shore kept us a-going—hiking. It seemed as though they had sent us to France to kinder test out the strength of them-there American military shoes.

JUNE 4TH

Mons Babert, France. Hiked here and we stayed a few Days.

And the boys were beginning to think by this time
that we weren't a-fightin' outfit at all. We were jes
sorter touring France—on the hoof. Ho! ho! I
didn't mind it much because I was used to hunting and
tramping over the mountains. But them-there Greeks
and Jews and Italians from the cities shore filled their
shoes full of blisters. But they kept a-going jes the
same. I'm a-tellin' you them boys were coming along
right smart. I was beginning to get kinder fond of
them. They were sorter human jes like the mountain
boys I had knowed all my life. Of course, they were
not as strong or as good hikers or shooters, but I was
beginning to larn they had a few things about them
which the mountain boys didn't have nohow. Them-
there city boys shore nursed their feet, jes about as
careful as I nursed my guns.

JUNE (no date)

Fressenneville, France. Went on to Fressenneville.

JUNE (no date)

Toul, France. Entrained for toul and we got to
toul and got off the train.

JUNE 20TH

Lucey, France. Hiked to Lucey.

Of course, ef a night time if we was near a town,
some of the boys got leave. Some of them got all

tanked up with vin rouge and cognac; and, being soldiers, they was right smart when it come to finding
them-there pretty French girls. Some of them shore
knowed more about hunting and finding them, too,
than I did about trailing coon and fox back there on
the mountains at home. They were fuller of fight than
ever. It was in them and it had to come out. They
couldn't get at the Germans yet, so they sorter prac-
tised out on themselves. There was a heap of Irish
and Poles in our platoon, and one night in one of the
cafés one of the Irish boys said he didn't believe the
Poles could fight nohow. Ho! ho! That shore started
it! They went at it with fists and belts. They turned
that café into a No Man's Land, only worse, and we
had to turn out the guard to stop it. I'm a-tellin' you
there was nothin' mean or bad about the boys. They
was jes sorter full of life.

I didn't go into the towns much. I had put all of
the drinkin' and fist-fightin' away behind me. I left it
back home on the Kentucky line. I didn't have a drink
all the time I was in France. I didn't have a fist fight
or an argument. I didn't swear or smoke either. I
wasn't any better'n any of the other boys. It was jes
my way of livin', that was all. They did what they
wanted to do. So did I. Our ways were different.
We let it go at that. I did a heap of reading from
the Bible. I read it through several times over there.
I worked on my little diary. I was a awful slow writer
and thinker. And though I didn't put much in it, it
tuk up plenty of time jes the same. I used to go
around, too, a little with Corporal Murray Savage.

About this time we were going in again for bayonet practice. We had to rush the dummies the instructors set up and stab bayonets into them and muss them up. That sorter set me to worrying agin. I knowed the time was coming when I might have to do the same thing to the Germans. And though I knowed now that we were fighting for peace, still it made me feel queer to think I might have to cut up human beings. I still didn't want to kill. I still did feel somehow that it was wrong—terrible wrong for human beings to take each other's life. I don't know why I still felt like this. But I did jes the same.

JUNE 26TH

Rambucourt, France. We hiked a little ways and then taken the train for a short ride and then we got of train and hiked to Rambucourt and we stayed at rambucourt until after Dark and then we went up and took over the front line trenches for the first time.

We were going in at last. We could hear the guns away in the distance now, jes like the thunder in the hills at home. We seed a right-smart lot of deserted trenches with wire entanglements, all snarled and mussed up. We seed gun emplacements half full of water. We passed an awful lot of graves, with little wooden crosses at their heads. I'm a-tellin' you that brought it home to us. And all the roads were sorter blocked up with troops coming and going and artillery and transports. As we got up closer we could hear the rifles barking and the machine guns spitting, and soon the bullets started coming over. They were stray bullets. The Germans were firing in the front line ahead of us and they were missing the parapet and coming right back among us. It was the first time that we were under fire, and of course we were a little nervous. The officers told us boys that it was all right; that they were only stray bullets; that they would not injure us, and not to mind them. And one of them-there Italian boys grinned and give as his opinion that it didn't matter whether they were strays or not, that if they hit us they would do jes as much damage as if they was aimed at us. As we got right up close some of the boys began to duck as the bullets come over. And then somebody else 'lowed that it weren't no use ducking nohow, because you never hear the one that hits you. We went in and takened over the front line at night time.

JUNE 27TH

Montsec Sector, France. And we releaved the 26th Div. Boys at night in the Montsec Sector at Rambucourt and we stayed there until the 4th of July.

It was a quiet sector where they put new troops into training before sending them out to No Man's Land. The Greeks and Italians and all of the other boys done fairly well. They shore were turning out to be the bestest soldiers. I was often out on No Man's Land.

I done done some patrolling. I handled an automatic squad. We were armed with French sho-sho rifles. They were sort of portable machine guns. They fired about eighteen shots without reloading. They were not much good nohow. They were big and clumsy. They were too heavy. They were not accurate or silent. You never could be shore you would hit what you fired at, no matter how good a shot you were. All you could do with them was make a lot of noise, and waste a heap of ammunition, and hope for the best. They weren't near as good as the sawed-off shotguns.

We had a heap of big stuff from the artillery coming over and some gas, and we had to put on them pesky gas masks agin. The German snipers were always after us. They were good marksmen. They could bust a periscope 'most every shot. They knowed how to keep our heads down, too. The bullets was always coming over, humming and buzzing around our ears, jes like a lot of mad hornets or bumble bees when you rob their nests.

I did a heap of thinking and praying at this time. And more'n ever I jes knowed I was going to get back all right. I believed in God and in His promises. And I knowed as long as I did that He would believe in and watch over me, and there one night in that old front-line trench, I wrote in my diary:

JULY 1ST

Montsec Sector, France. *A few words on Christian witness in war and why a Christian does worry.*

Yet there is no use worrying about anything except, the worry of So many Souls who have passed out into the Deep of an Unknown world and has left no testimony as to the welfair of their souls. There is no use of worrying a Bout Shells for you cant keep them from bursting in your trench nor you cant Stop the rain or prevent a light from a going up jes as you are half way over the parapet—So what is the use of worrying if you cant alter things just ask God to help you and accept them and make the best of them by the help of God; yet some men do worry and By Doing So they effectually distroy their peace of Mind without doing any one any good. Yet it is often the religious man who worries. I have even heard those whose care was for the Soldier Soul Deplore the fact that he Did not worry. I have heard it said that the Soldier is so Careless, realizes his position So little.

Up there in the front line I knowed as I had never knowed before what a comforting thing religion is. So I clung to my faith all the time. I read my Testament everywhere. I read it in the dugouts, in the fox holes, in the front lines and everywhere. Hit was my rock to cling to; hit and my diary.

The trouble with our boys when we went into this quiet sector was they would want to go out on top of the trenches and start something. They was wanting to get into it and get it over. I knowed now that the Greeks and Italians and Poles and New York Jews were fighters. Ho! ho! As right-smart fighters as

the American-borned boys. They didn't want to lay
around and do nothing. And they would even go on
top and get the Germans out. Once one of them come
up to me right there in the front line and asked me,
"Where is the war?"

They was always wanting to go over the top—and
keep a-going. They shore were ambitious.

Well, we would stay in a quiet sector for a few
days. Then we would pull out and hike off to another,
and then another, until we gradually worked our way
into the real fighting sectors.

JULY 4TH

Cormeville, France. Then we come out to Cormeville and stayed there until July 17th.

JULY 17TH

Rambucourt, France. Went Back in the Lines
again and stayed until July 25th.

JULY 25TH

Rambucourt, France. We come out.

AUGUST 2D

Mandres, France. We went in again in the sector at Mandres.

AUGUST 8TH

Mandres, France. Come out again.

While we were in these so-called quiet sectors four of our men were detailed to take the chow to the front-line outposts. It was night time, of course. They were given the necessary passwords. But one of them, on the return, got separated and also forgot the passwords. This was serious. Then he done something which sorter showed the kind of soldier he was. He waited quietly for about a half hour until another soldier come along. He then halted him in the customary way, advanced him, received the password, and let him pass by. He done pretended he was on guard duty and so done received the password and got back all right. He was a Greek and he spoke very little English, but that didn't stop him nohow. I'm a-telling you that's soldiering for you; that's using your head!

The Greeks and Italians and Poles and New York Jews. Ho! ho!—they were men. I was beginning to understand them.

AUGUST 14TH

Pont-à-Mousson, France. Went back to Pont-à-Mousson.

CHAPTER XXII

ST. MIHIEL

AUGUST 16TH

Pont-à-Mousson, France. Went to Pont-à-Mousson and stayed there in the front until August 24th.

To we-uns all dirty and tired from being in the front-line trenches and hiking all over France, Pont-à-Mousson was a kinder earthly paradise. It is in the valley on the banks of the Moselle River. It was late summer, jes the time when the fruit is ready for picking. The trees and vines were loaded with grapes and apples and everything. The gardens were all kept up nice, with everything kinder ripe and ready, and there was plenty of green grass and shade and cool, clean water. It was most hard for us to imagine that we were still in the war. The city wasn't mussed up at all. It hadn't been shelled nohow. We heard there had been a kind of agreement between the French and the Germans to leave it alone. So it had stayed there all by itself and unharmed for four years. We bathed and rested there. And got us some good fruit and laid out in the sunshine until we felt sort of re-made all over again.

AUGUST 24TH

Liverdun, France. Come out to Liverdun and stayed there until Sept. 1st.

SEPTEMBER 1ST

Pont-à-Mousson, France. Went back to Pont-à-Mousson.

When we entered the town this time we found that the French population had jes left before we arrived. Everything was left standing jes as it was. Even the tables were set and the food was still standing on the stoves. Some of us stole in and had the best food we done tasted for a long time. The beds were made; everything was clean and orderly. You see the French population had been done told that the drive was beginning, and they had lit out as fast as they could, only taking with them what they could tote in their arms. About this time the Germans started to send over some big shells. They done done a whole heap of damage to the nice little town and they done mussed up the orchards and done scattered the fruit all over the place. A little while later we heard the most awful explosion, jes as if an ammunition dump had been blowed up. We found out that our artillery done moved up some big naval guns. They were much bigger than tractors, and most awful long. They shore let the Germans have it. We could hear the big shells whinin' and whizzin' over our heads on their way to Metz, which was fifteen miles away.

We were now getting ready for the St. Mihiel drive, which was to be the first real battle we were in, and the first major offensive for the American Army. It done opened with a most awful barrage from our big guns. It was the awfulest thing you ever heard. It made the air tremble and the ground shake. At times you couldn't hear your own voice nohow. The air was full of airplanes, and most of them American planes. There must have been hundreds of them. They were diving and circling around all over the place like a swarm of birds. We seed several right-smart fights away up there above us. One day we was sitting in a trench, looking up and watching, when one of them-there East Side Jews 'lowed that he might be killed in a airplane accident, but if ever he was, the airplane would have to light on him. For a few days before the attack we waited on a little hillside jes outside of Pont-à-Mousson, on the banks of the river. Then we moved up into the front-line trenches. We waited in them about a day and a night until the artillery done done its work, and it done done it right smart, too.

SEPTEMBER 12TH

St. Mihiel, France. And the Big American Drive started and we went over the top the night of the 12th then we took a little town By the name of Norroy and went on to the top of a nother hill Beyond Norroy.

Early on the morning of the twelfth the guns let down a most awful heavy barrage, louder than a thun-

derstorm. And at daybreak we went over the top.
We cut our way through the barbed wire and advanced
on the little village of Norroy. But fast as we went
forward the Germans kept on moving backwards,
faster. They jes wouldn't stand and fight it out. Our
battalion was right in the thick of it, and some of the
other companies got mussed up right smart, but ours
never lost a man. I don't know why, but we didn't.
I'm a-thinking the Germans were in too much of a
hurry to take careful aim. There was a-plenty of
machine-gun and artillery fire, but it didn't seem to
find us. I done heard tell that it takes nearly a ton
of lead to kill a man in a war. I kinder believe it.
There were bullets and shells everywhere, but the boys
kept on a-going. None of them fell. There was no
holding that-there League of Nations of ours. They
wanted to push right on and not stop until they got to
Berlin. They cussed the Germans out for not standing and they kept yelling at them to wait and fight it
out. We continued from Norroy on to the top of the
hill beyond until we got in advance of our own flank
and the Germans were enfilading us. So we was ordered by our Captain to dig in until some of the other
troops got up.

When we captured Norroy we mopped up the houses
and went through the town looking for prisoners. A
lot of our boys takened prisoner several barrels of
wine. So they knocked the bungs out of them and
drinked a whole mess of it. Then they were fuller
of fight than ever. And there was one big house there,
all locked up. It looked like headquarters, but when

we done surrounded it and stormed it we found it was
a storehouse and it was full of Belgian hares. These
hares ran all over the place and our boys done chased
them. I'm a-telling you those barrels of wine and
them-there hares shore demoralized my Greeks and
Italians. And when we started back in the night one
of the boys takened a milk goat that was captured and
was leading it back to Pont-à-Mousson. And when the
officer done called to him and asked him what he was
doing with that goat, he answered: "Sir, I am jes going
back to put a little cream in my coffee."

When we dug in the hillside beyond Norroy we
seen a little vineyard. We were very hungry, and
them-there grapes jes natcherly made our mouths
water. So we begun to slip back after the grapes,
but the Germans had an observation balloon, one of
those big sausage balloons, up in the air, and they seed
us and directed the German artillery to tech us off.
So we had orders not to go back there any more. But
that night I decided to go back and get me some of
them grapes. I jes stalked back and was keeping very
quiet so I wouldn't be seen when a shell landed near
and I jumped and ran and I done run right into my
own Captain, Captain Danforth of Augusta, Ga. He
liked grapes, too—ho! ho!—and we both fled.

The Germans threw a lot of gas shells into Norroy,
and we had to wear our gas masks for several hours.
I had been made corporal before this battle. So I
led the squad. I kinder think they almost led me. I
mean I was supposed to be in the front and they were
supposed to follow. But no matter how fast I went

they wanted to go faster, so that they could get at the Germans. The Greeks and Italians, the Poles and the Jews and the other city boys were still firing pretty wild. They were still mostly hitting the ground or the sky. They burned up a most awful lot of Uncle Sam's ammunition. But they kept on a-going jes the same. They were that full of fight that wild cats shore would have backed away from them.

The St. Mihiel offensive must have been as complete a drive and as well arranged as ever could have been by any general of any army. It was a great success. The feeling of the majority of the boys was one hundred per cent. for General Pershing. As a whole the Army was back of him, believed in him, and would follow him anywhere. They seemed to think as a general he was a right-smart success. After a few days in the front lines we were takened out to rest in a little valley jes back of Pont-à-Mousson. But I never did hear of that-there goat any more. I don't know whether the boy got the cream for his coffee or not.

CHAPTER XXIII

THE ARGONNE

SEPTEMBER 17TH

St. Mihiel, France. We come out to some woods
and camped there and got us something to eat.

SEPTEMBER 23D

St. Mihiel, France. We come on back to some
more woods and then we stayed a few days.

SEPTEMBER 24TH

St. Mihiel, France. We started for the Argonne
forest.

We takened a little narrow gauge railroad to a
place somewhere in France. We didn't know where
it was. I don't think anybody except the officers
knowed that. Here we come upon about one hundred
old French buses. They were big and painted white.
The drivers were Chinese and most of them spoke
French. I done never seen Chinaman before, and I
jes couldn't keep my eyes off them. Some of our boys
afterwards done told the story, I don't know how true
it was, that one of them-there Chinamen kept a-pes-
terin' one of our doughboys for a souvenir. The
doughboy took a Mills grenade out of his pocket—one

of them pesky little things. You pull the lever and in
five seconds it explodes. Well, he pulled the lever and
then handed it to the Chinaman and told him to put
it to his ear and listen to it tick. Ho! ho!

Them Chinamen were the awfulest drivers you ever
seed. They must have sorter had the idea they had to
get us there before they even started. The way they
done tore and bumped those old French buses over
those old French roads was enough to make your hair
stand up straight. I'm a-thinking we were in more danger from them than we were from the Germans when
we were in the front line. Two of the trucks turned
over, but nobody was mussed up bad. It now seemed
to me that we had most all of the nationalities in the
world around, and there were all them-there different
races in my platoon. There were the American-borned
and the foreign-borned boys; there were the French
and those Chinese drivers and the Germans over the
way. Hit shore was a lot of travelling and meeting
people for a mountain boy who never travelled more'n
a few miles before he left home.

The war brings out the worst in you. It turns you
into a mad, fightin' animal, but it also brings out something else, something I jes don't know how to describe,
a sort of tenderness and love for the fellows fightin'
with you. It's sort of clean, like a fire of pine logs on
a frosty night. I had kinder got to know and sorter
understand the boys around me. I knowed their weakness as well as their strength. I guess they knowed
mine. If you live together for several months sharing
and sharing alike, you learn a heap about each other.

It was as though we could look right through each
other and knowed everything without anything being
hid. I'm a-telling you I loved them-there boys in my
squad. I had forgiven them for their bad shooting.
I had forgiven it if they drank and tore things up before going to the front. Anyway, that was their own
business. It was no affair of mine. If they got happiness that way, it was all right with me. I guess they
sorter figured they were going to be mussed up and
maybe killed when they got into the trenches, so they
figured they might jes as well enjoy things while they
had the chance. If that's the way they figured it out,
it was all right with me. If they cussed a whole lot,
I don't think they meant it to be as bad as it sounded.
It was their own way of expressing themselves; that's
all. Even if a fellow doesn't drink or smoke or cuss,
like me for instance, he has no right to find fault with
others, provided they don't interfere with him. He
has no right to pass judgment, and I didn't nohow. I
kinder think away down underneath I sorter loved
them for their weakness most of all. They were my
buddies. That's a word that's only understood by
soldiers who have lived under the same blankets, gathered around the same chow can, and looked at death
together. I never knowed I loved my brother-man so
much until I was a doughboy. I knowed men could
be strong and rough, but I never understood before
that they could be so tender and loving, and I jes
couldn't baar to think of anything happenin' to them.
It was too awful to think of them-there boys being
wounded or killed. I kinder did a lot of thinking and

praying about these things as we moved out into the
Argonne. Somehow, I seemed to jes know that we
were going to get into it right, in them-there woods.

OCTOBER 3D

Zona Woods, France. We camped over night on
a high hill in the woods.

OCTOBER 4TH

Argonne Forest, France. We had went on into
the Argonne Woods where we stayed over night.

The battle of the Argonne started the night of
the 25th of September, but we were sorter in reserve. We camped each night well back in the woods
and moved up a little bit at a time. At first we noticed the woods hadn't been shot up much. We hadn't
reached the main battlegrounds. But as we got closer,
I'm a-telling you we knowed there was a war on. The
woods were all mussed up and the ground was all torn
up with shells.

OCTOBER 5TH

Argonne Forest, France. We went out on the
main road and lined up and started for the front
and the germans was shelling the road and airo-
planes was humming over our heads and we were
stumbling over dead horses and dead men and shells
were Bursting all around me and then it was that I
could see the Power of God helped man if he would

only trust him.   Oh it was there I could look up and
say:

> O Jesus, the great rock of foundation
> Where on my feet were set with sovereign grace;
> Through Shells or Death with all their agitation
> Thou wilt protect me if I will only trust in thy Grace
> Bless thy holy name.

OCTOBER 7TH

Argonne Forest, France.   We layed in some little holes on the roadside all Day that night we went
and stayed a little while and come Back to our little holes and the Shells Bursting all around us.   I
seen men just Blowed up By the Big German Shells
Which Were Bursting all a round us.   So the order
came for us to take hill 223 and 240 the 8th.

It was raining a little bit all day, kinder drizzly
and very damp.   Lots of big shells bursting all around
us.   We were not up close enough for the machine
guns to reach us, but airplanes were buzzing overhead
'most all the time, jes like a lot of hornets.   Lots of
men were killed by the artillery fire.   And lots were
wounded.   We seed quite a lot of our machine-gun battalion across the road from us blowed up by the big
shells.   The woods were all mussed up and looked as
if a terrible cyclone done swept through them.   But
God would never be cruel enough to create a cyclone as
terrible as that Argonne battle.   Only man would ever
think of doing an awful thing like that.   It looked like
the "Abomination of Desolation" must have been.

And all through the long night those big guns flashed and growled jes like the lightning and the thunder when it storms in the mountains at home. And oh, my! we had to pass the wounded. And some of them were on stretchers going back to the dressing stations and some of them were lying around moaning and twitching. And oh, my! the dead were all along the road and their mouths were open and their eyes, too, but they couldn't see nothing no more nohow. And it was wet and cold and damp. And it all made me think of the Bible and the story of the anti-Christ and Armageddon. And I'm a-telling you the little log cabin in Wolf Valley in old Tennessee seemed a long, long way off.

CHAPTER XXIV

THE ARGONNE FIGHT

OCTOBER 8TH

Argonne Forest, France. So the morning of the 8th just before daylight we started for the hill at Chatel Chehery. So before we got there it got light and the germans sent over a heavy Barrage and also gas and we put on our gas mask and just Pressed right on through those shells and got to the top of hill 223 to where we was to start over the top at 6:10 A.M.

All day long on October 7th we laid out there in the rain and the mud along the main army road running from Varennes to Fléville, and watching the attack of the First Battalion, which takened Hill 223 in the afternoon. Shells were bursting all around and a whole heap of stray bullets were buzzing through the air. Airplanes were fighting overhead. It was all most awful.

Through most of the night we laid out there, too. It was that dark you couldn't see nothing nohow. Lights were flashing from the gun fire. There were all sorts of sounds and noises. It was raining worse'n than ever. The ground was soft and mucky and all cut up. We were wet through and dirty and kinder

217

tired. About 3 A.M. in the morning, the morning of
October 8th, our Captain, Captain Danforth, come to
us and told us we were to move on to Hill 223, which
was to be the jumping-off place for our attack, which
was to be at daybreak. Our objective was the Decauville Railroad, which was about three kilometres to
the northwest of the hill, and further on almost in the
centre of the Argonne Forest. We were to bust that
old railroad so as to stop the Germans from sending
in their troops and supplies. With the Captain leading, we marched over the Aire River on a little shaky,
wooden bridge which the engineers had thrown up for
us, on through the town of Chatel Chehery and on
up to Hill 223. It was so dark and everything was
so mussed up and the going was so rough that it was
most awful hard to keep contact and to find the hill.
But we done kept on a-going jes the same. We were
marching, I might say floundering around, in column
of squads. The noise were worse than ever, and everybody was shouting through the dark, and nobody
seemed to be able to hear what anybody else said.
We should have reached the hill before daybreak.
But we didn't. It weren't nobody's fault. The going
was too tough. So as soon as they were able to see the
German artillery lit into us with a heap of big stuff.
One of their shells bust plumb in the middle of one of
our squads, and wounded or killed every man. They
done laid down the meanest kind of a barrage too, and
the air was jes full of gas. But we put on our masks
and kept plugging and slipping and sliding, or falling
into holes and tripping over all sorts of things and

getting up again and stumbling on for a few yards and then going down again, until we done reached the hill. The First Battalion had takened it the day before, but they hadn't mopped it up. And there were some snipers and German machine guns left there hidden in the brush and in fox holes.

And they sniped at us a whole heap. I guess we must have run over the top of some of them, too, because a little later on we were getting fire from the rear. We were to go over the top at 6:10 A.M. and push on across the valley and work our way across the ridges to that-there old railroad. The Captain's orders was for two of our platoons to go over the top first and advance as a front wave with the other two platoons in support following about one hundred yards behind the front wave. I was in the left supporting platoon. Hit was the extreme left of our division and was supposed to keep contact with the Twenty-eighth Division, which was on our left, but we never did see anything of them all that morning. I guess they must have run into some awful tough fighting and been held up for a while.

Well, at the zero hour, which was 6:10 A.M., with fixed bayonets, we done went over the top, as ordered.

OCTOBER 8TH

Argonne Forest, France. And they was to give us a Barrage. So the time came and no Barrage and we had to go with out one. So we started over the top at 6:10 A.M. and the germans was Putting their machine guns to working all over the hill in front of us and on our left and right. So I was in suport and I could see my pals getting picked off until it almost looked like there was none left.

I don't know what happened to our artillery support, but we didn't get none nohow, except from a lieutenant from the Third Battalion. He done stood near six-foot-six tall. And he come up on top of the hill, dragging what looked like a toy cannon with him. It was a trench mortar. He did the best he could with it, but it didn't help much nohow. The Germans met our charge across the valley with a regular sleet storm of bullets. I'm a-telling you that-there valley was a death trap. It was a triangular-shaped valley with steep ridges covered with brush, and swarming with machine guns on all sides. I guess our two waves got about halfway across and then jes couldn't get no further nohow. The Germans done got us and they done got us right smart. They jes stopped us in our tracks. Their machine guns were up there on the heights overlooking us and well hidden, and we couldn't tell for certain where the terrible heavy fire was coming from. It 'most seemed as though it was coming from everywhere. I'm a-telling you they were shooting straight, and our boys jes done went down like the long grass before the mowing machine at home. Our attacks jes faded out.

We had to lie down flat on our faces and dig in. And there we were out there in the valley all mussed up and unable to get any further with no barrage to help us, and that-there German machine-gun fire and all sorts of big shells and gas cutting us to pieces. There was scarcely none of our front wave left. Lieutenant Stewart, who was leading the platoon in front of where I was lying, went down with a shot through the leg, but got up again and rallied the few men he had left and led them forward until he fell dead with a bullet through the head. I couldn't see Captain Danforth. He was on the other side of the hill on the right. I could hear shells and machine guns there, too, and I knowed he was getting it jes as bad as we was.

The German machine guns had done stopped our attack. We jes couldn't go on. We could scarcely even lift up our heads as we laid flat on the ground. But all the time we knowed we had to get through to that railroad somehow. We jes had to.

About this time we figured that the worstest machine-gun fire was coming from a ridge over on our left front. We knowed then that them-there machine guns would have to be put out of action before the advance could go on. We also knowed that there was so many of them and they were in such commanding positions that a whole battalion couldn't put them out of action nohow by a frontal attack. I doubt if a whole division could get to them that way. But they had to be takened somehow.

Our platoon sergeant, Harry M. Parsons, from Brooklyn, N. Y., done exposed himself again and again, trying to locate exactly where the machine guns over there on the left front were firing from. He hadn't no chance nohow of getting in touch with the

Captain. He had to use his own judgment. He done done it. He ordered the left half of our platoon to crawl back a little and try and work out way down around on the left and then push on through the heavy underbrush and try and jump the machine guns from the rear. He didn't know how many of them there were. He didn't know for sure where they were hid. But he figured it was the only chance. So three squads of us done dropped back and made our way around on the left. Sergeant Bernard Early was in charge and Corporal Murray Savage and Corporal William Cutting and myself each led our squads. The privates under us were:

Dymowski
Weiler
Waring
Wins
Swanson
Muzzi
Beardsley
Konotski
Sok
Johnson
Saccina
Donohue
Wills

So you see there were just seventeen of us.

OCTOBER 8TH

Argonne Forest, France. So there was 17 of us Boys went around on the left flank to see if we couldnt put those guns out of action.

According to orders, we got around on the left and in single file advanced forward through the brush towards where we could hear the machine-gun fire. We done went very quietly and quickly. We had to. We kept well to the left and deep in the brush. At first we didn't see any Germans and we were not under heavy fire. Jes a few stray bullets. Without any loss and in right-smart time we done skirted the left side of the valley and were over on the hill somewhere near where the German machine guns were placed. The heavy brush and the hilly nature of the country hid us from the enemy. We were now nearly three hundred yards to the left and in front of our own front line. When we figured that we were right on the ridge that the Germans were on, we done stopped for a minute and had a little conference. Some of the boys wanted to attack from the flank. But Early and me and some of the others thought it would be best to keep on going until we were well behind the German lines, and then suddenly swing in and try and jump them from the rear. We done decided to try and do this. We opened up in skirmishing order and sorter flitted from brush to brush, using all the cover we could and pushing on as fast as possible. We had now sorter encircled the German left end and were going away in deep behind them without them knowing anything about it.

OCTOBER 8TH

Argonne Forest, France. So when we went a round and fell in Be hind those guns we first seen to germans with a Red Cross Band on their arm.

So we ask them to stop and they did not so some one of the Boys shot at them and they run Back to our right. So we all run after them . . .

They jumped out of the brush in front of us and run like two scared rabbits. We called to them to surrender, and one of our boys done fired and missed. And they kept on a-going. And we kept on after them. We wanted to capture them before they gave the alarm. We now knowed by the sounds of the firing that we were somewhere behind the German trench and in the rear of the machine guns that were holding up our big advance. We still couldn't see the Germans and they couldn't see us. But we could hear them machine guns shooting something awful. Savage's squad was leading, then mine, and then Cutting's. Sergeant Early was out in front, leading the way.

OCTOBER 8TH

Argonne Forest, France. . . . And when we jumped across a little stream of water that was there they was a Bout 15 or 20 Germans jumped up and throwed up their hands and said Comrade So the one in charge of us Boys told us not to shoot they was going to give up any way.

It was headquarters. There were orderlies, stretcherbearers, runners, a major and two officers sitting or standing around a sort of small wooden shack. They seemed to be having a sort of conference. And they done jes had breakfast too. And there was a mess

of beefsteaks, jellies, jams, and loaf bread around.
They were unarmed. All except the major. And
some of them were in their shirt sleeves. By the way
they were going on we knowed they never even
dreamed that there were any Americans near them.

Of course, we were 'most as surprised as they were,
coming on them so sudden. But we kept our heads
and jumped them right smart, and covered them and
told them to put up their hands and to keep them up.
And they done done it. And we fired a few shots
just to sorter impress them. I guess they thought
the whole American Army was in their rear. And
we didn't stop to tell them any different. Sergeant
Early, who was in command of us, told us to hold
our fire, as we had them, but to keep them covered
and to hurry up and search and line them up. Just
as he was turning around from giving this order and
we were moving forward to obey, some machine guns
up on the hill in front of us and between us and the
American lines, suddenly turned around and opened
fire on us. Early went down with five bullets through
the lower part of his body and one through his arm.
Corporal Savage was killed. He must have had over
a hundred bullets in his body. His clothes were 'most
all shot off. And Corporal Cutting was also all shot
up. Six of the other boys were killed or wounded.
That machine-gun burst came sorter sudden and unexpected. And it done got us hard. The moment it
begun the German prisoners fell flat on their faces.
So did the rest of us American boys who were still
standing. You see, while we were capturing head-

quarters the German machine gunners up there on the hill seed us and done turned their guns around and let us have it.

After the first few bursts a whole heap of other machine guns joined in. There must have been over twenty of them and they kept up a continuous fire. Never letting up. Thousands of bullets kicked up the dust all around us. The undergrowth was cut down like as though they used a scythe. The air was just plumb full of death. Some of our boys done huddled up against the prisoners and so were able to get some protection and at the same time guard the prisoners. Some others crawled under cover, or jumped up and got behind trees. I was caught out in the open, a little bit to the left and in front of the group of prisoners and about twenty-five yards away from the machine guns which were in gun pits and trenches upon the hillside above me. I was now in charge.

OCTOBER 8TH

Argonne Forest, France. So by this time some of the Germans from on the hill was shooting at us. Well I was giving them the Best I had and by this time the Germans had got their machine guns turned around and fired on us so they killed 6 and wounded 3. So that just left 8 and then we got into it right By this time So we had a hard Battle for a little while . . .

But I hadn't time to give no orders nohow. There was such a noise and racket all around that I would not have been heard even if I had done given them. I had no time nohow to do nothing but watch them—there German machine gunners and give them the best I had. Every time I seed a German I jes teched him off. At first I was shooting from a prone position; that is lying down; jes like we often shoot at the targets in the shooting matches in the mountains of Tennessee; and it was jes about the same distance. But the targets here were bigger. I jes couldn't miss a German's head or body at that distance. And I didn't. Besides, it weren't no time to miss nohow. I knowed that in order to shoot me the Germans would have to get their heads up to see where I was lying. And I knowed that my only chance was to keep their heads down. And I done done it. I covered their positions and let fly every time I seed anything to shoot at. Every time a head come up I done knocked it down.

Then they would sorter stop for a moment and then another head would come up and I would knock it down, too. I was giving them the best I had. I was right out in the open and the machine guns were spitting fire and cutting up all around me something awful. But they didn't seem to be able to hit me. All the time the Germans were shouting orders. You never heard such a racket in all of your life. I still hadn't time or a chance to look around for the other boys. I didn't know where they were now. I didn't know what they were doing. I didn't even know if they were still living. Later on they done said that in the thick of the fight they didn't fire a shot.

Of course, all of this only took a few minutes. As soon as I was able I stood up and begun to shoot off-hand, which is my favourite position. I was still sharpshooting with that-there old army rifle. I used up several clips. The barrel was getting hot and my rifle ammunition was running low, or was where it was hard for me to get at it quickly. But I had to keep on shooting jes the same.

In the middle of the fight a German officer and five men done jumped out of a trench and charged me with fixed bayonets. They had about twenty-five yards to come and they were coming right smart. I only had about half a clip left in my rifle; but I had my pistol ready. I done flipped it out fast and teched them off, too.

I teched off the sixth man first; then the fifth; then the fourth; then the third; and so on. That's the way we shoot wild turkeys at home. You see we don't want the front ones to know that we're getting the back ones, and then they keep on coming until we get them all. Of course, I hadn't time to think of that. I guess I jes naturally did it. I knowed, too, that if the front ones wavered, or if I stopped them the rear ones would drop down and pump a volley into me and get me.

Then I returned to the rifle, and kept right on after those machine guns. I knowed now that if I done kept my head and didn't run out of ammunition I had them. So I done hollered to them to come down and give up. I didn't want to kill any more'n I had to. I would tech a couple of them off and holler again.

But I guess they couldn't understand my language, or else they couldn't hear me in the awful racket that was going on all around. Over twenty Germans were killed by this time.

OCTOBER 8TH

Argonne Forest, France. . . . and I got hold of a german magor and he told me if I wouldn't kill any more of them he would make them quit firing. So I told him alright if he would do it now. so he blew a little whistle and they quit shooting and come down and give up.

I think he had done been firing at me while I was fighting the machine guns—I examined his pistol later and sure enough hit was empty. Jes the same, he hadn't pestered me nohow. After he seed me stop the six Germans who charged with fixed bayonets he got up off the ground and walked over to me and yelled "English?"

I said, "No, not English."

He said, "What?"

I said, "American."

He said, "Good Lord!" Then he said, "If you won't shoot any more I will make them give up."

I told him he had better. I covered him with my automatic and told him if he didn't make them stop firing I would take his head next. And he knowed I meaned it. So he blowed a little whistle and they come down out of the trench and throwed down their guns and equipment and held up their hands and begun to gather around. I guess, though, one of them thought he could get me. He had his hands up all right. But he done had a little hand grenade concealed, and as he come up to me he throwed it right at my head. But it missed me and wounded one of the prisoners. I hed to tech him off. The rest surrendered without any more trouble. There must have been about fifty of them.

OCTOBER 8TH

Argonne Forest, France. So we had about 80 or 90 Germans there disarmed and had another line of Germans to go through to get out. So I called for my men and one of them answered from behind a big oak tree and the others were on my right in the brush so I said lets get these germans out of here. So one of my men said it is impossible so I said no lets get them out. So when my men said that this german magor said how many have you got and I said I have got a plenty and pointed my pistol at him all the time—in this battle I was using a rifle or a 45 Colts automatic pistol. So I lined the germans up in a line of twos and got between the ones in front and I had the german magor before me. So I marched them straight into those other machine guns and I got them.

The German major could speak English as well as I could. Before the war he used to work in Chicago. When the prisoners in the first trench surrendered I yelled out to my men to let's get them out. And one of my men said it was impossible to get so many prisoners back to the American lines. And I told him to shut up and to let's get them out. Then the German major became suspicious and wanted to know how many men I had. And I told him I had a-plenty. And I told him to keep his hands up and to line up his men in a column of two and to do it in double time. And he did it. And I lined up my men that were left on either side of the column and I told one to guard the rear.

Sergeant Early and Corporal Cutting then come up towards me. Corporal Cutting said: "I am hit and hit bad." He was wounded in the arm. He done had all the buttons shot off his uniform and there was a great big "X" shot in his helmet. Sergeant Early said: "York, I am shot and shot bad. What shall I do?" I knowed by the look of him that he was very badly wounded. He was dazed and in most awful pain. I done told them they could come out in the rear of our column with the other boys.

I ordered the prisoners to pick up and carry our wounded. I wasn't a-goin' to leave any good American boys lying out there to die. So I made the Germans carry them. And they did. And I takened the major and placed him at the head of the column and I got behind him and used him as a screen. I poked the Colt in his back and told him to hike. And he hiked. I guess I had him bluffed. It was pretty hard to tell in the brush and with all the noise and confusion around which way to go. The major done

The Boys Shot at them
and they run Back to
our right so we all
run after them and
When we jumped a cross
a little Stream of water
that was then they was
a Bout 15 or 20 Germans
jumped up and throwed
up their honds and said
comrade so the one in
charge of us Boys told us
not to Shot they was
going to give up—any
Way so By this time
some of the germons
from on the hill was
Shooting at me well
I was giving them the

(15)

Best I had and By this
time the germans had
got their machine guns
turned around and fired
on us so they killed
6 and wounded 3
so that just left
8 and then we got
in to it right By this
time so we had a hard
Battle for a little while
and I got hold of a german
mager and he told me
if I wouldent kill eny
more of them that he
would make them
quit firing so I told
him alright if he would
Doit now so he Blew

(19)

in the training camps, on the crowded transports and in the fox
date. In these two pages which are word for word reproductions
guns in the Argonne.

suggested we go down the gully. Then I knowed that was the wrong way. And I told him we were not going down any gully. We were going straight through the German front-line trenches back to the American lines. It was their second line that I had captured. We sure did get a long way behind the German trenches. And so I done marched them straight at that old German front-line trench. And some more machine guns swung around to fire. I told the major to blow his whistle or I would take his head and theirs too. So he blowed his whistle and they all done surrendered. All except one. I made the major order him to surrender twice. But he wouldn't. And I had to tech him off. I hated to do it. I've been doing a tol'able lot of thinking about it since. He was probably a brave soldier boy. But I couldn't afford to take any chance, and so I had to let him have it. There was considerably over a hundred prisoners now. It was a problem to get them back safely to our own lines. There was so many of them there was danger of our own artillery mistaking us for a German counter-attack and opening up on us. I sure was relieved when we run into the relief squads that had been sent forward through the brush to help us.

OCTOBER 8TH

Argonne Forest, France. So when I got back to my magors P.C. I had 132 prisoners.

We marched those German prisoners on back into the American lines to the Battalion P. C. and there we come to the Intelligence Department and Lieutenant Woods come out and counted them and counted 132. We were ordered to take them out to Regimental Headquarters at Chatel Chehery; and from there all the way back to Division Headquarters and turn them over to the Military Police. We had such a mess of German prisoners that nobody seemed to want to take them over. So we had to take them back a right-far piece ourselves.

On the way back we were constantly under heavy shell fire and I had to double-time them to get them through safely. There was nothing to be gained by having any more of them wounded or killed. They done surrendered to me and it was up to me to look after them. And so I done done it. I had orders to report to Brigadier General Lindsay, our brigadier commander, and he said to me, "Well, York, I hear you have captured the whole damned German army." And I told him I only had 132.

CHAPTER XXV

OFFICIAL STORY OF FIGHT

I DIDN'T want to kill a whole heap of Germans nohow. I didn't hate them. But I done it jes the same. I had to. I was cornered. It was either them or me, and I'm a-telling you I didn't and don't want to die nohow if I can live. If they done surrendered as I wanted them to when I hollered to them first, and kept on hollering to them, I would have given them the protection that I give them later when I tuk them back. But they wouldn't surrender, and there was no way out for me but to tech them off.

Jes the same I have tried to forget. I have never talked about it much. I have never told the story even to my own mother. For years I done refused to write about it for the newspapers, and wasn't at all pleased when others wrote about it.

But now that the story is coming out I want it to come out right, and I want everything brought out. Everything. There were others in that fight besides me. Some of them, Sergeant Early for instance, and others too, played a right-smart part in things until they were shot down. I'm a-telling you they're entitled to a whole heap of credit. It isn't for me, of course, to decide how much credit they should get.

236

But jes the same, I'm a-telling you a heap of those boys were heroes and America ought to be proud of them.

So, I'm a-going to publish the documents and I'm a-going to do it right here. They speak for themselves.

I might add that if there are any differences in them it is kinder well to remember that no two people ever see the same thing alike. It is also true that people who are not trained to write down what they have seed and been through—and most of them-there boys were not trained that way—ain't always in agreement when they write about the same thing. Jes the same, the documents give a right-smart account of the goings-on in the forest that awful morning.

Most all of the documents are copied from the originals in the War Department in Washington, or in the possession of Major George Edward Buxton, Jr., the official historian of the Eighty-second Division.

Here is the account of Captain Danforth, our company commander, of what he knowed of the fight:

At 6 A.M. on the morning of October 8, 1918, the 2d Battalion, 328th Infantry, attacked from Hill 223, in the direction ten degrees north of west, with its objective, the Decauville Railroad, about three kilometres away. The battalion had moved into the Argonne sector with other units of the 82d Division on the night of October 6th and 7th. All day of October 7th we lay along the main Army road, running from Varennes to Fléville, and watched the attack of the 1st Battalion, which in the early afternoon gained the height of Hill 223.

About 3 A.M., October 8th, the regimental commander sent for the company commanders of the 2d Battalion and issued instructions for the attack of the battalion to be made from Hill 223 at 6 A.M. I was in command of Company G of this battalion and immediately upon receiving these instructions began moving my company across the Aire River to the designated jump-off line on Hill 223.

I reached this hill at 5:50 A.M. and deployed my company for assault in two waves, two platoons in the front wave and two platoons in the supporting wave. The left support platoon was commanded by Sergeant Harry M. Parsons, one of his corporals being Alvin C. York.

At zero hour we began the advance, moving down the slope of Hill 223 and across the five-hundred-yard open valley toward a steep wooded hill to our immediate front. On our right was E Company, 328th Infantry; on our left Unit 5 of the 28th Division, though throughout the entire day we had no contact whatsoever with these troops on our left.

Upon reaching about the centre of this valley we were stopped by a withering fire of machine guns from the front, from the unscalable heights of the Champrocher Ridge on our right and from a heavily wooded hill on the left. From this point the advance was very slow, the men moving by rushes from shell hole to shell hole a few feet at a time. At some time during the morning the fire from the left flank slackened and we were enabled to gain the hill to our immediate front, capturing a great many machine guns and driving the enemy to the west. During the progress of the fighting across this valley, I was with the assault waves and gave no orders for the employment of the support platoons, which had been ordered to follow at three hundred yards.

About noon I left the assault wave and with one runner returned to bring up my support platoons, running into a group of forty-four Germans in the edge of the woods just outside our left flank, which group surrendered to my runner and me without firing a shot at us. I sent these prisoners to the rear, located my support platoons, returned with them to the front lines, and at 4 P.M. continued the advance to the corps objective with the other companies of the 2d Battalion. This objective—the Decauville Railroad—we took about 5 P.M. With the handful of men that were left we organized a position and held it throughout the night of October 8th and 9th.

On the morning of October 9th at about ten o'clock Corporal York with seven men reported to me on the railroad. Corporal York, when questioned about his whereabouts and activities during the previous day's fighting, said that he had been sent with a detachment to silence some machine gun nests on the left of the valley, that this detachment had become heavily engaged, losing half its strength, and that he had captured about one hundred and fifty prisoners. He stated that all non-commissioned officers of the detachment had been killed or wounded, that he had taken command and had shot a number of Germans during the engagement and that he had carried his prisoners from headquarters to headquarters, finally delivering them to the military police many miles to the rear. His statement to me on the morning of October 9th was the first time that I knew anything of his fight on our left flank and offered the best explanation of why the fire from that point had slackened on the morning of the 8th.

After coming out of the lines I fully investigated this detachment's fight and recommended Corporal York for the Distinguished Service Cross and later, after a more careful study, for the Congressional Medal of Honour.

E. C. B. DANFORTH, JR.

While Captain Danforth was fighting hard to lead the front wave forward, our own platoon commander, Sergeant Harry M. Parsons, was left in charge of us boys on the extreme left:

State of New York,
County of Kings.

Harry Parsons of the City of New York and County of Kings, State of New York, being duly sworn, deposes and says:

I was the platoon sergeant of the 1st Platoon, G Company, 2d Battalion, 328th Infantry, 82d Division; we had no commissioned officer, and I was in charge of the platoon. The platoon was made up of Greeks, Slavs, Swedes, Jews, Irish, Germans, and Italians, all American citizens, of course. There were also a number of farmers and a few mountaineers, one of whom was Alvin C. York. On the morning of October 8, 1918, we marched through the town of Chatel Chehery, and up on to Hill 223, where we waited for the zero hour. Without artillery support we went over the top at about daylight. Our platoon was upon the extreme left flank of the division, and was in the second wave, about one hundred yards in the rear of the first. The Germans quickly opened on us with machine guns, securely entrenched in the ridges and brush on our front and left flank. Our first line was mowed down; Lieutenant Stewart was killed and the survivors were forced to dig in. The machine-gun fire was something terrible. If the advance was to be continued, somehow or other the machine guns would have to be put out; and I knew the advance had to be continued at all costs. Our company commander, Captain Danforth, was over on the right, on the other side of the hill, fighting against desperate odds. I had no opportunity of getting in touch with him and he had no chance whatever of getting over to us. But I figured at all cost the machine guns had to be silenced. It was an awful responsibility for a non-commissioned officer to order his men to go to what looked to be certain death. But I figured it had to be done. I figured they had a slight chance of getting the machine guns. So I made the decision—and I now know that it was the wisest decision I ever made. I ordered the left half of my platoon, what remained of four squads, to deploy through the heavy brush on the left and work their way over the ridges to where the German machine guns were firing—and then attack the machine guns and put them out of commission. Sergeant Early was in charge of the four sections, and Corporal York, Corporal Cutting, and Corporal Savage were in charge of the squads. The thirteen private soldiers were privates Dymowski, Wiley, Waring, Wins, Swanson, Muzzi, Beardsley, Konotski, Sok, Johnson, Sacina, Donahue, and Wills. Lead by Sergeant Early, as ordered, the men immediately advanced through the brush on our left flank and disappeared. A few minutes later we heard heavy firing from the direction which they had taken; and shortly after the German machine-gun fire ceased. It was after this that Corporal York and seven privates returned with 132 German prisoners. Corporal York marched in front of the prisoners and was in absolute command. Unquestionably, the silencing of these machine guns played a tremendous part in our success in finally reaching our objective.

HARRY MASON PARSONS.

Subscribed and sworn to before
me this the 1st day of May 1928.
Bessie M. Swan, Notary Public
My commission expires on the
29th day of March, 1929.

Here is Sergeant Bernard Early's own account of how he led us behind the German lines:

Bernard Early of the City and County of New Haven, State of Connecticut, being duly sworn, deposes and says:

As senior non-commissioned officer in charge of the left half of 1st Platoon, G Company, 2d Battalion, 328th Infantry, 82d Division, on the morning of October 8, 1918, I led what remained of our squads, totalling seventeen men, from the valley under Hill 223 in the Argonne Forest around our left flank in an attempt to silence German machine guns which were holding up my battalion's advance to the Decauville Railroad which was our objective.

My command was on the extreme left of our division. I led my men through the thick undergrowth about half a mile toward where we figured the German machine guns were. Then I decided to swing in behind and attack them from the rear. On account of the nature of the country the Germans were unable to see us, just as we were unable to see them. So far we had no casualties. When we were well behind the German lines, we surprised a German stretcher bearer who immediately ran and we trailed him through the undergrowth deeper in behind the German lines.

We jumped a little stream and suddenly unexpectedly discovered the headquarters of a German machine-gun regiment. There must have been at least one hundred Germans, including three officers and several non-commissioned officers. There were also runners, orderlies, and others. They were having breakfast and we completely surprised them. We fired several shots to intimidate them and rushed them with fixed bayonets. I was out in front leading them and, seeing the Germans throwing up their hands, I ordered my men to cease fire and to cover and close in on them. I then ordered my men to line them up preparatory to marching them back to our P. C.

In the act of turning around issuing this order, a burst of machine gun bullets struck me. I fell with one bullet through my arm and five through the lower part of my body. I called on Corporal Cutting to take command and get the prisoners out and if possible later on come back and get me.

A little later Corporal Cutting was wounded and Corporal York took command.

I was carried back with the German prisoners to our first-aid station. There I was operated on and some of the bullets were taken out and I was sent to the hospital.

This statement was read to Bernard Early after being taken and he stated the same was correct.

BERNARD EARLY.

State of Connecticut ⎱
County of New Haven⎰ *ss.*

New Haven, April 11, 1928

I certify that the above is the statement made by Bernard Early of said City and County of New Haven, State of Connecticut, to which he made oath, before me.

LEWIS L. FIELD,
Commissioner of the Superior
Court for New Haven County.

Here is the official affidavit of Private Percy Beardsley:

2d Bn. 328th Inf.

82d Div. American E. F.

Frettes, France, Feb. 21, 1919.

Affidavit of Private Percy (1,910,246) Beardsley.

Personally appeared before me the undersigned, Private Percy (1,910,246) Beardsley, first being duly sworn according to law, says that he was present with Sergeant Alvin C. (1,910,426) York, northwest of Chatel Chehery on the morning of October 8, 1918, and testified to the distinguished personal courage, self-sacrifice, and presence of mind of Sergeant Alvin C. (1,910,426) York, as follows:

On the morning of the 8th of October, 1918, Sergeant York was a corporal in G Company, 328th Infantry, and I was a member of his squad. Our battalion, the 2d Battalion of the 328th Infantry, was attacking the ridge northwest of Chatel Chehery. The battalion had to manœuvre across the valley under heavy machine-gun fire which came from our right and left as well as in front of us. Very heavy fire came from a hill on our left flank. Sergeant Parsons was our platoon leader and he told acting Sergeant Early to take three squads and go over and clean out the machine guns that were shooting at our left flank. He circled the hill first in a southerly and then in a southwesterly direction until the noise of the machine guns sounded as if the guns were between us and our battalion. We went down the west slope of the hill into a ravine filled with heavy underbrush and there found two Germans and fired at one of them when he refused to halt. We were following the one who

ran and came onto a battalion of Germans grouped
together on the bottom and slope of the hill. Those
nearest us were surprised, and, thinking they were
surrounded, started to surrender, but a lot of machine
gunners halfway up the hill turned their machine guns
on us, killing six and wounding three of our detachment. All three of our other non-commissioned officers were shot and there was left only Corporal York
and seven privates. We were up against a whole battalion of Germans and it looked pretty hopeless for us.
We were scattered out in the brush, some were guarding a bunch of Germans who had begun to surrender,
and three or four of us fired two or three shots at the
line of Germans on the hillside. The German machine
gunners kept up a heavy fire, as did the German riflemen on the hillside with the machine gunners. The
Germans could not hit us without endangering the
prisoners whom we had taken at the very first. A
storm of bullets was passing just around and over us.
Corporal York was nearest the enemy and close up to
the bottom of the hill. He fired rapidly with rifle and
pistol until he had shot down a German officer and
many of his men. The officer whom Corporal York
shot was leading a charge of some riflemen with
bayonets fixed down the hillside toward us. Finally
the German battalion commander surrendered to Corporal York, who called the seven privates remaining
up to him and directed us to place ourselves along the
middle and rear of the column of prisoners, which we
assisted him in forming. When we moved out some
Germans on a near-by hill continued to fire at us.

Corporal York was at the head of the column where he placed two German officers in front of him. A considerable number of German prisoners were taken on our way back over the hill. Corporal York made them surrender by having the German battalion commander call to them to give themselves up.

PRIVATE PERCY BEARDSLEY.

Sworn to and subscribed before me at Frettes, France, this 26th day of February, 1919.
Edwin A. Buckhalter,
1st Lieut. 328 Inf. Bn. Adjt.

Private George W. Wills, first being duly sworn, according to law, also signed exactly the same document, word for word.

Here is the official affidavit of Private Joseph Konotski:

American E. F.
Frettes, France
February 6, 1918.

Affidavit of Private Joseph (1,910,336) Konotski (his X mark).

Personally appeared before me the undersigned Private Joseph (1,910,336) Konotski, who, first being duly sworn according to law, says that he was present with Sergeant Alvin C. (1,910,426) York, west of Chatel Chehery, on the morning of October 8, 1918, and testified to the distinguished and personal bravery and self-sacrifice of Sergeant Alvin C. (1,910,426) York, as follows:

On the morning of October 8, 1918, west of Chatel Chehery, Sergeant York performed in action deeds of most distinguished personal bravery and self-sacrifice. His platoon had been sent to the left flank of the assaulting wave, which was then exposed, to clear out some machine guns. Encountering a large machine-gun nest, all but seven men of his platoon were killed or wounded and all non-commissioned officers, except Sergeant York, who was at that time a corporal. His comrades had lost hope but Sergeant York kept his usual balance and self-control. He rallied the men and closed in on the enemy, using his rifle as long as he could conveniently reach his ammunition. He then resorted to his pistol with which he killed and wounded no less than fifteen of the enemy. After this intense fight Sergeant York succeeded in taking prisoner the battalion commander. Then, instructing his seven men, he took the remainder of the enemy prisoners in an exceedingly tactful manner. In lining the prisoners up preparatory to taking them to the Battalion P. C., Sergeant York displayed decided decision by placing the officers at the head of the column with himself next in line and the remaining men distributed in the line, making it impossible for the enemy to kill any of his men without killing a German.

On the way in to the Battalion P. C. a number of the enemy made their appearance and were taken prisoners. When Sergeant York arrived at the Battalion

P. C. he turned over 132 prisoners, of whom three were officers, one being a field officer.

JOSEPH KONOTSKI (his X mark),
(1,910,336)

Subscribed and sworn to before
me at Frettes, France, this 6th
day of February, 1919.
Edwin A. Burkhalter,
1st Lieut. 328th Inf., Bn. Adjt.

Privates Patrick Donohue, Theodore Sok and Michael Saccina, first being duly sworn, according to law, also subscribed to exactly the same document, word for word.

The above two affidavits, together with the statements of Captain Danforth, Sergeant Parsons, and Sergeant Early have never before been made public. They are published in this book for the first time.

Major George Edward Buxton, Jr., who was the first commander of our battalion, and he later on became divisional inspector, also took the affidavits of Privates Percy Beardsley, Michael A. Saccina, George W. Wills and Patrick Donohue:

Hq. 82d Div., American E. F., France,
26 January, 1919.

Private Percy (1,910,246) Beardsley, Company G, 328th Infantry, being duly sworn, made the following affidavit:

On the 8th day of October 1918, I was a member

of Corporal York's squad in G Company, 328th Infantry. When we were sent under acting-Sergeant Bernard Early to clean out the machine guns on our left, I was following behind Corporal York. I saw two Red Cross Germans and when they started to run, we fired at them. One of them stopped and gave himself up. We followed after the other German and about twenty paces from where we had first sighted these two Red Cross Germans, we ran into a bunch of Germans all together in an underbrush on the slope of the hill. When we appeared, Germans came running out of the brush and machine-gun trenches in every direction. There seemed to be about one hundred of these Germans. Some of them held up their hands and shouted "Kamerad" and gave themselves up. A few shots were fired at us and a few men on our side fired back. After this, all the Germans in sight stopped firing and came in around us, having thrown down their arms and equipment. Before we could line them up in column and move them out, German machine gunners, whom we had not seen before this, commenced firing down the hill at our men. This fire came mostly from opposite our own right flank. We had six men killed and three wounded in a very short time.

I was at first near Corporal York, but soon after thought it would be better to take cover behind a large tree about fifteen paces in rear of Corporal York. Privates Dymowski and Waring were on each side of me and both were killed by machine-gun fire. When the machine-gun fire on each side of my tree stopped,

I came back to where the Germans were and fired my pistol two or three times. I saw Corporal York fire his pistol repeatedly in front of me. After I came back from the tree I saw Germans who had been hit fall down. I saw German prisoners who were still in a bunch together waving their hands at the machine gunners on the hill as if motioning for them to go back. Finally the fire stopped and Corporal York told us to have the prisoners fall in columns of twos and for me to take my place in the rear.

This statement was read to Private Beardsley after being taken, and he stated the same was correct.

I certify that the above is statement made by Private Percy (1,910,246) Beardsley, Company G, 328th Infantry, to which he made oath before me.

G. EDWARD BUXTON, JR.
Major, Inf., U. S. A.,
Division Historical Officer.

Hq. 82d Div., American E. F., France.
26 January, 1919.

Private Michael A. (1,910,393) Saccina, Company G, 328th Infantry, being duly sworn, made the following affidavit:

On the 8th day of October, 1918, I was a member of Corporal Cutting's squad in G Company, 328th Infantry. When we were sent under acting-Sergeant Bernard Early to clean out the machine guns on our left, I was following behind Corporal Cutting. I saw two Red Cross Germans, and when they started to run, we fired at them. One of them stopped and gave himself up. We followed after the other German, and about twenty paces from where we had first sighted these two Red Cross Germans, we ran into a bunch of Germans all together in an underbrush on the slope of the hill. When we appeared, Germans came running out of the brush and machine-gun trenches in every direction. There seemed to be about one hundred of these Germans. Some of them held up their hands and shouted "Kamerad" and gave themselves up. A few shots were fired at us and a few men on our side fired back. After this, all the Germans in sight stopped firing and came in around us, having thrown down their arms and equipment. Before we could line them up in column and move them out, German machine gunners, whom we had not seen before this, commenced firing down the hill at our men. This fire came mostly from opposite our own right flank. We had six men killed and three wounded in a very short time. I fired three shots when we saw the Germans.

I was guarding the prisoners with my rifle and bayonet on the right flank of the group of prisoners. I was so close to these prisoners that the machine gunners could not shoot at me without hitting their own men. This, I think, saved me from being hit. During the firing, I remained on guard watching these prisoners and unable to turn around and fire myself for this reason. From where I stood, I could not see any of the other men in my detachment because they were hidden from me by the German prisoners. From this point I saw the German captain and had aimed my rifle at him when he blew his whistle for the German firing to stop. The whistle sounded like the whistle on a peanut stand. I then saw Corporal York, who called out to us, and when we all joined him, I saw seven Americans besides myself. These men were Corporal York, Private Beardsley, Private Donohue, Private Wills, Private Sok, Private Johnson and Private Konotski. The column of prisoners was then started and we moved out. I was guarding near the rear of the column. A number of Germans who did not give themselves up fired at us as we left. We never captured these men.

This statement was read to Private Saccina after being taken, and he stated that same was correct.

I certify that the above is statement made by Private Michael A. (1,910,292) Saccina, Company G, 328th Infantry, to which he made oath before me.

G. EDWARD BUXTON, JR.
Major, Inf., U. S. A.,
Division Historical Officer.

Hq. 82d Div., American E. F., France.

26 January, 1919.

Private George W. (1,910,418) Wills, Company G, 328th Infantry, being duly sworn, made the following affidavit:

On the 8th day of October, 1918, I was a member of Corporal Cutting's squad in G Company, 328th Infantry. When we were sent under acting-Sergeant Bernard Early to clean out the machine guns on our left, I was following behind Corporal Cutting. I saw two

Red Cross Germans and when they started to run, we fired at them. One of them stopped and gave himself up. We followed after the other German and about twenty paces from where we had first sighted these two Red Cross Germans, we ran into a bunch of Germans all together in an underbrush on the slope of the hill. When we appeared, Germans came running out of the brush and machine-gun trenches in every direction. There seemed to be about one hundred of these Germans. Some of them held up their hands and shouted "Kamerad" and gave themselves up. A few shots were fired at us and a few men on our side fired back. After this, all the Germans in sight stopped firing and came in around us, having thrown down their arms and equipment. Before we could line them up in column and move them out, German machine gunners, whom we had not seen before this, commenced firing down the hill at our men. This fire came mostly from opposite our own flank. We had six men killed and three wounded in a very short time.

When the heavy firing from machine guns commenced, I was guarding some of the German prisoners. During this time I only saw Privates Donohue, Saccina, Beardsley and Muzzi. Private Swanson was right near me when he was shot. I closed up very close to the Germans with my bayonet on my rifle and prevented some of them who tried to leave the bunch and get into the bushes from leaving. I knew that my only chance was to keep them together and also to keep them between me and the Germans who were shooting. I heard Corporal York several times shouting to the machine gunners on the hill to come down and surrender, but from where I stood, I could not see Corporal York. I saw him, however, when the firing stopped and he told us to get along the sides of the column. I formed those near me in columns of twos.

This statement was read to Private Wills, after being taken, and he stated that same was correct.

I certify that the above is statement made by Private George W. (1,910,418) Wills, Company G, 328th Infantry, to which he made oath before me.

G. EDWARD BUXTON, JR.
Major, Inf., U. S. A.,
Division Historical Officer.

Hq. 82d Div., American E. F., France.
26 January, 1919.

Private Patrick (1,910,305) Donohue, Company G, 328th Infantry, being duly sworn, made the following affidavit:

On the 8th day of October, 1918, I was a member of Corporal Cutting's squad in G Company, 328th Infantry. When we were sent under acting-Sergeant Bernard Early to clean out the machine guns on our left, I was following behind Corporal Cutting. I saw two Red Cross Germans, and when they started to run, we fired at them. One of them stopped and gave himself up. We followed after the other German, and about twenty paces from where we had first sighted these two Red Cross Germans, we ran into a bunch of Germans all together in an underbrush on the slope of the hill. When we appeared Germans came running out of the brush and machine-gun trenches in every direction. There seemed to be about one hundred of these Germans. Some of them held up their hands and shouted "Kamerad" and gave themselves up. A few shots were fired at us and a few men on our side fired back. After this, all the Germans in sight stopped firing and came in around us, having thrown down their arms and equipment. Before we could line them up in column and move them out, German machine gunners, whom we had not seen before this, commenced firing down the hill at our men. This fire came mostly from opposite our own right flank. We had six men killed and three wounded in a very short time.

During all this shooting, I was guarding the mass of Germans taken prisoners and devoted my attention to watching them. When we first came in on the Germans, I fired a shot at them before they surrendered. Afterward I was busy guarding the prisoners and did not shoot. From where I stood, I could only see Privates Wills, Saccina, and Sok. They were also guarding prisoners, as I was doing. Later, when we were moving the prisoners out of the woods, I saw Private Moreau, but I do not know where he was or what he was doing during the fight. The men I have mentioned above were all members of Corporal Cutting's squad, and our squad had each fired at least one shot when we first saw the Germans and before Corporal Cutting told us to stop shooting.

I was wounded slightly on the shoulder at the first-aid station, to which I helped Corporal Early, and continued on duty until that night, when the doctor evacuated me.

This statement was read to Private Donohue after being taken, and he stated that same was correct.

I certify that the above is statement made by Private Patrick (1,910,305) Donohue, Company G, 328th Infantry, to which he made oath before me.

G. EDWARD BUXTON, JR.

Major, Inf., U. S. A.,

Division Historical Officer.

Captain Joseph Woods met me at Battalion Headquarters, when I reported with the prisoners the morning of the fight. Here is his account of it:

2d Bn. 328th Inf.,

82d Div., American E. F.,

Frettes, France, Feb. 21, 1919.

Affidavit of 1st Lieut. Jos. A. Woods, Inf., U. S. A.

Personally appeared before me 1st Lieut. Jos. A. Woods, Inf., U. S. A., who made the following affidavit:

On the morning of Oct. 8, 1918, I was battalion adjutant, 2d Battalion, 328th Infantry. The Battalion P. C. had been moved forward from Hill 223 to a hillside across the valley and just west of Hill 223, the jumping-off place. We heard some heavy and almost continuous firing on the other side of our hill and in the direction taken by Sergeant Early, Corporal York and their detachment. Some time later

I personally saw Corporal York and seven privates returning down the hillside on which our P. C. was located. They had 132 prisoners with them, including three German officers, one a battalion commander. I personally counted the prisoners when Corporal York reported the detachment and prisoners. Corporal York was in entire charge of this party and was marching at the head of the column with the German officers. The seven men with Corporal York were scattered along the flanks and rear of the column. Sergeant Early and Corporal Cutting, both severely wounded, were being assisted at the rear of the column.

Jos. A. Woods,
1st Lieut. Inf., U. S. A.

Sworn to and subscribed before
me at Pratthay, France, 23 Feb., 1919.
R. L. Boyd, Maj. A.G.D.,
Adjutant 82d. Div.

Here is another official check of his:

27 January, 1919.

I certify that I personally counted the prisoners reported to the P. C. of the 2d Battalion, 328th Infantry, by Corporal Alvin C. York, Company G, 328th Infantry, on Oct. 8, 1918, and found them to be 132 in number.

Jos. A. Woods,
1st Lieut., Inf., U. S. A.
Asst. Div. Inspector.

Here is Captain Bertrand Cox's account of what the battlefield looked like just after the fight:

> 2d Bn., 328th Inf.,
> 82d Div., American E. F.,
> Frettes, France, February 21, 1919.

Affidavit of Capt. Bertrand Cox, 328th Inf.

Personally appeared before me the undersigned, Capt., Bertrand Cox, who made the following affidavit:

On the morning of October 8th, I commanded a support platoon of F Company, 2d Battalion of the 328th Infantry. Shortly after Corporal York and his detachment of seven men succeeded in capturing the greater part of a German battalion, I advanced with my platoon and passed the scene of the fight, which took place before this capture was accomplished. The ground was covered with German equipment and I should estimate that there were between 20 and 25 dead Germans on the scene of the fight.

> BERTRAND COX,
> Captain 328th. Inf.

Sworn to and subscribed before me at Frettes, France, this 26th day of February, 1919.
Edwin A. Burkhalter,
1st Lieut. 328th Inf. Bn. Adj.

CHAPTER XXVI

OFFICIAL STORY OF FIGHT
(*Continued*)

THE complete official record of the story has to include one more document. My own account as it was takened down at Divisional Headquarters a short time after the fight. I don't much care to publish the first part of it. But it is a part of the document and is an exact copy of the original, which is in the War Department in Washington, and I ain't got no right to leave any of it out. I have to publish it all or not at all. So I have no choice but to put it all in. I might say that this is the first time that this document has ever been published.

The records of the 82d Division reveal no more extraordinary act of individual gallantry and achievement than is accredited, after careful investigation, to Sergeant Alvin C. (No. 1,910,426) York, Co. G, 328th Infantry. York is a farmer, 31 years old, whose home is located at Pall Mall, Tenn., in the mountainous and northeastern corner of the state.

On the 8th of October, 1918, York was a corporal in G Company, 328th Infantry. This company was the left assault company of the 2d Battalion, which jumped off from the crest of Hill 223 just north of Chatel Chehery and attacked due west, with its objective, the Decauville Railroad, two kilometres due west. The success of this assault had a far-reaching effect in relieving the enemy pressure against American forces in the heart of the Argonne Forest. The local success achieved by this battalion was, in itself, of outstanding proportions. About 300 prisoners were taken and nearly 200 dead Germans left on the ground and material captured which included four 77's, a trench mortar battery, a complete signal outfit and 123 machine guns. The attack was driven through in spite of resistance of a very savage character and most destructive enemy machine gun and artillery fire. The battalion suffered enfilade fire from both flanks.

The part which Corporal York individually played in this attack is difficult to fully estimate. Practically unassisted, he captured 132 Germans (three of whom were officers), took about 35 machine guns and killed no less than 25 of the enemy, later found by others on the scene of York's extraordinary exploit. York is well known in his section of Tennessee for his remarkable skill with both rifle and pistol.

The following story has been carefully checked in every possible detail from headquarters of this division and is entirely substantiated.

Although Sergeant York's statement tends to underestimate the desperate odds which he overcame, it has been decided to forward to higher authority the account given in his own words:

"Sergeant Harry M. Parsons was in command of a platoon of which my squad was a part. This platoon was the left support platoon of G Company, my squad forming the extreme left flank of the platoon. The valley was covered by machine-gun fire from the right [pointing at the map], from the front, and from the left front. Machine guns from the left front were causing a great deal of damage to our troops advancing across the valley. Sergeant Parsons was ordered to advance with his platoon and cover our left flank. As the fire was very hot in the valley, we decided to skirt the foot of the hill on our left and thereby gain some protection. We had advanced a little ways up to about here [pointing at the map] when we were held up, by machine guns from our left front here [pointing at the map]. Sergeant Parsons told Sergeant Bernard Early to take two squads and put these machine guns out of business, my squad, being the left squad, was one of those chosen.

"We advanced in single file. The undergrowth and bushes here were so thick that we could see only a few yards ahead of us, but as we advanced, they became a little thinner. In order to avoid frontal fire from the machine guns, we turned our course slightly to the left, thereby working around on the right flank of the machine guns and somewhat to their rear, which caused us to miss these forward guns [pointing at the map]. As we gained a point about here [pointing at the map and designating a point somewhat in the rear of the machine guns], we turned sharply to the right oblique and followed a little path which took us directly in rear of the machine guns. As we advanced we saw two Boche with Red Cross bands on their arms. We called to them to halt, but they did not stop and we opened fire on them. Sergeant Early was leading and I was third.

"As I said before, we were proceeding in single file. We immediately dashed down a path, along which the Boche were running, and crossed this stream [pointing at map]. The Boche then turned to the right and ran in the direction from which we had come. When we reached the point where they turned, we stopped for half a second to form a skirmish line. I jumped about four paces away from a sergeant and we told the other men to scatter out because we thought there was going to be a battle and we did not want to be too close together. As soon as we formed our skirmish line we burst through the bushes after the Boche.

"This little stream of which I spoke runs through a gulch into the valley. On either side of the stream there was a little stretch of flat level ground, about twenty feet wide, which was covered with extremely thick bush. On the east bank of the stream was a hill having an exceedingly steep slope. This hill was somewhat semi-circular in shape and afforded excellent protection to anyone behind it. Along the top of the hill were the machine guns firing across the valley at our troops.

"We burst through the undergrowth and were upon the Germans before we knew it, because the undergrowth was so thick that we could see only a few yards ahead of us. There was a little shack thrown together that seemed to be used as a sort of a P. C. by the Germans. In front of this, in a sort of a semi-circular mass, sat about seventy-five Boche, and by the side of a chow can, which was near the P. C., sat the commanding officer and two other officers. The Boche seemed to be having some kind of conference.

"When we burst in on the circle, some of the Boche jumped up and threw up their hands, shouting 'Kamerad.' Then the others jumped up, and we began shooting. About two or three Germans were hit. None of our men fell.

"Sergeant Early said: 'Don't shoot any more. They are going to give up anyhow,' and for a moment our fire ceased, except that one German continued to fire at me, and I shot him. In the meantime, the Boche upon the hill with the machine guns swung the left guns to the left oblique and opened fire on us. I was at this time just a few paces from the mass of Boche who were crowded around the P. C. At first burst of fire from the machine guns, all the Boche in this group hit the ground, lying flat on their stomachs. I, and a few other of our men, hit the ground at the same time. Those who did not take cover were either killed or wounded by the Boche machine-gun fire, the range being so close that the clothes were literally torn from their bodies. Sergeant Early and Corporal Cutting were wounded, and Corporal Savage was killed. In this first fire we had six killed and three wounded. By this time, those of my men who were left had gotten behind trees, and two men sniped at the Boche. They fired about half a clip each. But there wasn't any tree for me, so I just sat in the mud and used my rifle, shooting at the Boche machine gunners. I am a pretty good shot with the rifle, also with the pistol, having used them practically all my life, and having had a great deal of practice. I shot my rifle until I did not have any more clips convenient and then I used my pistol.

"The Boche machine-gun fire was sweeping over the mass of Germans who were lying flat, and passing a few inches over my head, but I was so close to the mass of Germans who were lying down that the Boche machine gunners could not hit me without hitting their own men. There were about fifty Boche with the machine guns and they were under the command of a lieutenant. By this time, the remaining Boche guns had been turned around and were firing at us, and the lieutenant with eight or ten Germans armed with rifles rushed toward us. One threw a little grenade, about the size of a dollar and with a string that you pull like this when you want to explode it, at me, but missed me by a few feet, wounding, however, one of his own men.

"I just let the Boche come down the hill and then poured it into them with my pistol, and I am, as I said before, a pretty good shot with the pistol. I shot the lieutenant, and when he was killed the machine-gun fire ceased. During the fight, I kept hearing a pistol firing from the midst of the Boche who were lying on the ground. This was evidently the commanding officer shooting, as he was the only one in the crowd armed with a pistol, and all of his clips were empty when I examined them later.

"When the machine guns ceased firing the commanding officer, who spoke English, got off the ground and walked over to me. He said: 'English?' I said:

'No, not English.' He said: 'What?' I said: 'American.' He said: 'Good Lord.' Then he said: 'If you won't shoot any more, I will make them give up,' and I said: 'Well, all right, I will treat you like a man,' and he turned around and said something to his men in German, and they all threw off their belts and arms and the machine gunners threw down their arms and came down the hill.

"I called to my men and one of them answered me from over here, another from over here, and another here (they were pretty well scattered), and when they all come to me, I found that there were six left besides myself.

"We searched the Boche and told them to line up in a column of twos. The Boche commanding officer wanted to line up facing north and go down through the valley along the road which runs by the foot of the hill, but I knew if they got me there it would be as good as they wanted on account of the machine guns on the opposite slope, so I said, 'No, I am going this way,' which was the way I had come, and which led through the group of machine guns placed here [pointing at the map], which seemed to be outpost guns. We had missed this machine-gun nest as we advanced, because we had gone further to the left.

"When we got the Boche lined up in a column of twos, I scattered my men along and at the rear of the column and told them to stay well to the rear and that I would lead the way. So I took the commanding officer and the two other officers and put one in front of me and one on each side of me, and we headed the column. I did that because I knew that if I were caught on the side of the column, the machine gunners would shoot me, but that if I kept in the column, they would have to shoot their officers before they could kill me. In this manner we advanced along a path and into the machine-gun nest which is situated here [pointing at the map].

"The machine gunners, as I said before, could not kill me without killing their officers, and I was ready for them. One aimed a rifle at me from behind a tree, and, as I pointed my pistol at him, the commanding officer said: 'If you won't shoot any more, I will tell them to surrender.' He did and we added them to our column.

"I then reported with the prisoners to the Battalion P. C. They were counted there and there were 132 of them. I was there ordered to deliver the prisoners to Brigade Headquarters, which I did, and returned to my company the next morning."

It is further interesting to note that Sergeant York was a member of the Church of Christ in Christian Union. During the training days at Camp Gordon, Atlanta, Ga., he informed his company commander of his church affiliations, and was seriously troubled by the fact that one of the fundamental tenets of this faith is a pronounced opposition to war. This continued to cause York the most genuine perplexity, although he carefully refrained from accepting the military status of conscientious objector, declaring that he proposed to obey all orders while a member of the

Army. His mental doubts were finally dissipated by his company commander in a long interview before embarking at Camp Upton, N. Y., at the end of which York stated that the purposes of American participation were of such a character that he felt himself able to take his part with a clear conscience.

Supplementary statement by Sergeant Alvin C. (1,910,426) York, Company G, 328th Infantry:

"After the German captain had made the Germans remaining on the hill surrender and the firing stopped, Corporals Early and Cutting came up toward me. Corporal Cutting said: 'I'm hit and hit bad,' and Corporal Early said: 'York, I am shot, and shot bad. What shall I do?' I told him: 'You can come out in the rear of our column with the other boys.' Private Donohue helped Corporal Early out to the edge of the woods, where they met a stretcher bearer from G Company with a stretcher, and Corporal Early was carried back to Chatel Cheherry, when the German prisoners carried him to the ambulance. Corporal Early was shot through the lower body. Corporal Cutting was shot three times in the left arm. Private Muzzi was shot in the shoulder. Corporal Cutting and Private Muzzi walked out themselves. No German wounded, as far as any of us know, came out with our prisoners. The wounded German lieutenant was brought out, I think, afterwards by German prisoners who went back for him. When we got back to the Battalion P. C., the prisoners were counted by Lieutenant Woods and Lieutenant Garner. Lieutenant Woods told us to take them to the Battalion P. C. and Colonel Wetherill told us to take them to Brigade Headquarters at Varennes. Another group of prisoners were added to those we had and I turned over at Varennes 208 prisoners to the Military Police, and a receipt was given to Corporal Clark, who had joined us after the fight was over. The prisoners which were captured and which were counted at the Battalion P. C. by Lieutenants Woods and Garner, I am told, amounted to 132. I counted them roughly by myself and thought there were about 146."

Here is the official list of the men participating in action of October 8th, 1919, capturing 132 prisoners.

KILLED

Corp. Murray	(1,910,237)	Savage—328th Inf.
Pvt. Maryan E.	(1,910,254)	Dymowski—Corp. Savage's Squad Inf.
Pvt. Ralph E.	(1,910,415)	Weiler—Corp. Savage's Squad Inf.
Pvt. Fred	(1,910,411)	Waring—Corp. Cutting's Squad Inf.
Pvt. William	(1,910,224)	Wins—Corp. Cutting's Squad Inf.
Pvt. Walter E.	(1,909,768)	Swanson—Corp. York's Squad Inf.

WOUNDED

Sgt. Bernard	(1,910,216)	Early—
Corp. William S.	(1,910,252)	Cutting—
Pvt. Marie	(1,896,622)	Muzzi—Corp. York's Squad Inf.

SURVIVORS

Corp. Alvin C.	(1,910,426)	York—
Pvt. Percy	(1,910,246)	Beardsley—Corp. York's Squad Inf.
Pvt. Joe	(1,910,336)	Konotski—Corp. York's Squad Inf.
Pvt. Feodor	(1,908,791)	Sok—Corp. Cutting's Squad Inf.
Pvt. Thos. C.	(3,624,156)	Johnson—Corp. York's Squad Inf.
Pvt. Michael A.	(1,910,393)	Saccina—Corp. Cutting's Squad Inf.
Pvt. Patrick	(1,910,305)	Donohue—Corp. Cutting's Squad Inf.
Pvt. George W.	(1,910,418)	Wills—Corp. Cutting's Squad Inf.

CHAPTER XXVII

ABOVE THE BATTLE

ABOUT ten o'clock on the morning of October 9th I reported to Captain Danforth at the railroad. On account of the long distance we had to go back from where we handed over the prisoners and the most awful rough nature of the country and the mix-up and confusion everywhere, it takened me 'most all night to get back to him again. The company done been all mussed up and there were only a few left, but they kept on a-going through everything, and they done busted that old railroad. The Captain asked me where I had been. I told him of the fight with the machine guns around on the left flank; of how the other non-commissioned officers had been killed or wounded; and how I had takened command and marched them prisoners away back behind the lines to Divisional Headquarters. He asked me why I hadn't handed them over at Battalion Headquarters and then pushed on and joined him. I told him that there was a whole heap of prisoners and nobody would take them from me and I had to take them all the way back. He asked me how many prisoners there were and when I told him one hundred and thirty-two, he looked at me with a funny-like expression in his face. He seemed kinder surprised.

I had been away from Captain Danforth and the

company for over twenty-four hours, and I knowed he needed me most awful bad now. He needed every man he could get, because there was only a few left. Jes the same I had been doing a heap of thinking about the boys we had left behind in the fight. There was jes a chance that some of them might be only wounded and still lying out there in pain and needing help something terrible. I felt I jes had to go and look for them. So I asked the Captain if I couldn't take some stretcher bearers and orderlies and go back and look around, and though he needed me most awful bad he said it was all right, I could get the detail and go back.

So I got me two stretcher bearers and led them back to the place where I done fought the German machine guns. When we got there the Salvage Corps had already done come and cleaned up the place; they packed up the equipment and takened it away. And they done buried the dead, our own boys, and the Germans. The ground there all around looked like the most torndowndest place I ever had seen. There was an old canteen lying within a few inches of where I stood. It had eighteen bullet holes in it. There was a shrapnel helmet a couple of feet away, and it was all sorter sieved, jes like the top of a pepper box. The ground in front and on both sides of where we done stood was all soft and torned up with bullets. The brush on either side was also torned up and there was a sort of tunnel cut in the brush behind me. Everything destroyed, torned up, killed—trees, grass, men. Oh, my, it was a terrible sight. But we didn't find no wounded nowhere. We not only searched with our eyes, we searched with

our voices. We yelled, thinking that maybe someone
was in the bushes. But no one yelled back. There
weren't no wounded that we could see; neither American nor German. There weren't no bodies around
neither. All was terribly quiet in the field. And I jes
couldn't help thinking of the boys that only the day before was alive and like me. Dymowski—dead. Weiler
—dead. Waring—dead. Wins—dead. Swanson—
dead. Corporal Murray Savage, my best pal, dead.
Oh, my, it seemed so unbelievable. I would never see
them again. I would never share the same blanket with
Corporal Savage. We'd never read the Bible together
again. We would never talk about our faith and pray
to our God. I was mussed up inside worser than I had
ever been. I'm a-telling you when you lose your best
buddie and you know you ain't never going to see him
again, you sorter know how terrible cruel war is.
There was nothing I could do now for Corporal
Murray Savage or any of the other boys that done lost
their lives. I could only pray for their souls. And I
done that. I prayed for the Greeks and Italians and
the Poles and the Jews and the others. I done prayed
for the Germans too. They were all brother men of
mine. Maybe their religion was different, but I reckon
we all believed in the same God and I wanted to pray
for all of them.

So we went back, and I remember the boys that got
wounded, and was a-hoping and praying they would get
well. Early got five bullets in the body and one in the
arm. And Cutting was bunged up right smart. His
helmet was broken. The buttons were shot off'n his

uniform, and he was hit in the arm. Well, I had come through it all without even a hair of my head being harmed. It seemed sorter hard to believe that I done come through alive. Two men on both sides of me and two others right behind me were killed, and I hadn't been touched. I tried to figure it out how it come that everybody around me who was exposed done got picked off or wounded and that I alone come out unharmed. I have been trying to figure it out ever since. And the more I figure the more I am convinced that it wasn't no mere luck or jes an accident. It must have been something more and bigger than that.

The officers and the experts who went over the battleground afterwards, some of them several times, and who takened the statements of all of us who came through the fight, have tried to give their own explanations of how I come through.

Some of them say that for fear of hittin' their own men who were prisoners the German machine gunners had to raise their fire and shoot high, and so the bullets done passed just a few inches over my head. I'm admittin' that that's a right-smart lot of reasonin', but jes the same they didn't fire too high when they opened on us. They hit a whole heap of other boys all around me. They cut up the ground at my feet when they riddled that old canteen and shrapnel helmet.

Others say that the German machine gunners were surprised and kinder rattled. They hadn't even dreamed that there were any Americans behind them or even near them. Then when we burst in on them they thought that we were the advance units of a big

American attacking force which done either got in behind them or surrounded them. And that made them panicky. And they sorter got mixed up and didn't know what to do. I'm admittin' that that's good reasonin' too. There can be no doubt at all but what we did surprise them. We takened headquarters with only a few shots fired. But jes the same the German machine gunners were quick and were used to being in tight quarters. These were veteran troops that we done run into. They had been in the war a long time and done fought through many battles. They knowed what it was all about. Then there was so many of them and they had such a whole heap of machine guns that it don't stand to reason that they all sorter lost their nerve and give up. I can't admit that nohow. I know different. They fought like a heap of wild cats. I mean the machine gunners did. They kept up a continuous fire for several minutes. They killed and wounded a whole heap of our boys. They were surprised and some of them might have been panicky. But not all of them.

Some of the officers have sorter suggested that I was the "right man in the right place." They done tried to make the point that I was a right-smart sharpshooter; that I knowed how to handle weapons; that I could shoot equally well with rifle or pistol; that I could shoot from either hand, or from any position; and that this jes happened to be my favourite distance. They also claimed that I always was cool and deliberate under fire. I ain't so foolish as to deny that I know a whole heap about guns. I do. I know, too, that I am a tol'able good shot. But I don't care how good a shot man is, hit ain't in the nature of things for one man with an army rifle and a pistol to whip thirty-five machine guns that can each fire over six hundred shots a minute; from a p'int-blank range of between twenty and thirty yards.

Some of them officers have been saying that I being a mountain boy and accustomed to woods and nature done all these things the right way jes by instinct, like an animal when it is cornered. There may be something in that. I hain't never got much larnin' from books, except the Bible. Maybe my instincts is more natural than of men who ain't been brunged up like I was in the woods and in the mountains. But that ain't enough to account for the way I come out alive, with all those German soldiers and machine guns raining death on me.

I am willing to admit that all of these explanations have a whole heap of truth in them. I am willing to admit that maybe I had all the breaks, and had them right. Jes the same, there was something else. There had to be something more than man power in that fight to save me. There can't no man in the world make me believe there weren't. And I'm a-telling you the hand of God must have been in that fight. It surely must have been divine power that brought me out. No other power under heaven could save a man in a place like that. Men were killed on both sides of me and all around me and I was the biggest and the most exposed of all. Jes think of them thirty machine guns raining fire on me p'int-blank from a range of only twenty-five yards and all of them-there rifles and pistols besides, and those bombs, and then those men that charged with fixed bayonets, and I never receiving a scratch, and bringing in one hundred and thirty-two prisoners. I have got only one explanation to offer, and only one: without the help of God I jes couldn't have done it. There can be no arguments about that. I am not going to believe different as long as I live. I'm a-telling you that God must have heard my prayers long before I done started for France. I'm a-telling you He done give me my assurance that so long as I believed in Him He would protect me. That's why when I bade my mother and Gracie and all my brothers and sisters and Rosier Pile good-bye before sailing for France I told them all not to worry, I would be safe, I would come back.

I done settled it all with my God long ago before I went overseas. I done prayed and prayed to Him; He done given me my assurance that so long as I believed in Him He would protect me, and He did.

OCTOBER 8TH

So you can see here in this case of mine where God helped me out. I had been living for God and working in the church work sometime before I come to the army. So I am a witness to the fact that God did help me out of that hard battle; for the bushes were shot off all around me and I never got a scratch. So you can see that God will be with you if you will only trust him and I say that He did save me——— Now He will save you if you will only trust Him.

132 prisners so you can see here in this case of mine Where god helped me out I had Ben living for god and Working in church Work some time Before I come to the army So I am a witness to the fact that god did help me out of that hard Battle for the Bushes wer shot off all a round me and I never got a scratch So You can see that god will Be with You if You will only trust him and

(99)

THE FAITH THAT MOVETH MOUNTAINS

In this extraordinary entry in his war diary, scribbled the night after the fight, Sergeant York says that God helped him in his fight with the German machine guns.

After the armistice Brigadier General Lindsay and some other generals and colonels takened me back to the Argonne Forest and went up the scene of the fight with me. They measured and examined the ground and asked me a whole heap of questions. Brigadier General Lindsay asked me to take him out like I did the captured German major. And I did. And then the General said to me: "York, how did you do it?" I told the General that it was not man-power but hit was divine power that saved me. I told him that before I went to war I prayed to God and He done gave me my assurance that so long as I believed in Him not one hair of my head would be harmed; and even in front of them-there machine guns He knowed I believed in Him. The General put his arms around my shoulders and said very quietly: "York, you are right."

I know, of course, that people will say that if He protected me, why didn't He protect the other American boys who were killed, and the Germans, too? He was their God as well as mine, and if He was a just and righteous God, why didn't He protect them? I can't answer that. I ain't a-going to try to. I don't understand the way in which He works "His marvels to perform." I ain't a-questioning them nohow. I jes accept them and bow my head and bless His holy name, and believe in Him more'n ever.

CHAPTER XXVIII

THE ARMISTICE

BUT the fightin' hadn't done stopped yet. There was some more big battles ahead, terrible battles. And I was only wishing and praying that a good God would bring all this man-killing desolation to an end.

OCTOBER 9TH

Argonne Forest. Well now as we went on fighting our way through the thick forest of the Argonne woods we could hear the cryes of our boys who were getting shot and oh my we had to sleep by the dead and with the dead. But when we were seeing so many of our boys being shot all we could say is just to say as we seen our fallen Comrades Good by pal; I don't know where you is camping now:

> Whether you've pitched your tent 'neath azure skies;
> Or whether o'er your head the bleak storm winds blow
> I only know that when your final call come for you
> It almost broke my heart to see you go.

But I trust pal that you was ready to meet that last call. Yes, and now you be carefull that the last final call don't find you not ready to meet your God in peace.

OCTOBER 10TH

Fléville, the Argonne Forest. We got to Fléville.

OCTOBER 12TH

Somerance, the Argonne Forest. We had got to
Somerance and during this time we had lost heavy
on our men and was still losing them as you know
that you cant fight in war without losing men and
the Germans was shelling us awfull with big shells
also gas and the boys laying there that they couldn't
burry. Oh my I cant tell you how I felt and when
those big shells would come over and burst then I
heard my comrades crying and mourning. All we
could do was to trust God to protect us and look up
and say:

> Good by old pal, your body sleeps heer 'neath the sod,
> Your soul I pray has gone home to God.

But yet I cant know the greenwood tree that leads
into the vale beyond. Not yet. So close by this
pal, my solitary bunk I had to make to stay over
night and oh how lonely how sad no tongue can
tell. But yet God was with me. Is God with you
if not please don't do as many others have done—
Put it off to long.

So we stayed in the front at Somerance untill we
git releaved by the 80th Div. boys.

We stayed in actual fighting in the Argonne from
the time we went in, which was the morning of Oc-

tober 8th to November 1st. Over three weeks. Fighting in the front line all the time and through those terrible woods. And we were both mussed up right smart. The woods and us. Those old woods were all ruined. And we were all shot to pieces. There were not many of them-there Greeks and Italians left. But what was left were still fighting like a sackful of wildcats. I shore did like those boys now. They were my buddies. Yes; they were still burning up a most awful amount of ammunition. But they always kept on a-going. Always. The nearest I come to getting killed in France was in an apple orchard in Somerance in the Argonne. It was several days after the fight with the machine guns. We hed a very heavy barrage from the Germans suddenly drop down on us, and we were ordered to dig in and to lose no time about it. Some of us were digging in under an apple tree. The shells were bursting purty close. But we didn't take much notice of them. Jes kept right on a-digging. It's funny, after you've been at the front a right-smart while you can almost tell where the shells are going to burst and what size they are. It is a sort of soldier's instinct. And this morning they were close, but not close enough to scare us. And then they got closer. And we dug faster. I have dug on farms and in gardens and in road work and on railroad, but it takes big shells dropping close to make you really dig. And I'm a-telling you, the dirt was flying. And then bang!— one of the big shells struck the ground right in front of us and we all went up in the air. But we all come down again. Nobody was hurt. But it sure was close.

NOVEMBER 1ST

Argonne Forest. So we came out of the lines to
a germans rest camp and there we got something to
eat. . . .

I was made a sergeant just as quick as I got back
out of the lines. But, oh, my! so many of my old buddies were missing and we scarcely seemed the same outfit.

NOVEMBER 2D

Argonne Forest. . . . And then we started out
and hiked to a French camp.

NOVEMBER 4TH

(No place given). We loaded on French busses
to go to French Camp.

NOVEMBER 5TH

(No place given). We got to a French camp.

NOVEMBER 7TH

Aix-les-Bains. I taken train for Aix-les-Bain.
I had a furlough for 10 days.

NOVEMBER 8TH

Aix-les-Bains. So I got to Aix-les-Bain and went
to the Hotel de Albion and I stayed at this hotel
from the 8th to the 16th and I went a round and
seen some fine scenery I got on a motor boat and

went over to Itala and there I seen some good
scenery.

There was a bunch of us had been given a ten-day
leave to Aix-les-Bains. We went down there for a
rest. We had been in the Argonne for several weeks
without any relief and were tired and worn out and
went down there to rest during the ten-day leave. We
were staying in private places. We jes went around
seeing the historical places, the old Roman baths and
up on the mountain.

NOVEMBER 10TH

Aix-les-Bains. I went to church. I think the man
gave us a very good talk his subject was the angle
helping the wounded to the aid station. And there
I also seen the old Roman baths that they said was
built 122 years before Christ.

And then it all come to an end. All of this killing
and destroying.

NOVEMBER 11TH

Aix-les-Bains. And the armistice was signed.
And they sure was a time in that city that day and
night. Yes. say did you think that the armistice
was sign on the 11th month on the 11th day and
the 11th hour of 1918. And a nother thing did you
ever know that the war just lasted 585 days from
the time that the President declared war a gainst
Germany until the armistice was signed and did you

ever know that in this little short time of 585 days
that the Americans was over here in France a holding a 77 mile frount in the Argonne forest.

I don't know that I can jes exactly tell my feelings
at that time. It was awful noisy, all the French were
drunk, whooping and hollering. The Americans were
drinking with them, all of them. I never done anything much. Jes went to church and wrote home and
read a little. I did not go out that night. I had jes
gotten back there and were all tired. I was glad the
armistice was signed, glad it were all over. There had
been enough fighting and killing. And my feelings
were like most all of the American boys. It was all
over. And we were ready to go home. I felt that
they had done the thing they should have done, sign-
ing the armistice.

CHAPTER XXIX

PARIS

THE rejoicings which followed the armistice lasted for several days. I didn't take no part in them. I don't know why. I kinder think I felt it all so much that I daresn't let myself go.

NOVEMBER 17TH

Champlitte, France. Well, I'll go on—so I stopped at Champlitte and the French had a dance that night and they had to go by my bed to where they was dancing and the girls would pull my feet until I couldn't sleep for them.

DECEMBER 25TH

Long, France. I went to see President Wilson and wife at Long where they had a review. So there was a large crowd there. I enjoyed myself very well But I didn't get any dinner So I was not enjoying a xmas dinner you see, ho ho. So I went back to my company that night and it was after dark. So Mrs. Wilson was dressed very nice and she had a smile on her face all the time. She was wearing a Smart Seal Skin Coat with a Big Fox Collar and a close fitting Seal Skin Toque with a bright red rose trimming on one side and a little bunch of holly at her throat. So she looked very pleasing and Mr. Wilson was wearing a large black silk hat with a light grey fur coat he also had a smile on his face So that cheered the boys to see Mr. and Mrs. Wilson and hear them talk, ho, ho.

In January I begun to travel over France and talk to the boys. I was travelling in and out of my Division Headquarters something like six weeks. I travelled by motor cycle and automobile. I would jes go to a place and the boys would come around and I would hold a meeting and talk to them. I spoke in the Y huts and out in the open to the battalions and to the assembled troops on the ground. I got good representation everywhere. Our division chaplain, Rev. C. Tyler, of Milwaukee, often travelled with me. He was a nice man and a powerful preacher. I first talked to the boys in our Eighty-second Division and then I went to other outfits.

On one of these trips they done drove me about eighty miles an hour on a motor cycle over those old French roads. It was asking too much of God, travelling like that. In front of the machine guns in the Argonne I couldn't protect myself. So I expected Him to look after me. And He done it and I come out unharmed. But there was no sense rushing like mad over those old roads on a motor cycle. So I wouldn't do it.

The boys were longing to get home. They felt they had done their jobs. The war was over. They were kinder restless. I was that way too. Now that there was nothing much to do I begun to get homesick again. I begun to think more and more of the log cabin in the Valley of the Three Forks of the Wolf at home in Tennessee, and of my little old mother, and of Gracie.

Oh, my! How slow those cold wet days in camp went by. There was nothing to do and so much time to do it in. I don't like fooling around like that nohow. I kinder think the waiting, waiting, waiting pestered me a heap more than the war itself did. It jes seemed as though that old ship to take us home would never come.

FEBRUARY 12TH

Prauthoy, France. I sit a Round all day didnt do anything.

FEBRUARY 13TH

Prauthoy. It was so cold and snowy that I never did anything but sit by the fire.

FEBRUARY 14TH

Prauthoy. Cold and snowy and never did anything.

FEBRUARY 15TH

Prauthoy. Cold and snowy and sit by the fire all day.

FEBRUARY 16TH

Prauthoy. I went to church. It was Sunday and a rainy day, and we had a nice talk.

FEBRUARY 17TH

Prauthoy. I never done anything much for I was not feeling good.

FEBRUARY 18TH

Prauthoy. I didn't do much.

FEBRUARY 26TH

Prauthoy. On the night of the 26th of February I taken the a vant and started for Bordeaux.

At last we moved on to Bordeaux.

(NO DATE)

En Route to Bordeaux. I was on the train and it came an awfull cold snow storm about 3 P.M. So we was in box-cars and it was cold and snowing and we had no fire. So it was pretty tough. But that was better than sleeping in those old French barnes where the cows sleep in the parlor and the chickens in the dining room, ho! ho!

It was even worse in Bordeaux. Jes cold, stormy days with nothing to do but sit around and think of home. Of course we did some drilling and marching. And there were guards and reviews which somehow now that the war was over didn't seem the same nohow. There was neither strength nor seasoning in them.

Once in a while though things did get a bit exciting.

One night the officers had a dance in the Y hut. The privates were not allowed to go, but they done got tanked up on some of that-there French cognac. Then they sorter pushed in on the dance. They picked out most of the pretty girls; and the girls were kinder willing, too, ho, ho. And they sorter crowded the officers. I'm a-telling you that made them-there captains and lieutenants mad. They ordered me to call out the guard and get the boys off the floor. But that was a harder job than busting the Hindenburg Line. The boys hung on to the girls and didn't want to give them up or stop dancing nohow. The officers were just as determined to keep the dance private, that is for themselves and their girls. So I sorter arranged an armistice between them. I roped off that old dance floor and stationed the guards along the rope. So the officers were able to dance at one end. And the boys kept some of the girls and danced at the other end.

Later on in March I got me a leave pass and went to Paris. The first time, I didn't do much but hike round and see the sights. I done heard a lot about that-there opera. I had never heard of the word before. All I knowed about it from what the boys told me was that it was music, a lot of them stringed instruments playing together, so I hiked me to the place and bought a ticket and they done charged four dollars for a seat! I sat through it all right. I liked the orchestra, but I don't think I'd ever again spend four dollars to see another opera like it. I went out to Versailles and wandered through the palaces there. I went to the tomb of Napoleon. I went to where they buried the unknown soldier but I didn't stay long because it sorter made me sad; and I didn't want to be sad in Paris; but I was sad jes the same. Of course I could have gone out like a whole heap of the boys and fooled around with the mademoiselles and the vin rouge; and sorter tried to forget the war and them-there Germans I done killed in the Argonne. But I didn't drink and I had a girl of my own back home in the mountains. So I hiked around all day and at night time I jes got out in the streets and mixed in the crowd and then went home to bed.

MARCH 28TH

Paris. I rode on the Paris wheel and took a train ride down to Se Louis 14 Plait at night.

I kinder think that bestest of all I enjoyed my ride on the Paris wheel. I'm a-telling you that when it started to go round and round with me on it and the sky and the ground all got mixed up I not only forgot the war I done forgot everything, ho! ho!

I went back to Paris again in April. I was ordered to represent my division as a non-commissioned officer at the first meeting of the American Legion. That was when it was formed.

APRIL 7TH

Paris. I arrived in Paris at 8.30 A.M. and 10.30 A.M. was our meeting. I was there on time at the Hotel de Gabriel. So we had the meeting all day until 5.30 P.M. the meeting adjourned.

ON THE S. S. *OHIOAN*

Sergeant York as he returned from France after accomplishing what was said to be the greatest individual feat of the war.

So you see I'm a charter member of the American Legion. It begun right there in Paris, at the Hotel de Gabriel. The meeting lasted all day until about 5.30 in the afternoon. I attended all the sessions. I jes knowed hit was going to grow into a big organization. It sorter seemed right that the buddies who fought together in France should have some sort of organization that would keep them together in peace.

Once I got lost tramping round the streets. That is the only time that I ever got bewildered as to direction. Right in the middle of that-thar old city the streets are all sorter mixed up. They seem to have no beginnings and no ends. And when they do have ends they sorter go plumb up against a blank wall. They call it a cul-de-sac. So I got lost. I tried to get my direction by the sun, but I could not see it. Ho! ho! I tried to remember some of the buildings. I couldn't. And I'm telling you I couldn't make heads nor tails out of the names of the streets. I didn't know where I was. All I knowed was I was in Paris. So I went up to a mademoiselle and I told her as well as I could that I was lost and would she be so kind as to tell me where my hotel was. She was a right-smart girl. She smiled and then takened me to a street car and put me on it and told the mademoiselle conductor where I wanted to go and to let me off when I got there. She sure did too. So you see I never takened any girls home in France but one of them had to take me home, ho, ho.

One day some of us boys heard that the Queen of Roumania was coming in on the train, so we hiked down to the station. And sure enough she come and when she seed us she smiled and waved her hand. I was fairly close to her. She looked very pretty and she sorter walked like a queen. She had on a black dress and a kind of black veil.

APRIL 8TH

Paris. I seed the Queen of Roumania. She is a very good-looking lady So I stayed in Paris until 8.26 on the night of the 9th.

I liked Paris all right. It was a right-smart city. Jes the same it sorter convinced me more than ever that cities don't mean much to me nohow. I knowed in my own heart that I wouldn't give up my mountains and the hunting and the shooting for all of the cities in the world. So soon as my leave was up I went back to the camp near Bordeaux. And I jes sat around there in the rain and the mud doing nothing and waiting for that-thar old ship to come and take us home. Oh, my! The days went by slower and slower. It jes seemed as if we would never get away from France. I'm a-telling you them were the homesickest days I ever had in my life.

At last we got ready to sail. The boat done came. I'm a-telling you I was tickled. So were the boys. But when we got down to the wharf and begun to load there were so many of us the boat wouldn't hold us all. And, oh, my! I had to stay behind with sixty-six others and do some more waiting. That was pretty tough I'm a-telling you. But the next day another old boat came along and we done sailed jes the same.

CHAPTER XXX

HOME

MAY 10TH

On Board U. S. S. *Ohio*. In the morning we went down to the docks and eat us a little and then we got on the U. S. A. Ohio boat at 2.26 P.M. we broke loose from the shores of France and by dark we was out of sight of land.

MAY 11TH

At Sea. Sunday. Sick. We had awfull rough seas.

MAY 12TH

At Sea. Awfull rough seas. Sick.

MAY 13TH

At Sea. Awfull rough. Sick.

MAY 14TH

At Sea. Awfull rough. Sick.

MAY 15TH

At Sea. Awfull rough.

293

We had about three or four days of storms and most awful rough seas. I was right-smart sick for several days. Had to stay down part of the time in my berth and part of the time on top of deck. I sure would have liked to see some trees or those old mountains. Oh, my, that sea! I didn't feel like talking or doing anything but lying down and being left tol'ably alone. And then I knowed, too, that they were going to give me a big reception when I arrived in New York. They done wired out at sea. And that hed me worried. I would hev got out and walked if I could hev.

MAY 16TH

At Sea. Nice.

MAY 17TH

At Sea. Nice.

MAY 18TH

At Sea. Was Sunday we had services in the aftternoon. We Sing Jesus Saviour Pilot me and the reading was the first psam.

MAY 19TH

At Sea. Had a storm and the sea was rough.

MAY 20TH

At Sea. Was nice.

MAY 21ST

At Sea. Was pretty.

MAY 22D

Hoboken, N. J. At 2 P.M. I landed and the ten-nessee society had a five-day furlough for me to see New York City. So I stopped at Waldorf Hotel.

Oh, my, I can't tell you how I felt when our ship steamed up New York Harbour and I seed the sky-scrapers sorter standing up against the sky. In the distance they looked jes a little like the mountains at home when you see them from a long way off.

Oh, my, I was so homesick!

I jes knowed I would never leave my country again. I didn't want to nohow. I stood there in the front of the ship as we steamed up the harbour and when we passed the Statue of Liberty I sorter looked her in the eyes and I kinder understood what the doughboy meant when he said: "Take a look at me, Old Girl. Take a good look at me, because whenever you want to see me again you will have to turn around."

I knowed, of course, that a committee from the Tennessee Society was going to meet my boat. And they did. They tried to make a most awful fuss over me. They seemed to think I done done something wonderful. I couldn't see it that way nohow. I done done my duty like most any other soldier would have done when he was up against the same thing.

The Tennessee Society met me at the boat with a

car. There was a right-smart heap of newspaper men there too and they made me stand around and have my picture taken. There were a whole heap of cameras. So you see I was under fire again. And they done questioned me. And by the time they had finished writing about me in their papers I had whipped the whole German Army single-handed. Ho, ho. Those newspaper men! But they were very nice.

They gave me a right-smart reception in New York City. They drove me through the streets in an open car; and the streets were so crowded we could only go slow. It seemed as most everybody knowed me. They throwed a most awful lot of paper and ticker tape and confetti out of the windows of those big skyscrapers. I wondered what it was at first. It looked like a blizzard. I didn't understand that it was for me until they told me. I thought that they did the same thing for 'most every soldier that came back. I thought it was a New York habit. And a very nice habit, too.

They takened me to the Waldorf Astoria, where they had a whole suite of rooms for me. There were two beds in my room. Twin beds. That kinder tickled me. I didn't know which one to sleep in. So I tried them both.

The Tennessee Society done give me a banquet and there were a whole heap of people sitting down to the big dinner. There were generals and statesmen all over the place. They asked me that many questions that I kinder got tired inside of my head and wanted to get up and light out and do some hiking. There were a heap of speeches. They seemed to be having a sorter competition saying nice things about me. They told me I was famous. And I thought to myself, if this is fame, having to stay at a big hotel with several rooms all to yourself and two beds to sleep in and a big banquet where there are so many people you couldn't remember them nohow, then fame ain't the sorter thing I used to think it was.

Of course, everybody was nice. But I'm a-telling you it was a tough corner for a mountain boy to be in. Between answering questions and kinder watching the people around me eat so I would know how to handle that old silverware without making too many bad breaks, I'm a-telling you I was busied a-plenty. But I got through it all right. I didn't know what all the plates and knives and forks and spoons were for. So I kinder slowed up and jes kept a couple of moves behind the others. So I knowed what to do. In the middle of that-there old banquet I got to kinder dreaming about home and the little log cabin and my mother and Gracie and them-there hound dogs of mine. I knowed I was to be with them soon, and I sorter couldn't think of anything else.

Jes the same, everybody was nice and meant well and they all done their best to give me a right-smart time.

Next day I hiked a-plenty all over that old city. So you see I was still hiking. I done more of that when I was in the Army than anything else.

I tried to get my mother over the long-distance telephone, but we couldn't get through. That made me homesicker than ever.

They told me I could have anything I wanted in New York City. I got to figuring it out—and I couldn't figure that I wanted anything special. Hit's kinder funny that when you can have anything you want, you don't seem to want anything. That's life. So hit seems to me hit ain't having things that matters so much; hits the wanting to have them that counts. They kept insisting. So I thought I would like to have a ride in the subway. You see I thought it was right smart to have them tunnels under the ground and be able to go all over New York City that way, so they done got a special train and rode me all over New York City in the subway. I liked that, ho, ho.

MAY 23D

New York City. I was looking at New York City. On the night of the 23rd I took the train for Washington, D. C. honorable hull had come to get me.

MAY 25TH

Washington, D. C. So I got to Washington this morning about 6 A.M. So we drove a car all over Washington almost looking at the city and I had the honor to meet Secretary Baker of war and shake hands with him.

Congressman Cordell Hull takened me in charge and showed me all over Washington, D. C. He tak-

ened me to the White House to meet the President,
but the President was done gone. So I met Secretary
of War Baker. And we talked about the war. And
he was most kind and considerate. I went to Congress.
They takened me there on the floor of the House.
And the members all come around me. And there was
more questioning and a whole heap of cheers and ap-
plause. By this time I was sorter feeling like a red
fox circling when the hounds are after it. I was beginning to wonder if I ever would get back to my own
home again.

The next day I went back to New York City again;
and they takened me to the stock exchange in Wall
Street. That didn't mean nothing to me nohow. A
country boy like me jes couldn't understand what it
was all about. Rifle-guns, hounds, foxes, coons, mountains, shootin' matches—I understand these things. I
belong to them and I'm a-thinking they belong to me.
But money and big business were things I jes didn't
understand nohow. The streets in that part of New
York City are most awful narrow and plumb full of
people. I figured it was sorter funny that people
would be willing to crowd together and work and live
in such cramped-up spaces when there's such a heap of
open country and grass and sky in other parts of America. But then you see I was a country boy and didn't
understand the city life.

About this time they begun to pester me with a
whole heap of officers to go on the stage and into the
movies. They offered so much money that it almost
takened my breath away. I thought to myself,

wouldn't I look funny in tights, ho, ho. Besides, I sorter felt that to take money like that would be commercializing my uniform and my soldiering. I knowed if I hadn't been to war and hadn't been a doughboy they never would have offered me nothing nohow. I also knowed I didn't go to war to make a whole heap of money, or to go on the stage or in the movies. I went over there to help make peace. And there was peace now. So I didn't take their thirty pieces of silver and betray that-there old uniform of mine. I would have been interested in helping to make the pictures if I didn't have to be in it myself and if they would do it, not to make a heap of money for themselves or for me but jes to show what the boys done done over there, and also to show what faith will do for you if you believe in it right. But I knowed they weren't interested in that. They jes wanted me to show how I done killed the Germans in the Argonne. So I wouldn't have nothing to do with them nohow. They also offered me a heap of money to write newspaper stories and to sign advertisements. But I didn't want to do that either.

I jes wanted to be left alone to go back to my beginnings. The war was over. I had done done my job and I had done it the bestest I could. So I figured I ought to be left alone and allowed to go home to the mountains where I belonged. I sorter felt, too, that if they wanted to do something right smart for me they might help me to get a soon-go for home. The Army officers understood me and I understood them and they sent me South to be demobilized as soon as they could get the papers fixed up.

I'm a-saying right here that they treated me right smart all the time that I was in the Army. They done played the game with me and they played square. So far as I am concerned the officers and everybody connected with the Army done done the right thing by me. They were right-smart folk.

In late May I got my transportation papers to Ft. Oglethorpe, Ga., and there I got my discharge papers and transportation home. But I can't tell you what I felt like when I got home in May, 1919. The mountains sure looked good to me. The mountain people, thousands of them, come from all over jes to say howdy. All of my big brothers were there and my sisters and my mother.

As soon as I got back to the little old log cabin in the Valley of the Three Forks of the Wolf I went a-hunting—not for coon, or possum or fox or squirrels —I went a-hunting for Gracie. I done found her too. And what I said to her and what she said to me and what we said to each other ain't nobody's business nohow.

Then I went out on the mountainside where I used to pray and when it was all quiet and there was nobody around nohow, I returned thanks to God. He had given me my assurance that even if I didn't think it right I should go jes the same; and would be protected from harm; and would come back without a hair of my head injured. I don't know what I said to

Him. I disremember. I don't know that I said any-thing. I jes felt.

And, oh, my, what a joyful time I had with them-there hound dogs of mine. I done set down and looked at them and patted them and they wagged their tails and licked my hands, and then, ho, ho, they bayed and sorter circled round, and sorter lit out for the woods; jes to sorter remind me that they hadn't been foolin' round nohow while I was away, and they still knowed where the coons and possums and the foxes were.

In a few days I had the old uniform off and the overalls on. I done cleaned up the old muzzle-loader. It was all over. I was home.

IN A PEACE-TIME SETTING

Sergeant Alvin C. York and his three sons in front of their home in the Valley of the Three Forks of the Wolf.

CHAPTER XXXI

A HEAP O' LARNIN'

NOTHING seemed to have changed much. The little old log cabin was still there at the head of the spring and the water in it was a-running and a-singing the same as ever. The razorbacks were rooting for acorns and hickory nuts jes as before. Their bells, and the cow bells, too, sounded much the same. The dogwood blossomed white and the red-bud pinkish-like, jes as they used to. Though I seemed to notice them more now. The hills were as they always were, blue and kinder dreamy. And the people hadn't changed nohow. They were putting in their crops, working from sunup to sundown.

The same crowd of mountain boys and girls were to be seen at the store. The little church on the hill was doing tol'able well. Rosier Pile held his Sunday school the same and the kiddies larned their lessons and some of them fell off to sleep jes about the same.

The war had come and gone. Millions of boys had been killed and wounded. Millions of dollars had been poured out jes like water. Homes all over the world had been desolated. Some of the old countries had been all mussed up and new ones had come up and sort of takened their places. The whole outside world seemed to have changed. But not our valley. Everything there was kinder the same.

But I knowed, though, that I had done changed. I knowed I wasn't like I used to be. The big outside world I had been in and the things I had fought through had teched me up inside a most powerful lot. The old life I had lived seemed a long, long way behind me. It seemed to be a sort of other life in another world. I knowed I had changed. I was sort of restless and full of dreams and wanting to be doing something; and I didn't understand. So I sat out on the hillside trying to puzzle it out.

Before the war I had never been out of the mountains. I had never wanted to be. I had sorter figured that them-there mountains were our shield against the iniquities of the outside world. They sorter isolated us and kept us together so that we might grow up pure-blooded and resourceful and God-loving and God-fearing people. They done done that, too, but they done more'n that. They done kept out many of the good and worthwhile things like good roads, schools, libraries, up-to-date homes, and modern farming methods. But I never thought of these things before going to war. Only when I got back home again and got to kinder thinking and dreaming, I sorter realized hit.

Then I knowed we had to have them. We jes had to. And the more I thought the more I kinder figured that all of my trials and tribulations in the war had been to prepare me for doing just this work in the mountains. All of my suffering in having to go and kill were to teach me to value human lives. All the temptations I done went through were to strengthen my character. All the associations with my buddies were to help me understand and love my brother man. All of the pains I done seed and went through were to help and prepare me. And the fame and fortunes they done offered me in the cities were to try me out and see if I was fitted for the work He wanted me to do.

Again the Devil taketh him into an exceedingly high mountain and showeth him all the kingdoms of the world, and the glory of them; and he said unto him, all these things will I give thee, if thou wilt fall down and worship me. Then saith Jesus unto him, get thee hence, Satan, for it is written, thou shalt worship the Lord thy God and Him only shalt thou serve.

So He was tempted. So everybody since, who is called on to do good, is tempted. So I, an unlarned mountain boy, was tempted too.

But I done come through it all all right. My prayers and the prayers of my mother and Pastor Pile and a whole heap of other friends were answered.

So I talked to Gracie about these dreams of mine. She understood. She done always understood. So we done got married. Governor Roberts, the Governor of Tennessee, done come down to our valley and performed the ceremony. Thousands of people come from all over Tennessee to see the goings-on. And the mountain people provided the vittles. They brought in goats and hogs and turkeys and slaughtered and dressed them right there on the hillside. They set up a table, the largest I ever seed, and they done piled hit up with all the meats and eggs there was and with sweet potatoes and cornbread and milk and jams and cakes and a whole mess of other things. We were married on the mountainside above the spring and under the shady trees and with the blue mountains and green grass and the flowers all around.

Then I begun what I felt was my life work. I went to the State Highway Department and asked them to build a road through the mountains. And they done done it. They built what we now call the York Highway right across our county. Then the other counties done noticed it and built roads on either end. And to-day we have a right-smart road running through this-here mountain country. And there were only mountain trails and old dirt roads that were no good nohow and creek beds here before. That was the beginning.

Then I begun to work for a school, an up-to-date school in our county. We done needed it most awful bad. We only had a few schools here. They were all frame buildings, and some of them were well-nigh uninhabitable. There was only one high school. Very few of the teachers were college graduates. So, you see, we needed new buildings and up-to-date teachers and equipment most awful bad. So I raised about $15,000 myself and the state and the county each put up $50,000. That gave me $115,000 to build new schools. I wanted a modern, up-to-date vocational school, which later on could be sorter developed into a mountain college. The Board they give me couldn't see things the way I did. So I have had a most awful hard fight, a much worser one than the one I had with the machine guns in the Argonne.

The politicians and the real estate people tried to use me. The small-town bankers tried to get in on it. Jealous factions wanted to get a-hold of it and handle it their way. So it done got held up. And oh, my, I had a terrible time. But I knowed I was in the right. So I kept on fighting jes the same. I done got the old Board put out. I done got the State Board of Education to handle the promotion. The school is a quasi-state institution to-day. And hit's a-coming. At this moment we have two fine new school buildings with right-smart teachers and up-to-date equipment in Jim-town. And that's only the beginnings.

As soon as I can get the money to make them self-supporting, and have proven that I can successfully look after them I'm a-thinking they're a-going to be handed over to me. And then I'm a-planning to sorter turn them into a mountain college for vocational education. I'm a-going to teach the mountain boys and girls the trades; dairying, wood-working, carpentering, fruit growing, the breeding of pure-bred livestock, dressmaking, and so on. I'm going to have them instructed in health and hygiene. I'm going to train them to be self-supporting.

If they're too poor to pay their way I'm a-going to give them a chance to work their way through. If they live back in the mountains where the roads are too bad to get out I'm a-going to build good roads to them. I don't know of no part of America nohow that needs all of this worser than we do. In our county alone there are over one thousand boys and girls between the ages of six and eighteen that can't even read and write. And I'm a-telling you it's not their fault.

Some of the boys and girls who are going to our two schools to-day walk two miles through the mountains out to the highway, where they catch the school buses and then ride fourteen miles to school; then after the school is over they have to return the same way. I kinder think that boys and girls who will do this day after day, week after week, right through the school year, want and deserve a chance to git larnin' most awful bad.

Whenever I go away on a trip for the schools they meet me as soon as I git back and ask me haven't I got more money, so that they can get more larnin'. I'm a-telling you hit kinder gives me my assurance again that I am right, dreaming and planning these things for them. That ain't all nohow. I'm a-planning playgrounds for the children, too, and libraries and a medical and nursing system.

Of course, in such things as electric lighting, sewage, water supply, and up-to-date homes our mountain towns and villages are sorter away behind the times. But I'm a-thinking if I can bring larnin' to the children they will grow up and change all these things. I can't influence the older people much nohow. They're sorter set in their ways. But if I can get the children to school and to college, the rest will come.

I ain't had much larnin' myself; so I know what an awful handicap that is. I'm a-trying all the time now to overcome that and improve myself. I ain't had much business experience neither, but I'm working hard to get that. I don't know much about finance, but I know I am honest and I am larnin' to handle money tol'ably.

I am blessed with a whole heap of most loyal and powerful friends all over America; and I still have and always will have my faith in God. I know He will not fail to help me. So I'm getting along tol'able well. Hit's a-coming—that dream of mine. I'm a-going some day to have roads all through these-here mountains; to have modern homes and all sorts of other improvements and sanitary arrangements in our towns and villages; and most of all, to have a heap of schools and a right-smart mountain college.

I ain't going to show any favouritism nohow. I fought with Catholics and Protestants, with Jews, Greeks, Italians, Poles, and Irish, as well as American-borned boys in the World War. They were buddies of mine and I larned to love them. If there is any of them in these-here mountains we'll make a place for them in these schools. I'm a-going to give all the children in the mountains the chance that's a-coming to them. I'm a-going to bring them a heap o' larnin'.

THE END

SGT YORK CENTER FOR PEACE AND VALOR

Alvin C. York's lifetime was spent in unwavering principled service to his nation and its people. In addition to his wartime efforts, it was his compassionate generosity that was Alvin Cullum York's true mark of heroic character. By the time of his death in 1964, he had nearly accomplished all he set out to do. The schools he envisioned, he built. The impact he hoped to make on the world—he made. York Agricultural Institute, he said, was his proudest accomplishment.

When in 1926, the York Historic School opened its doors, it did so to an eager, needy, and neglected community. Built by Sergeant York—Tennessee mountain boy, World War I hero, and true American treasure—the building exists today in Jamestown, Fentress County, Tennessee. Abandoned to deteriorate in the early 1980s, however, and scheduled for demolition as late as 2008, it still stands as a designated National Historic Landmark and a building of National Historic Significance. It exists still, a symbol of our most honorable national foundations, deteriorated but not lost—and it requires your support to shine again as the Sergeant York Center for Peace and Valor.

Just as it was intended, the Sergeant York Center for Peace and Valor will stand proudly for Peace amongst all people and the honorable tenants of the Medal of Honor: Courage, Commitment, Sacrifice, Patriotism, Integrity, and Citizenship. It will do so by sponsoring and providing space for educational activities and opportunities aimed at the betterment of all persons and the communities in which they live and strive to contribute.

Resolute against the passage of time, the values of our nation are nonetheless vulnerable to the steady attrition of competing priorities and personal interest before service to others. The Historic Building that is the Center for Peace and Valor was built on absolute principles. It remains a testament to our nation's founding values, a symbol of an honorable legacy, an instrument of a hopeful future.

Like its founder, Sergeant Alvin York, the Sergeant York Center for Peace and Valor, will serve to promote the values and the qualities of courage, sacrifice, patriotism, and peace through increased awareness, education, behavior, and example.

With your help, this historic project will continue as a matter of legacy, to serve as it was intended—as a sanctuary for those who might dare to dream and as a beacon for those who strive to understand and contribute to the world beyond their humble homes.

The old building's foundation runs deep—to bedrock. The old masonry walls remain true as the day they were laid. Few things these days can say they were built and still do stand as a matter of history. Of course, the likes of Sergeant Alvin C. York don't come along just every day.

To contribute to these efforts and help establish The Sergeant York Center for Peace and Valor, please consider donating to his Foundation, pledging your support, and lending yourself to this proud Legacy. Every bit helps. Please go to:

www.sgtyork.org to learn more and to donate today.

Sgt Alvin C. York, digging the foundation for York Historic School, circa 1924.

York Historic School as it was in the 1930's.

York Historical School, Home of the Sgt York Center for Peace and Valor, as it appears today—ready for rehabilitation.

Rendering of the Sgt York Center for Peace and Valor—as it will be with your help.

The Sergeant York Patriotic Foundation is a nonprofit organization begun as a measure to ensure the legacy of Alvin C. York is not lost or forgotten. Proceeds from this book go to support efforts to rebuild York Historic School, and create the Sgt York Center for Peace and Valor, of which we all may be proud. We thank you for your purchase and thus your support of the Sgt York Patriotic Foundation. We are proud to count you among the Sergeant's supporters. To join the foundation or find out more go to **www.sgtyork.org**.